IMAGES
of America

ALTURAS AND LAKE GARFIELD

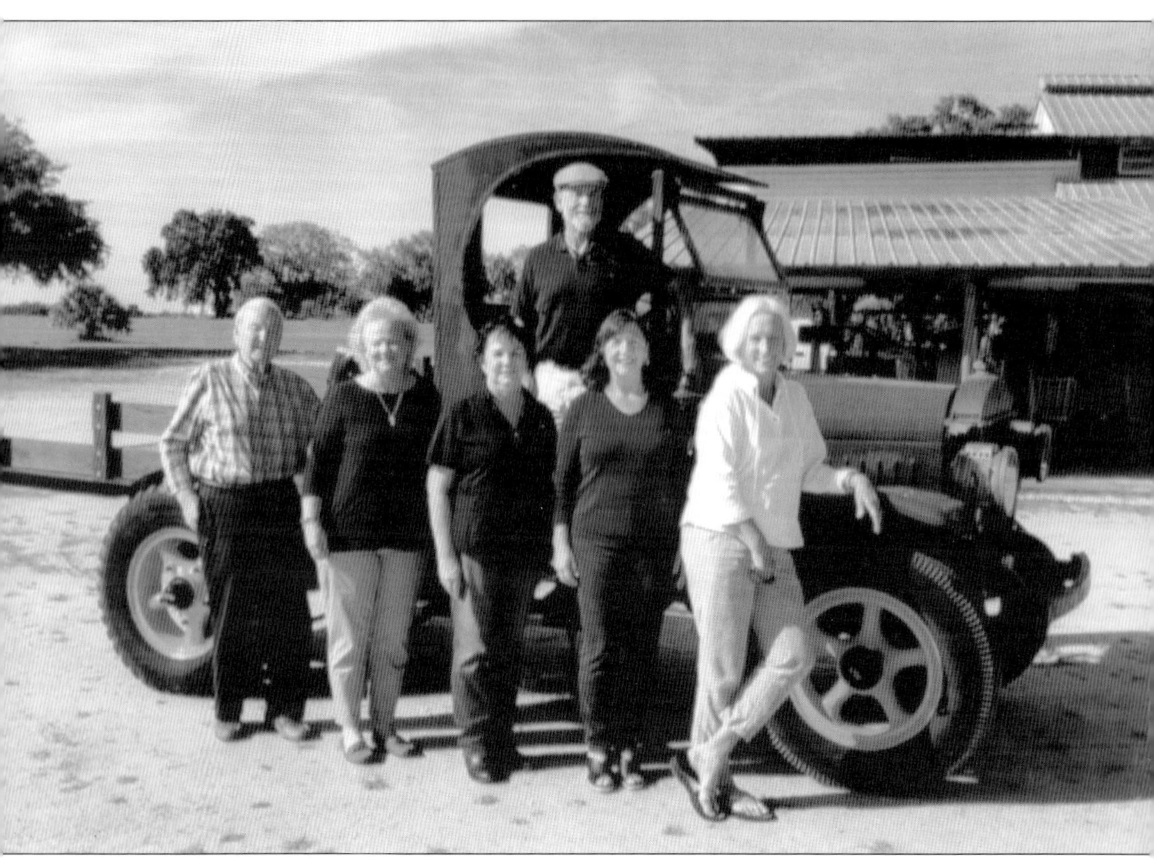

One day, six friends from Alturas and Lake Garfield, Florida, decided to write down the history of their hometowns. In 2021, that dream was realized in the book you are holding now. Scott (in truck), (from left to right) Pat, Christi, Cathy, Sherry, and Linda hope you enjoy reading this book as much as they enjoyed putting it together. Their desire was to give you a glimpse into the special places they called home. As Flavia Weedn once said, "Some people come into our lives and quickly go . . . others stay for a while, leave footprints on our hearts and we are never, ever the same." (Courtesy of Sherry Maberry.)

On the Cover: Four teenagers are "hitching" a ride to Alturas, Florida, in the 1940s. Ironically, the girls (pictured from left to right), Sylva Swartz, Millicent Rogers, Betty Mullins, and Jean McCourt, were residents of this small community and shared a strong friendship. The photograph was taken on the corner of Alturas Road and Tennessee Street just at the east end of Cox Road. In the distance one can see Star Lake, which was central to the Alturas community. (Courtesy of Karen Kelly.)

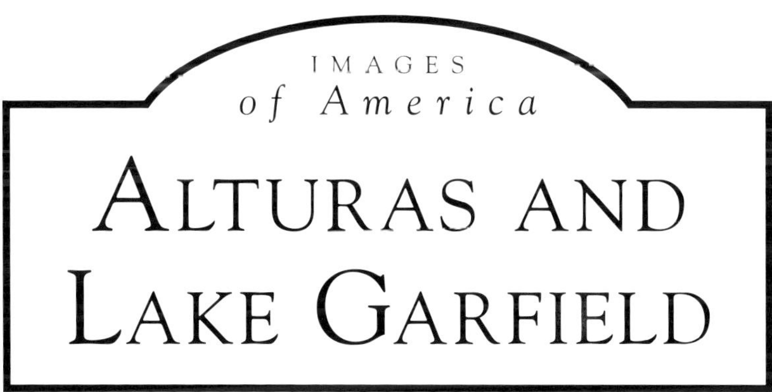

Sherry Hielscher Maberry,
Linda Smith King, Christi Voigt Adkins,
Cathy Frankenburger Curtis,
W. Patrick Huff, and D. Scott Young

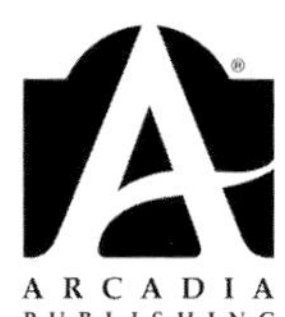

ISBN 978-1-4671-0563-7

Published by Arcadia Publishing
Charleston, South Carolina

Printed in the United States of America

Library of Congress Control Number: 2021936564

For all general information, please contact Arcadia Publishing:
Telephone 843-853-2070
Fax 843-853-0044
E-mail sales@arcadiapublishing.com
For customer service and orders:
Toll-Free 1-888-313-2665

Visit us on the Internet at www.arcadiapublishing.com

The six authors dedicate this book to their Alturas and Lake Garfield family and friends, past and present. It was a privilege to pay tribute to the pioneers who laid strong foundations for their future generations. The families who existed within these two secluded townships built homes, raised children, and met the challenges of a new way of life. They helped mold the meaning of "true community," where faith, friendship, and hard work had value and still does.

Contents

Acknowledgments

We, the authors, would like to extend appreciation to our families for patiently understanding that this "labor of love" was important, not only to us personally, but to the many families who value the preservation of the heritage of Alturas and Lake Garfield. We love you very much. We wish to thank Myrtice Young for encouraging us to actually begin this historical project in the first place. We want to thank Wayne Maberry and Amy Maberry for their endless hours of research, editing, running errands, and support. We deeply appreciate the long conversations with John Voigt, Leland Young, Flora Young Conley, and Imogene Brown Gandy. We thank them for sharing their collective memories that brought life to the history of these two communities. Lastly, we offer our special thanks to our editor at Arcadia Publishing, Caitrin Cunningham, for her expert guidance and encouragement to complete this book. We wish to apologize for any omissions or errors in this work, for we feel there may be many. It was not our intention to neglect the precious history of these townships or misrepresent facts in any way, but as the Bible says about Jesus's life in John 21:25, this book could not contain all the stories if every one of them were written down.

INTRODUCTION

There are two small townships in Polk County, Florida, nestled between Bartow and Lake Wales that sprang to life in the early 1920s. Yet a mere century later, very few even know of their existence. The hamlets of Alturas and Lake Garfield reside in the heart of Florida, near many wonderful attractions. There are spectacular beaches both to the east and west. Theme parks like Disney and Busch Gardens are simply an hour drive in either direction. Legoland, formerly the beautiful Cypress Gardens, is a quick seven-mile drive. Despite all the growth created in central Florida from these nearby attractions, Alturas and Lake Garfield remained small townships. Neither were ever incorporated.

Quietly situated among oaks, yellow pines, and beautiful natural lakes, the area attracted land seekers and developers in the late 19th century and the early 20th century. The land was purchased on May 29, 1883, by Robert A. Bridges. It changed hands several times. In 1905, some of the Alturas land was sold to the Polk Distillery. On February 15, 1906, the Sessons Investment Company of Jacksonville incorporated with the Southern Land Securities Company of Bartow to buy all the land in the Alturas and Lake Garfield areas for the purpose of real estate investment and development. The company held the land in reserve for the Seaboard Air Line Railway to lay tracks across this central section of Florida.

In 1911, the Southern Land Securities Company wanted this wilderness named. That task was given to the Seaboard Air Line Railway vice president, R.C. Hatton. He named the land with the highest elevation Alturas, which means "high place" in Spanish. Lake Garfield took its name from its largest lake.

In 1911, Alturas was earmarked to be developed as an extravagant Spanish villa surrounding the beautiful Star Lake. Surveyors were hired, and the land was platted for development. However, due to the land boom, other settlers moved to this area before the dream took hold. Amenities of civilizations, such as a railroad, paved roads, a hotel, multiple churches, and three packing houses, were built. These attracted hardworking farmers and citrus growers and supported an emerging citrus and agricultural industry. Alturas became the "Capital of Florida Agriculture."

Thus, the original anticipated metropolis never materialized but what remained was a quaint, quiet place off the beaten path, enduring the test of time as a wonderful location to enjoy a country lifestyle and raise children. Schools and educational institutions developed. Fine teachers and quality education insured that the youth of the area were well educated. In the late 1920s, a pewter sign was crafted to hang on a car's radiator. It proudly stated, "Alturas—the magic city."

In 1916, the Lake Garfield tract was earmarked by the Southern Land Securities Company to be sold to farmers and citrus growers. The company distributed a real estate pamphlet throughout the country inviting families and entrepreneurs to buy land in this area. The company's efforts did not return void as settlers were drawn to Florida's wonderful climate, which made it possible for year-round farming and ranching. Then the railroad came, and the little community began to flourish. Additionally, the Lake Garfield Packing House and the Roux Crate and Lumber

Company generated many job opportunities. Churches sprang up and provided for the spiritual guidance of the growing population. In January 1925, Vet L. Brown, speaker for the Lake Garfield Nurseries, announced the company would develop "Orange Terraces." These estates would border the "80-foot Road" while some of the home sites would border Lake Grizelle. Each property would consist of one acre of ground with 50 bearing orange and grapefruit trees that include lights, water, sewers, paved streets, sidewalks, and ornamental features. However, much like the Spanish villa that was engineered in the Alturas area during this time frame, the Orange Terrace development never transpired. In 1968, the International Mineral and Chemical Company (IMC) began mining for phosphate. This mining led to the destruction of much of the lovely lands and azure lakes. Big draglines dug away what was once a bustling township. Shortly thereafter, the sawmill and packing house closed. Today, the only evidence of its existence are the Lake Garfield Baptist Church and a few homes sprinklered here and there. However, those raised in the area still hold it close in their hearts and have fond memories of days gone by.

(Portions of the historical data were obtained in an article about Polk's past written by Martha F. Sawyer, printed in the *Lakeland Ledger*, Wednesday, June 13, 1984.)

One

The Beginnings

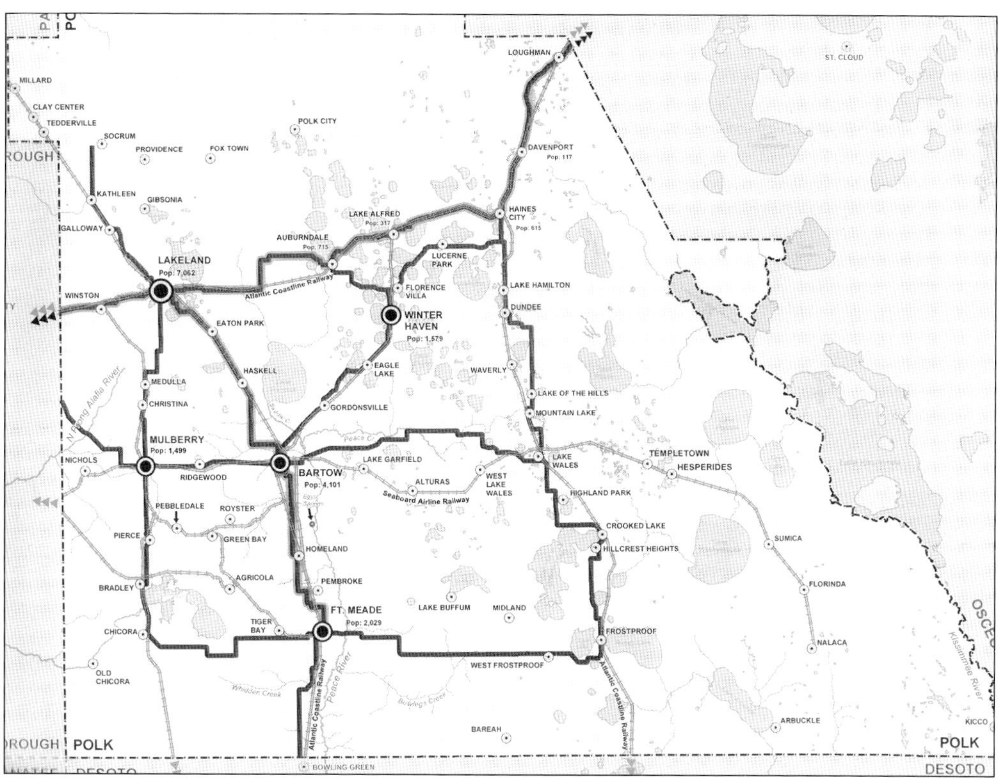

At the end of the Second Seminole War, Florida became a prime area for settlement as a result of the Armed Occupation Act of 1842. Early settlers migrating to the Alturas area in the 1860s included twins O.B. and E.B. Tyson, who were the first recorded family to come. Then the John Starling family and the Reynolds family came to the area. The Noah Waters family migrated to the Lake Garfield tract in 1870. This 1917 map from Polk County's transportation history shows the geographical proximity of the two small communities and where they are located in Polk County, Florida. (Courtesy of W. Patrick Huff.)

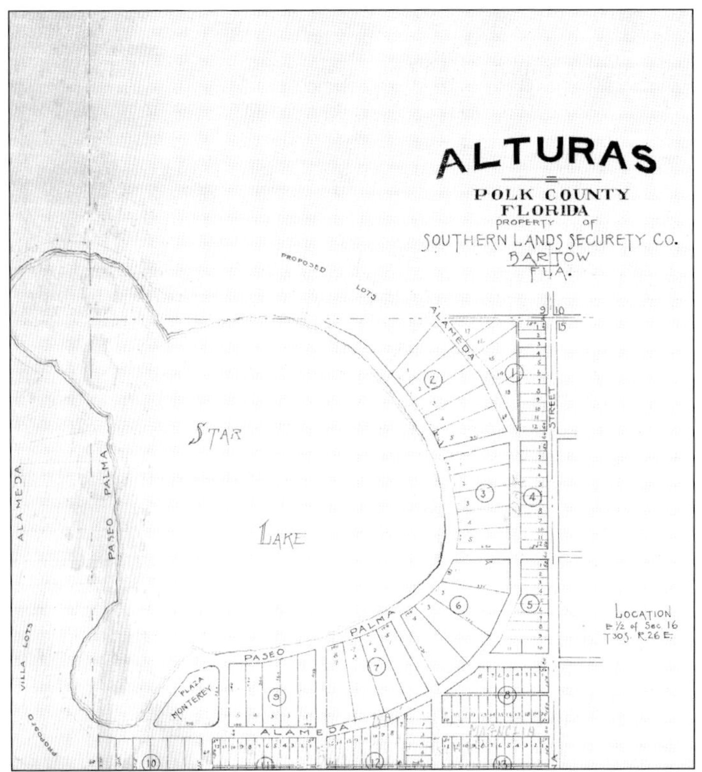

The beautiful pristine lands that surrounded Star Lake in central Florida were purchased by the Southern Land Securities Company of Bartow, Florida. Engineer A.C. Nydegger of Winter Haven, Florida, was hired to survey the land. This August 1911 plat shows the company's dream of creating a Spanish-influenced township surrounding the lake. Note that the names of the streets are in Spanish. The vice president of the company, R.C. Hatton, was given the task of naming the site, and since he spoke Spanish, he named the township Alturas, which means "high place." (Courtesy of Sherry Maberry.)

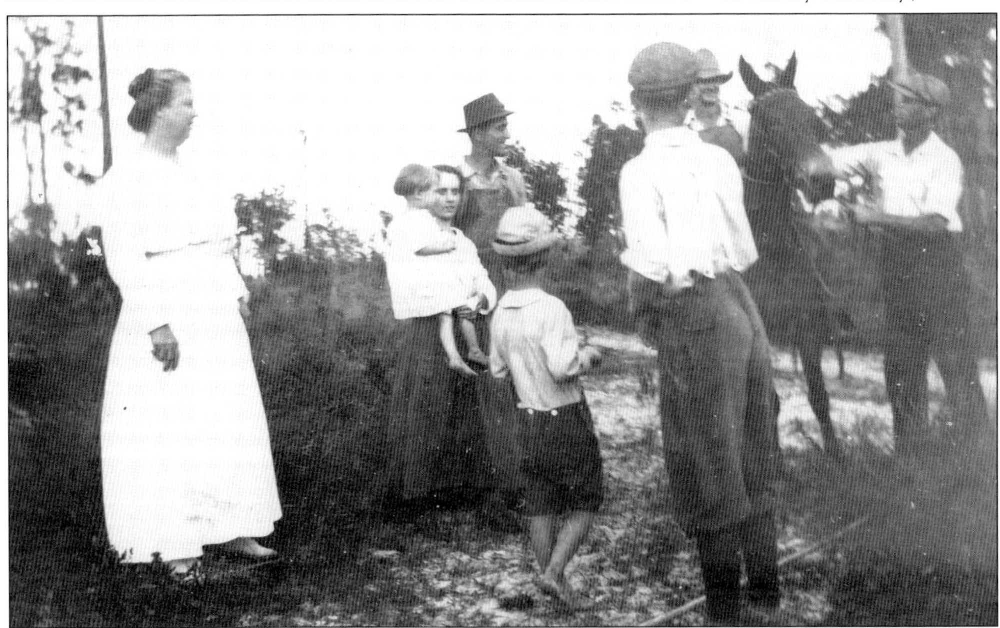

In October 1919, as new settlers arrived in Alturas and began planting groves, water was a necessity. Oliver Rothrock brought his mule and wagon to help the Wesley Gadau family sink a shallow well on the property. Pictured from left to right are Carrie Rothrock, Alvena Gadau (two years old), Tillie Gadau, Wes Gadau, Wendell Rothrock, Harold Rothrock, and Oliver Rothrock (holding the mule). (Courtesy of Linda King.)

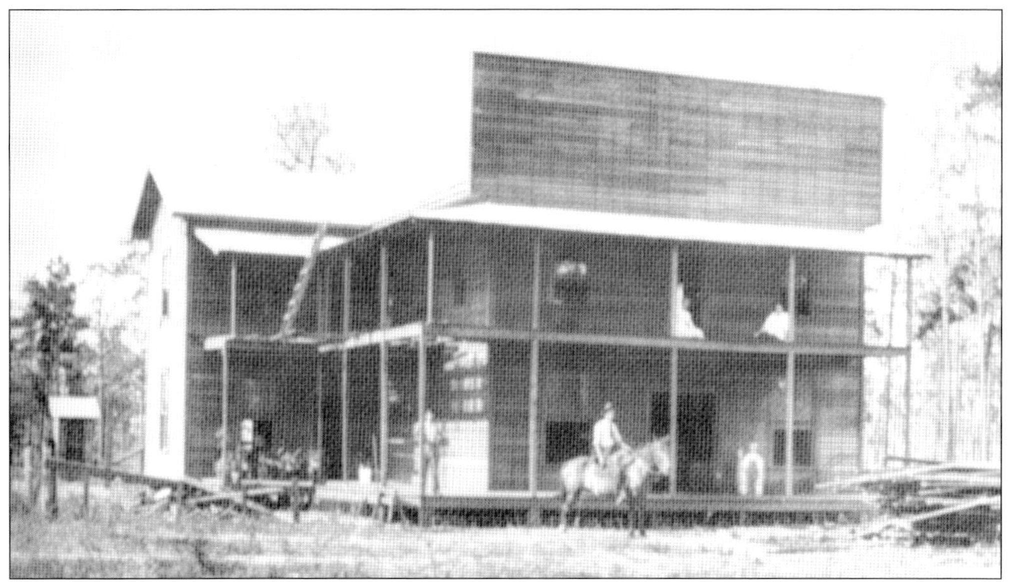

As the small community of Alturas began to flourish, construction on the Seiler Hotel began around 1910 by owner/proprietor George G. Seiler. The hotel was located near the north side of Perch Lake. The upper rooms were often used for community gatherings. Merchant Seiler also owned several citrus groves. Seiler and Harney Reynolds became the first mail carriers in 1911, when the post office opened in the Seiler Hotel. Mail carrier Harney Reynolds is sitting on the horse with the mail bag and preparing to depart on the first mail delivery on August 1, 1911. Later, in 1913, Seiler was commissioned as the first Alturas postmaster. (Courtesy of Fern B. Fletcher; donated to the US Post Office.)

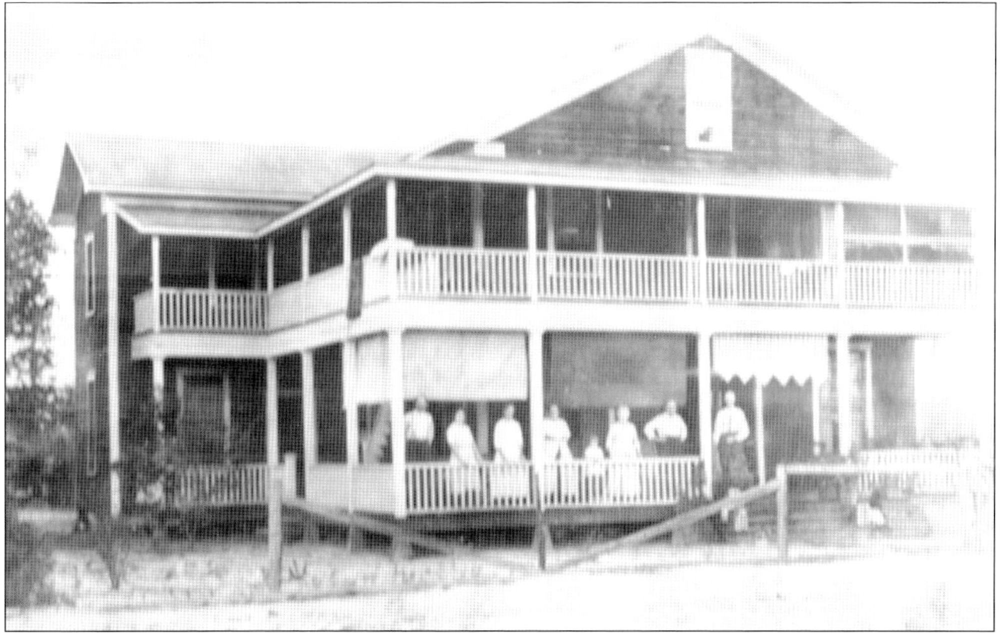

The image of the Seiler Hotel, now completed, shows George Seiler standing on the porch. His family is on the balcony. The hotel eventually burned down in the early 20th century. (Courtesy of Fern B. Fletcher; donated to the US Post Office.)

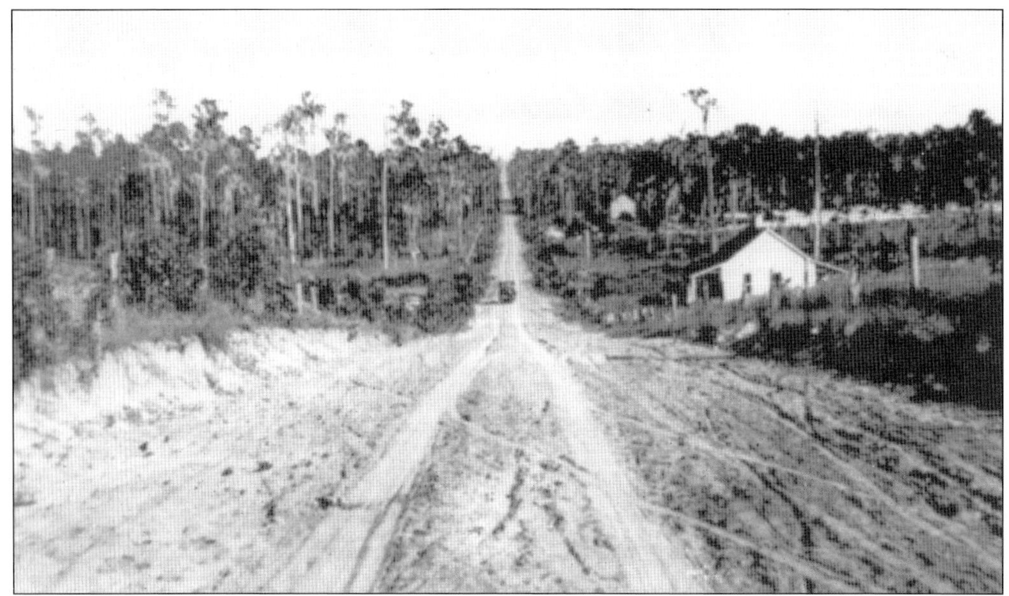

Construction of Cox Road has been started in this 1916 photograph. Contractors Roy and Joe Perdue had crews cut down trees, level the ground, and eventually pave it. The view is looking east from Patton Hill and Cox's Corner. The completion of the road connected the communities of Lake Garfield to the west and Alturas to the east. At the bottom of the "pocket" is a small settlement of Lake Garfield sawmill workers' homes. (Courtesy of W. Patrick Huff.)

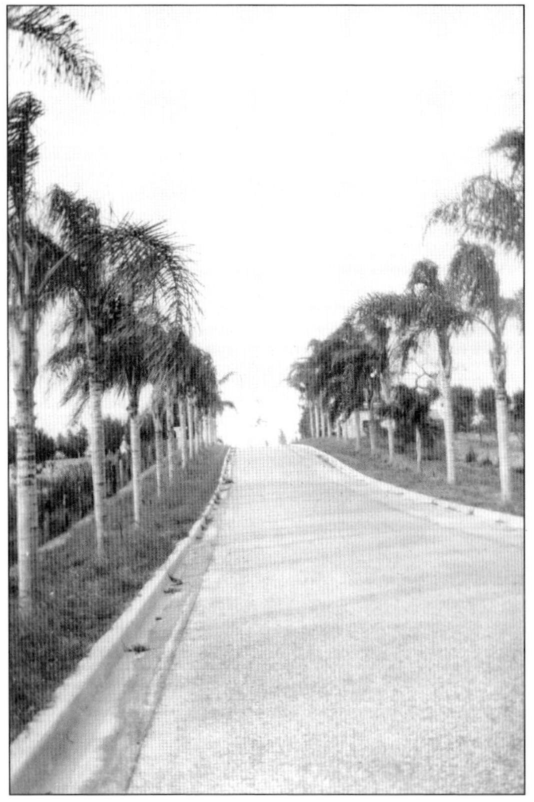

Unfortunately, the Southern Land Securities Company's dream to build a luxurious Spanish township never came to fruition. The draw to the lucrative citrus and cattle industry brought others to this fertile area. Yet in this 1928 photograph of Oak Avenue (Alameda on the plat seen on page 10), one can see the Mediterranean Revival influence on the lovely promenade lined with palm trees. It is believed that early Alturas pioneer Victor Voigt grew these beautiful palm trees. (Courtesy of Linda King.)

Rosalie Francois Adelaide Caroline Therese Eugenie Marie, Countess de Mercy Argenteau, Princess Montglyon of Belgium (1862–1925), known as the "Gold Rose of Paris," moved to Alturas, Florida, in 1911 and lived there until 1918 seeking seclusion. She had been a familiar presence among the royalty of Europe and wealthy elite of her day, but failed marriages and financial setbacks forced her relocation to the United States. She raised Buff Orpington poultry for profit. She raised, judged, and showed champion canine collies and chows and introduced the Russian Samoyed breed to America. Locals referred to her simply as "The Princess." After her home, which was located on the east side of the lake called Lake Garfield, burned, she relocated to Tampa until her death in 1925. (Courtesy of William Lloyd Harris.)

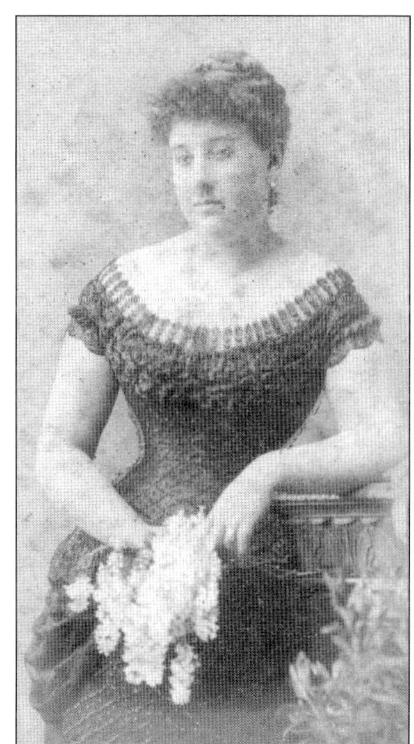

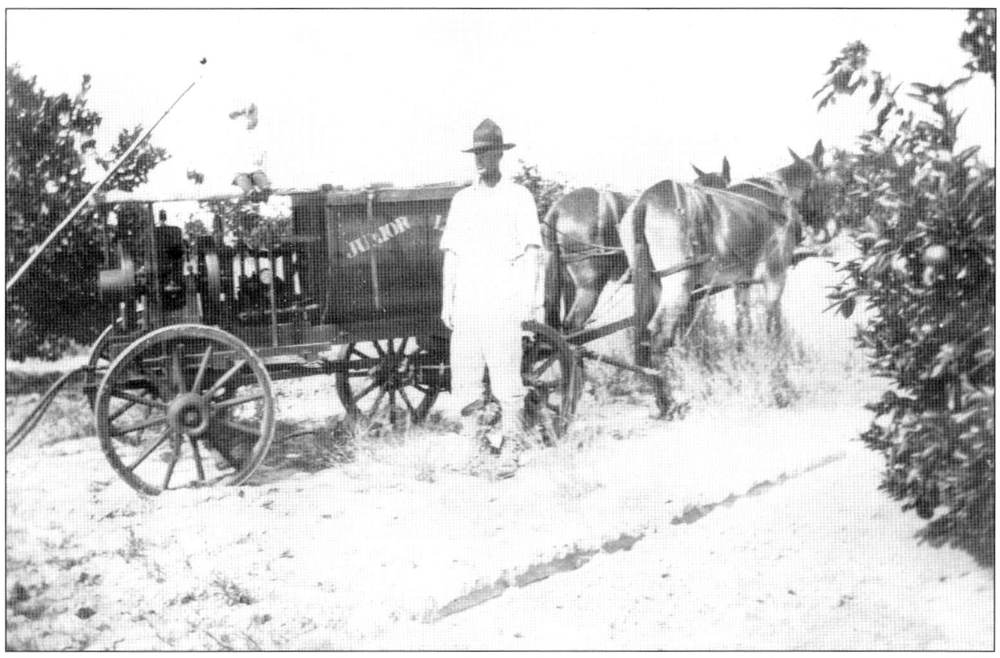

Oliver Rothrock is standing by his twin mules in the Gadau Grove in Alturas. A young child, Alevna Gadau, is crawling on top of the water sprayer waiting for a ride. The sprayer machine was used to irrigate the young citrus trees. Sandy, grove soil made it necessary to use metal wheels to drive through the rows of tress for cultivation as seen in the 1919 photograph. (Courtesy of Linda King.)

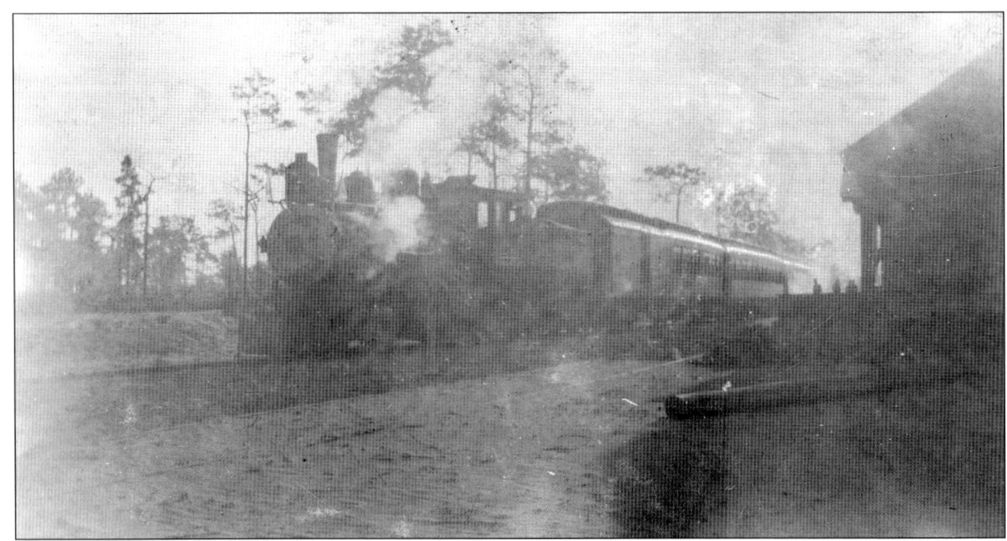

The Seaboard Air Line laid railroad tracks past Alturas the week of September 20, 1914. The first full freight car, loaded with fertilizer, was dumped at the Hatton switch near Alturas. In this photograph, taken on April 15, 1915, the first round-trip Seaboard Air Line passenger train arrived at the recently constructed Alturas Depot. The train line originated in Tampa and terminated in West Lake Wales. The route closed in 1983, and the tracks were eventually removed. (Courtesy of Scott Young.)

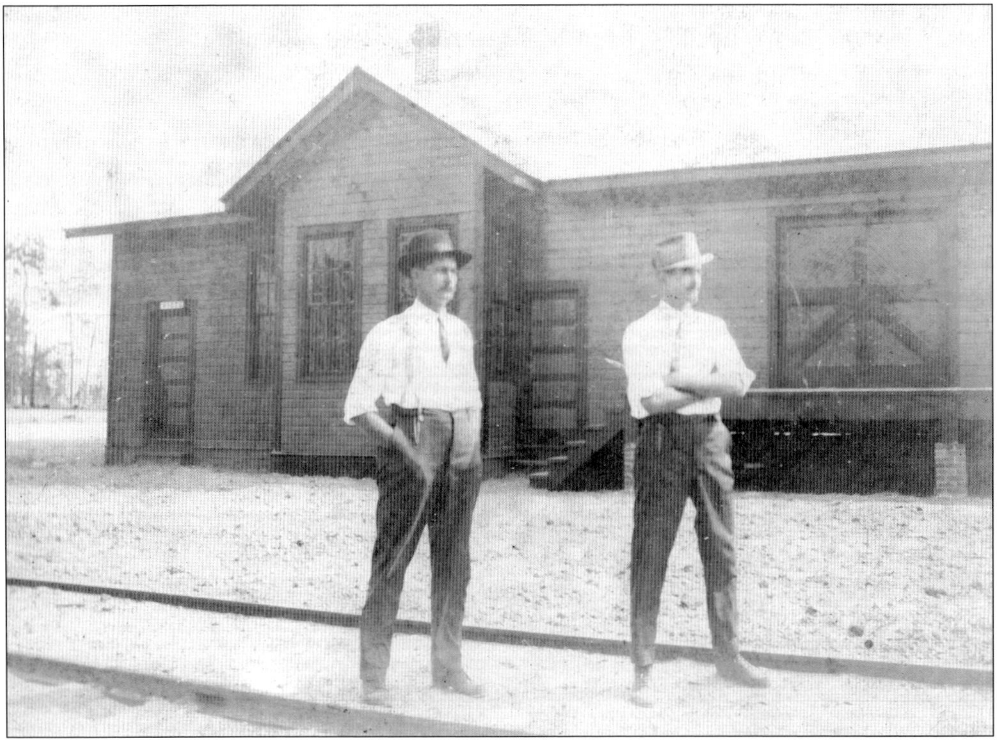

At the Alturas Depot on April 15, 1915, brothers Wes and George Gadau are awaiting the arrival of the first passenger train to Alturas. Until 1951, the passenger train would stop twice a day at the depot on its way to Tampa and back. (Courtesy of Alturas Postal Service.)

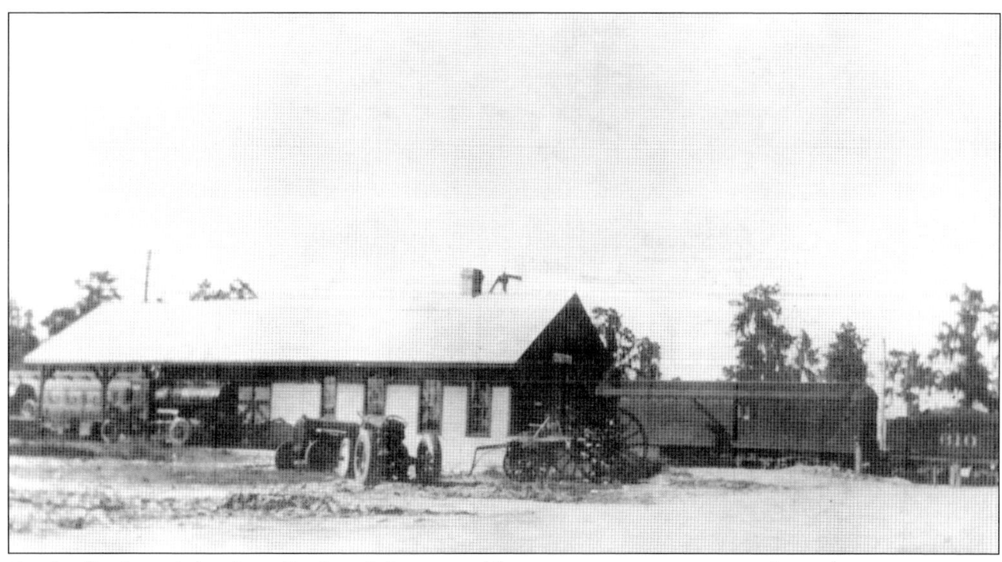

At the Seaboard Air Line Railroad depot in Alturas, one can see an eastbound passenger train as it awaits departure in 1915. The words "Air Line," in the railroad's herald, meant a high-speed direct rail line. The locomotive coal tender box is visible in this photograph. This picture also shows the large depot platform (left) that was used for citrus workers to load their fruit onto freight cars and where passengers waited with their luggage. (Courtesy of Scott Young.)

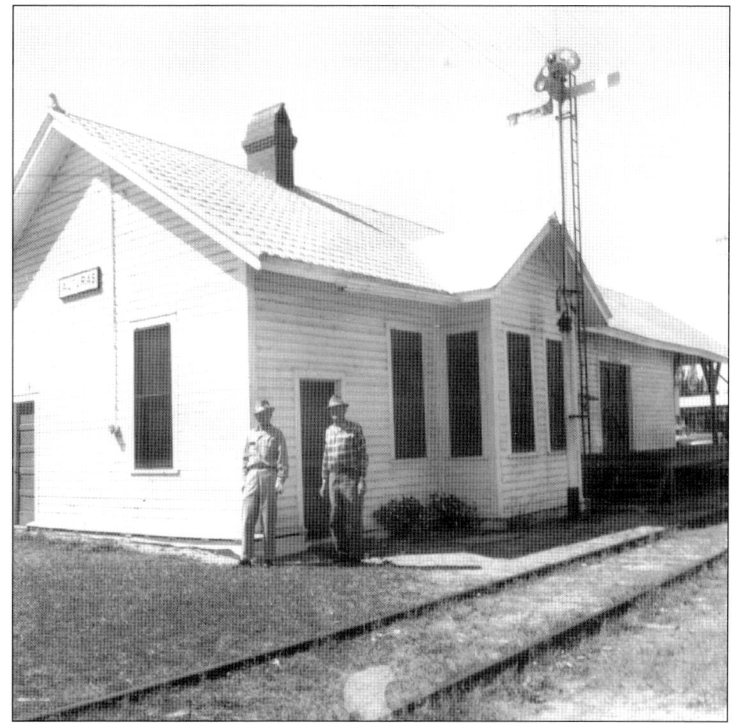

The year 1953 marked the end of era for the Seaboard Air Line Railroad Alturas Depot, as it closed its doors for the last time. Agent William B. Miller and Alturas resident Wes Gadau are bidding farewell to an Alturas institution. The building was then used to house the Alturas Grove Service Company, whose owners were Beverly and Doug Smith. (Courtesy of Linda King.)

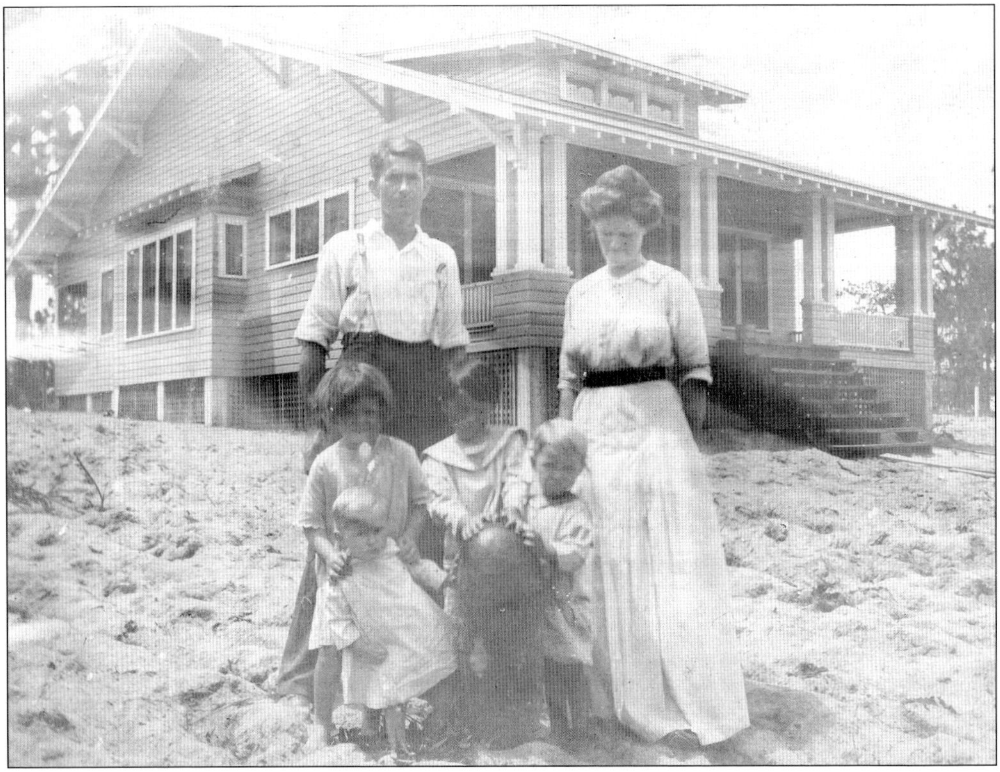

Rudolph A. Voigt; his wife, Bertha; and their children Carlton, Marvin, Verdon, and Robert are standing in front of their new home in 1919. It was built by Alturas carpenters Wes and George Gadau and Oliver Rothrock. Voigt moved to Alturas from Illinois around 1908. Josey Kreps moved into this home sometime in the late 1920s or early 1930s, and from then on, many referred to the house as the Kreps Place, no matter who lived in it. A noteworthy detail is that in 1988, this was the home where convicted murderer George Trepal lived when he poisoned his next-door neighbors. The case became headline news throughout the United States. (Courtesy of Linda King.)

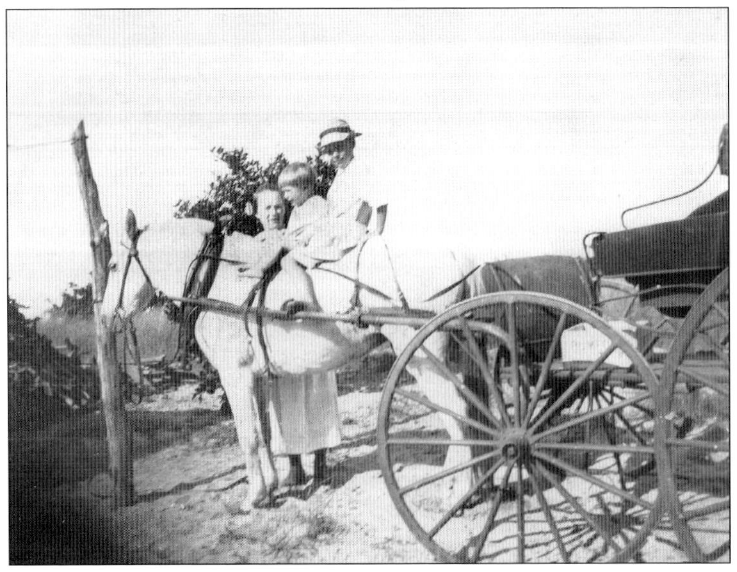

Wendell Rothrock drove his horse and buggy to visit neighbors Ethel Gadau and her two-year-old daughter Alvena in 1919, as this was the typical mode of transportation in rural Alturas at that time. The Gadau and Rothrock families worked side by side throughout many years as grove owners and carpenters. (Courtesy of Linda King.)

The Southern Land Securities Company had big dreams of selling property around the beautiful Lake Garfield. In this 1916 promotional pamphlet, the company enticed entrepreneurs nationwide to buy land for ranching and farming and to grow citrus crops. However, the area had slow growth until the Roux Crate and Lumber Sawmill Company came in 1915. The community retained the same name as the lake near it, Lake Garfield. The township of Alturas was only five miles east of this new community. (Courtesy of W. Patrick Huff.)

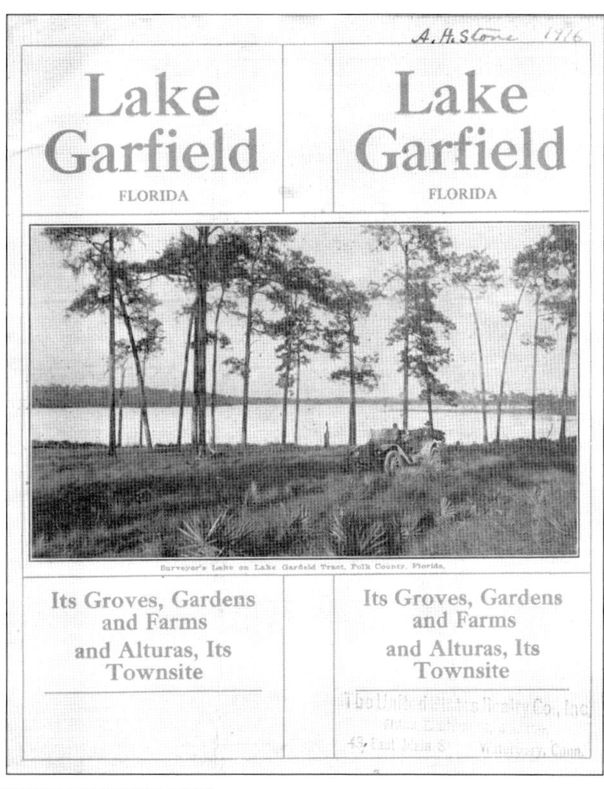

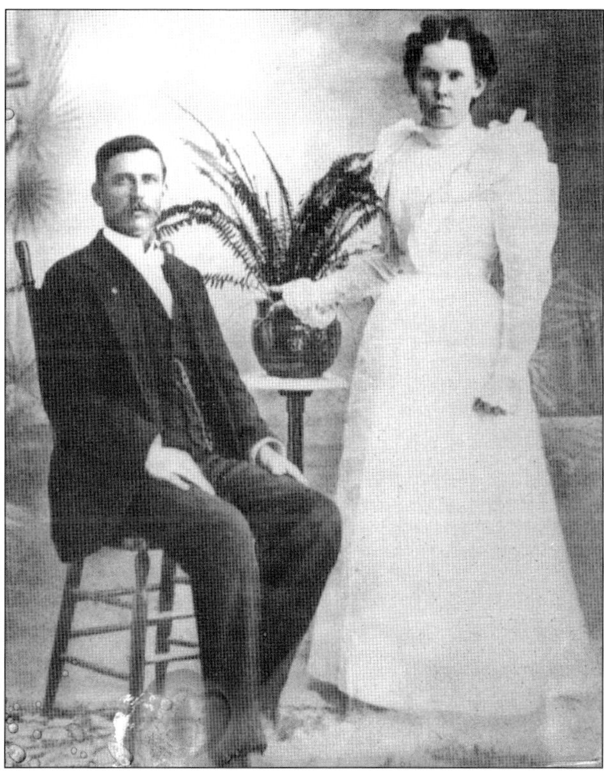

This late-1800s wedding photograph of William Noah Waters and his bride, Frances Adeline Mobley, was taken in Bartow, Florida. William's grandfather Noah Waters was among the first to settle in the Lake Garfield area around 1870. Their first homestead was located on the north/west shoreline of Lake Garfield, where they planted one of the first seedling orange groves and raised cattle. The descendants of Will and Addie continue to live and raise cattle and citrus in this area for seven generations. (Courtesy of Ned Waters.)

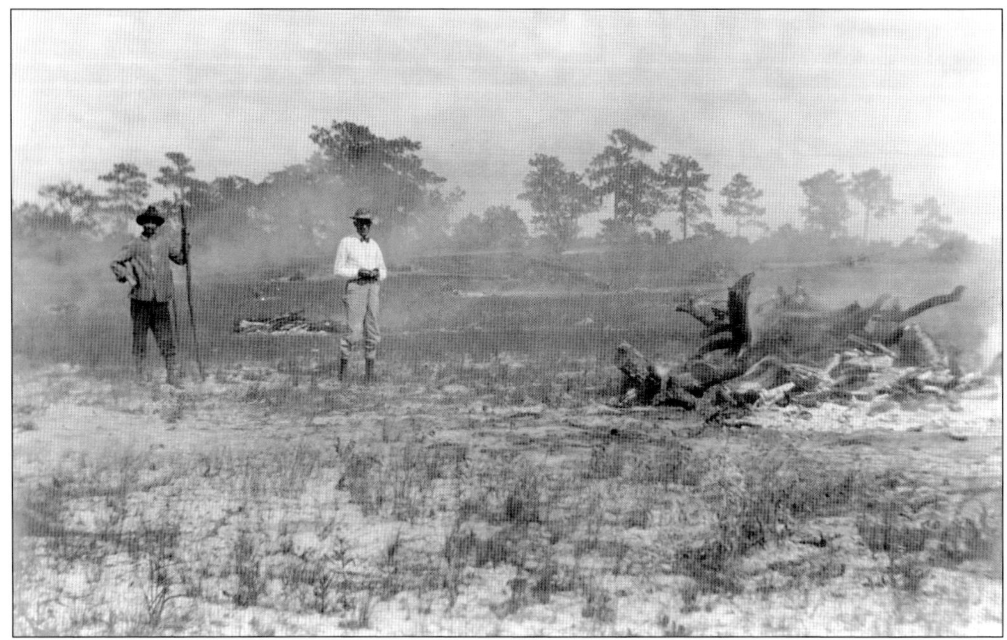

As some of the first settlers, John George Stenger Sr. and his wife, Olga, moved to the Lake Garfield tract from Cincinnati, Ohio, in 1912. This is a photograph of "Pop" Stenger, as he was affectionately called, and an unidentified worker. They are clearing the land to plant citrus trees. The lumber cut from the land was used to build their home. The Stengers raised a family of five boys on the property—Ralph, Louis, Max, Raymond, and John Jr. (Courtesy of Jackie Stenger Stoltz.)

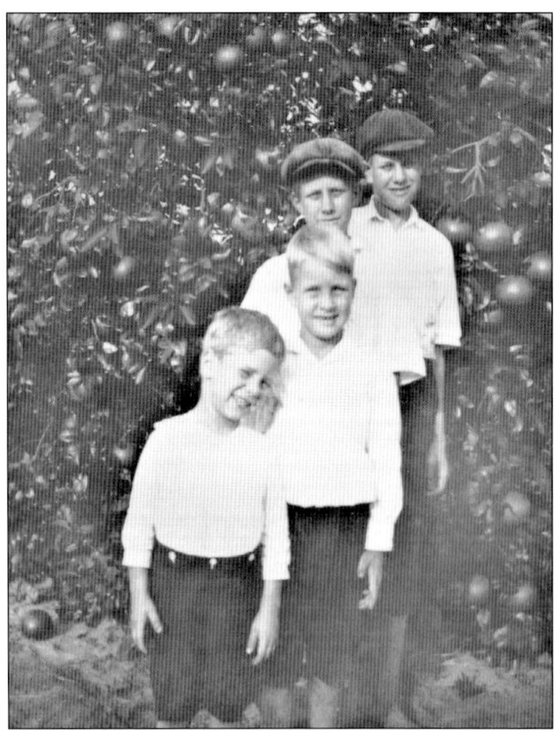

John and Olga Stenger raised a family of five boys on their Lake Garfield homestead. Four of the five boys are pictured here in this 1930s photograph. From front to back are Raymond, Max, Louis, and Ralph. The youngest child, John Jr., had yet to be born. Legend has it that the brothers, who were notorious for pulling pranks on one another, talked John Jr. into jumping off the barn with a carriage umbrella. Needless to say, it was not a good ending. (Courtesy of Jackie Stenger Stoltz.)

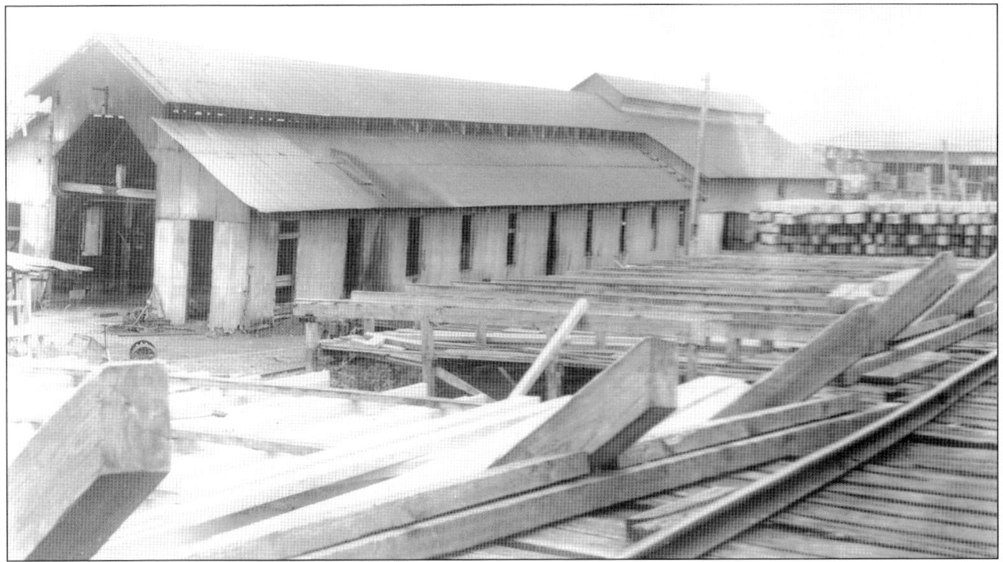

The Roux Crate and Lumber Company maintenance shop had a railroad spur that ran into this building (above). The company locomotives were driven into the shop for both major and minor repairs. Sawmill master mechanic J.W. Huff and his crew were responsible for repairing everything in the mill. The ramp in the foreground was used for unloading logs from the railcars. (Courtesy of W. Patrick Huff.)

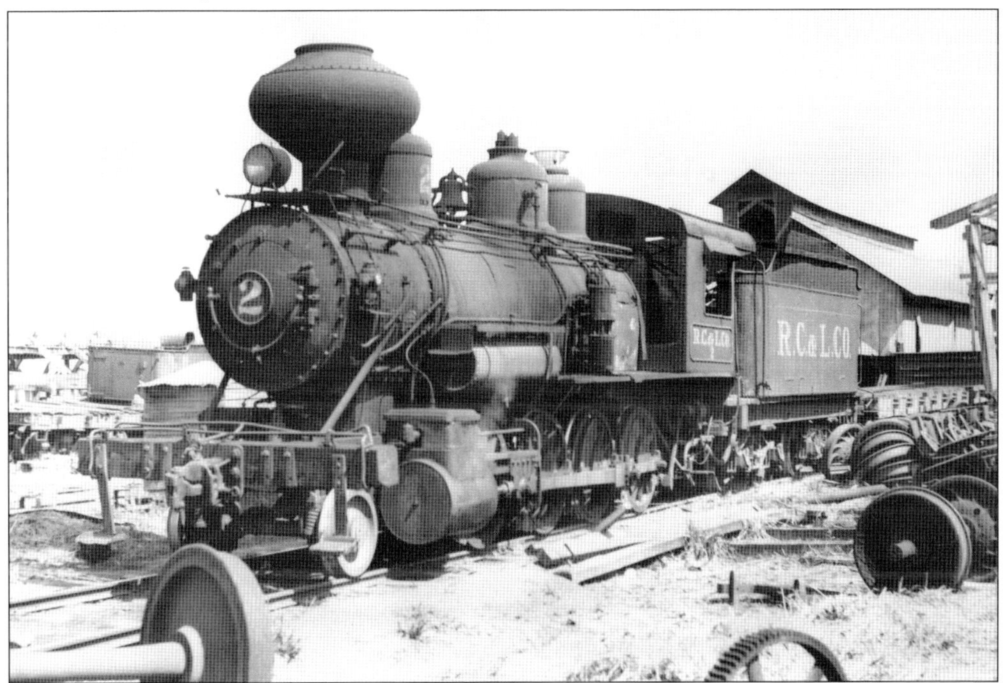

Around 1930, the Roux Crate and Lumber Company's steam engine No. 2 sits idle as it waits for empty train cars. The engine would then pull the empty cars back to the woods to load more timber for the sawmill. The locomotive is a product of Baldwin Locomotive Works. They were wood burners using scraps from the mill as fuel. This photograph pictures the engine in the final years of the mill's operation in Lake Garfield. (Courtesy of Scott Young.)

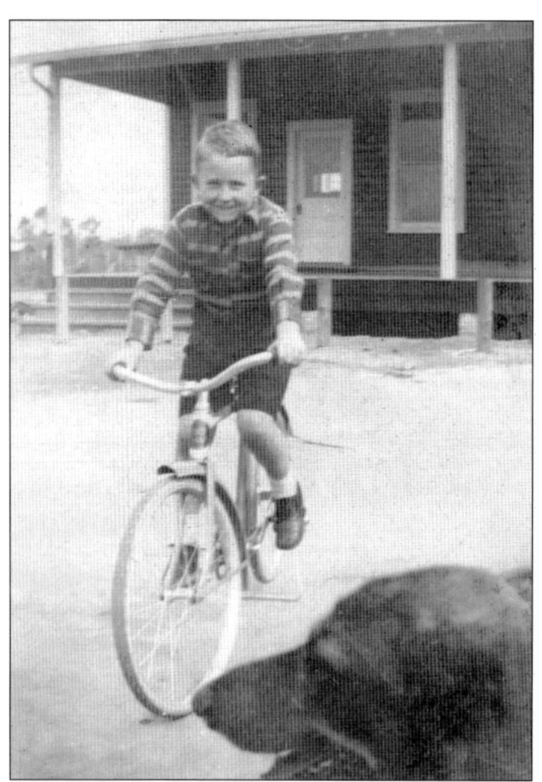

Albert Askew Beach was born on July 23, 1924, in Lake Garfield, Florida. Seven-year-old Beach is pictured here on a bicycle in 1930. His parents, Montford and Birdie Beach, a music teacher, were early settlers in Lake Garfield. Beach grew up to become a distinguished gentleman and a well-known composer and lyricist. (Courtesy of Christine and Keith Miller.)

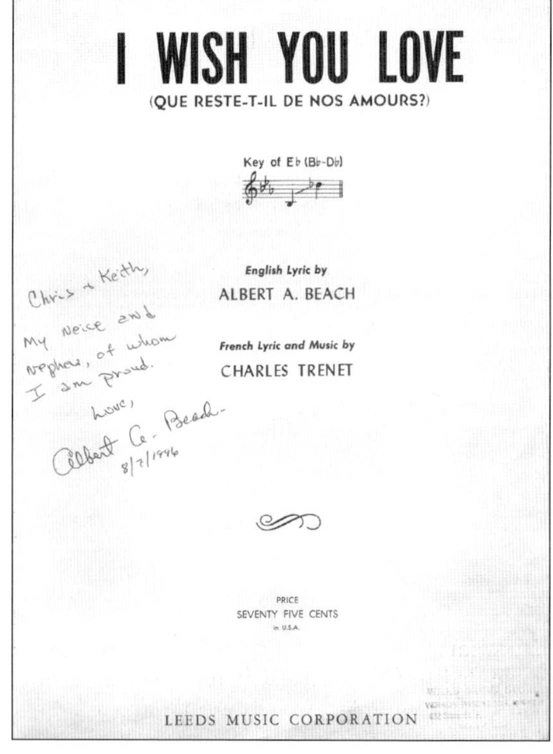

Lyrics to the famous sheet music "I Wish You Love," written by Albert A. Beach in 1946, are pictured here. Charles Trenet is credited with the melody. Over 70 artists recorded this song, including Michael Bublé, Dean Martin, Frank Sinatra, and Natalie Cole. Other songs by Beach are "The Wedding, Back Track!" (sung by Sammy Davis Jr.), "Stairway to the Sea," and "The Heel." (Courtesy of Keith and Christine Miller.)

Two

The Families

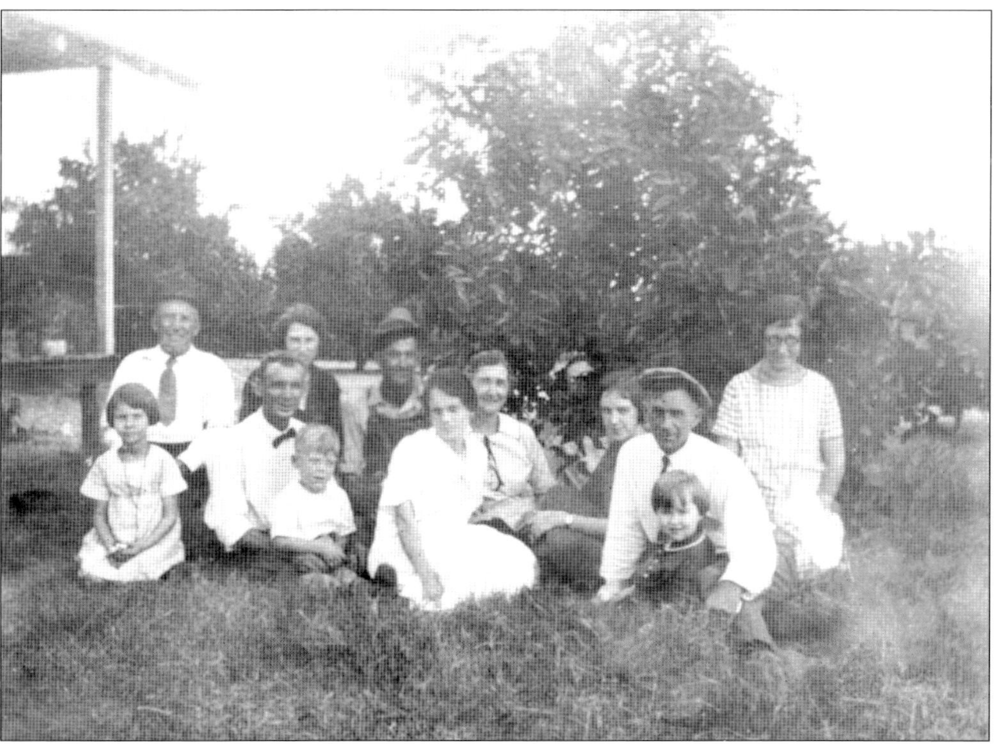

The families of Alturas and Lake Garfield have been intertwined for over 100 years. They came together to build communities rooted in faith and hard work, and friendships were forged for a lifetime. Pictured here is the Wes Gaudau family on Christmas day in the 1920s after they went for a swim in Star Lake. Pictured from left to right are (first row) Alvena Gadau, Bert Newcome, Noble Gadau, Tillie Gadau, Charlie Wiley, and Betty Thompson; (second row) Frank W. Korman, a Mrs. Thompson, Wes Gadau, Annie Newcome, Gwendolyn Boyd, and Vivian Wiley. (Courtesy of Linda Smith.)

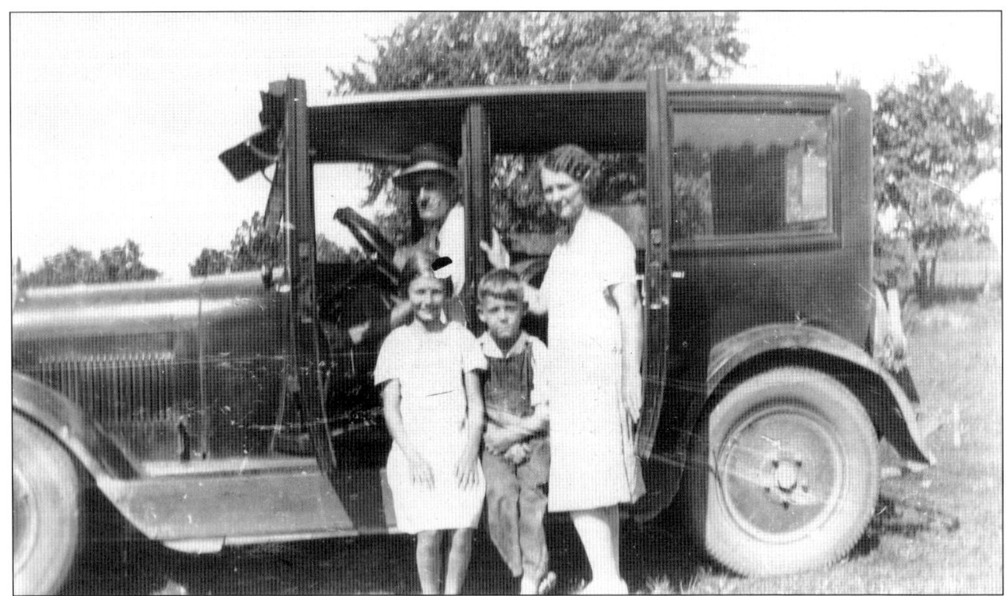

Wesley Nathaniel Gadau was so proud of his brand new four-door sedan, which he was able to afford from the sale of his profitable citrus harvest in 1928. Prior to the purchase of this vehicle, Gadau's regular mode of transportation was with his mule and wagon. Pictured in the photograph are his wife, Ethel, and his children, Alvena (11 years old) and Noble (eight years old). (Courtesy of Linda King.)

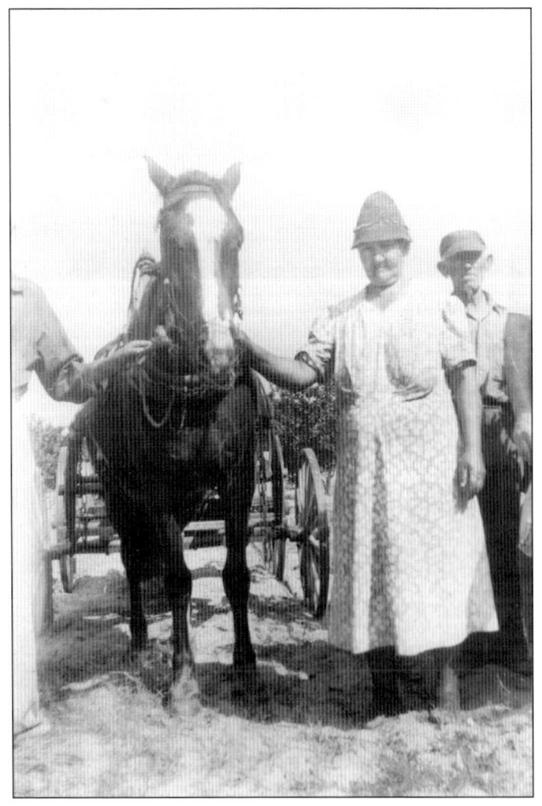

William and Rosalie Wojteczko are pictured here in 1940, working in their citrus groves. Like them, many Polish families moved to Alturas around 1910. They settled near Walker Lake, in southern Alturas. Some of the families were the Wojteczkos, Barushes, Golens, Lozarkos, Gornokskis, Odowskis, Serdynskis, Petrenkos, and the Aprilettis. Andrew Lozarkos purchased property in Alturas sight unseen in the early 1920s. William Serdynski and Amedeo Apriletti owned a service station at the "Y" on Alturas Babson Park Cut-off Road during the 1930s. Many of the families raised cattle, grew citrus, and were successful pioneers of the Alturas community. (Courtesy of Mary Lou Young.)

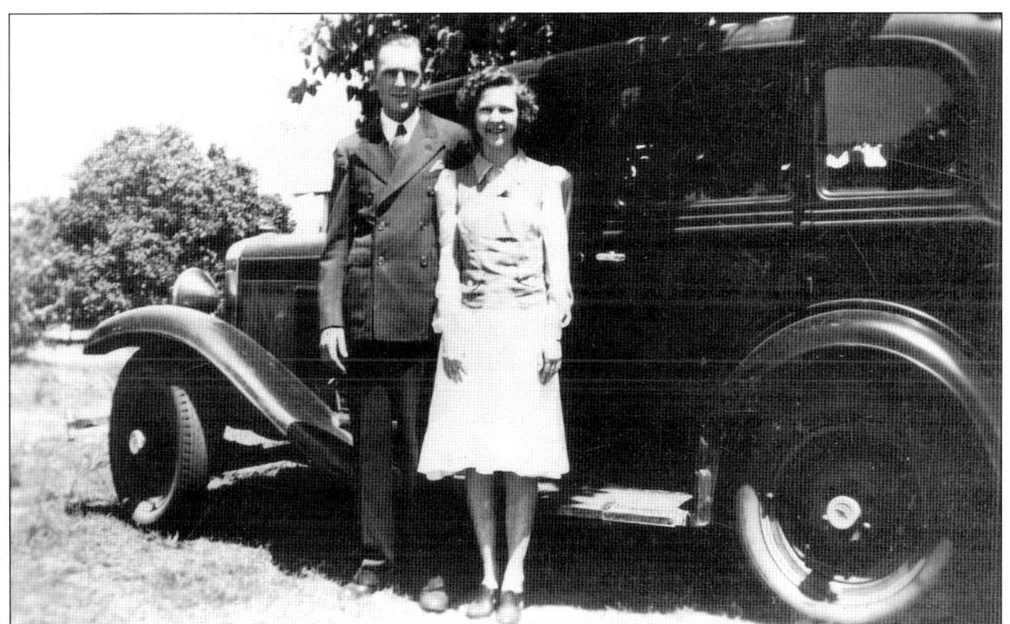

Both William (Wincenty—his Polish name) Wojteczko and his wife-to-be, Rosalie Oswieski, came from Russian Poland in 1890 but met later in Pittsburg at a fair, marrying three days later. Due to the bad environment from the coal mines, Rosalie's first six children died young. The doctor told the Wojteczkos to move if they planned to have more children. After a real estate agent showed them land in Alturas, Florida, they moved to the area around 1912. Rosalie had five more healthy children: Adam, Adolph, Alice, Mary, and Joseph. (Courtesy of Mary Lou Young.)

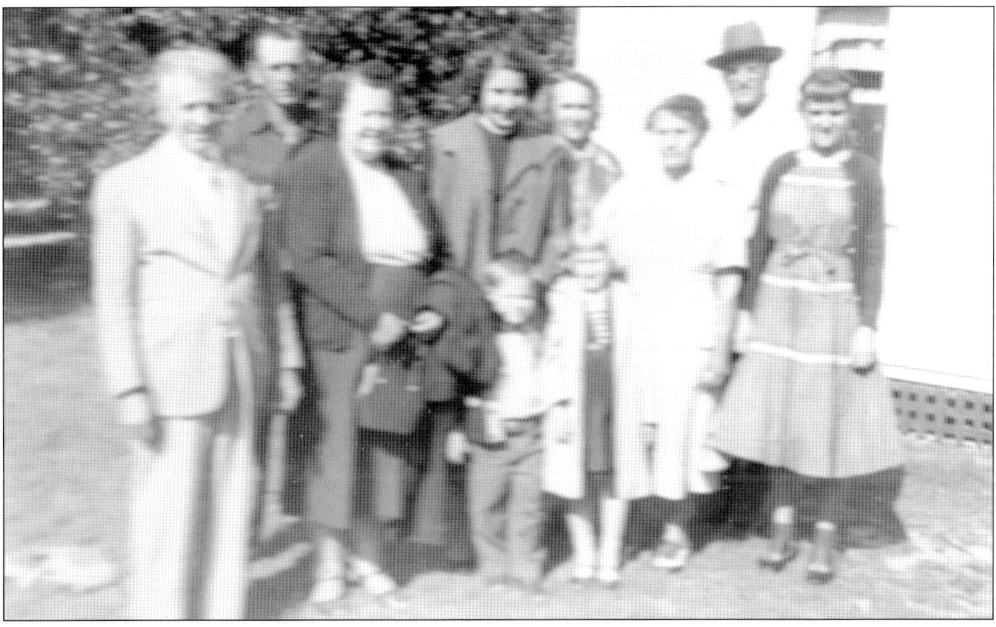

In April 1955, siblings Mary Lou and Bobby Werner of Alturas were baptized at the Catholic church in Bartow. Pictured from left to right are Amedeo Apriletti, Adolph Wojteczko, Mary Lazarko Apriletti, Marion Apriletti, Alice Petrenko, Mary Barush, John Petrenko, and Blanche Petrenko. Bobby and Mary Lou Werner are the children in front. (Courtesy of Mary Lou Young.)

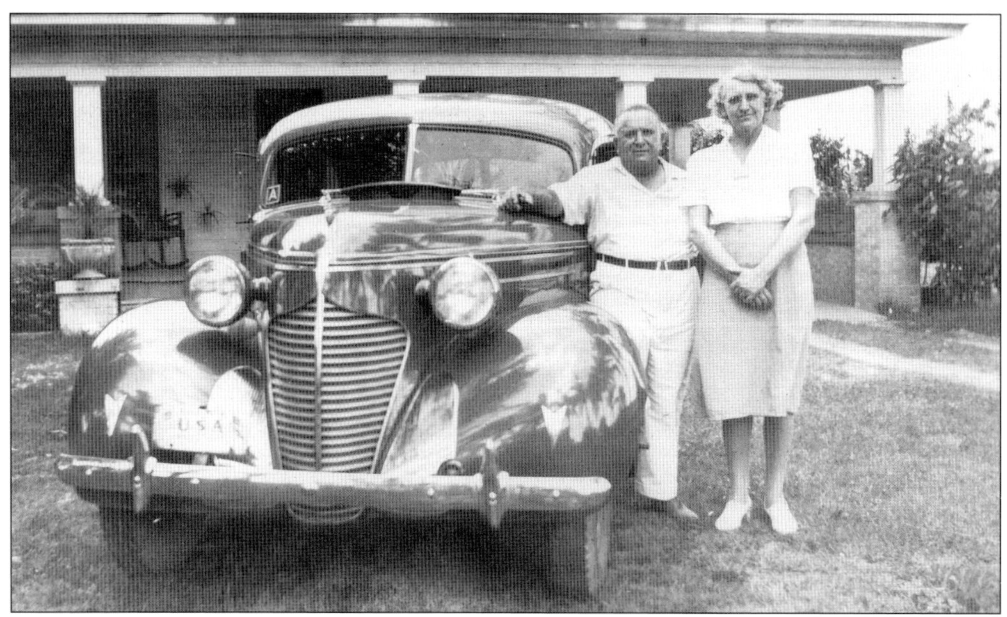

Victor Voigt turned his sights toward Alturas in 1908 when he traveled to the area from West Salem, Illinois, with a real estate tour, led by a good friend. Recently widowed, he found inspiration in the land and possibilities for the future, purchasing 20 acres while in Florida. Over the next 12 years, he made trips to Alturas as often as possible and began preparations to relocate to the area. Ultimately, he sold the original acreage and chose a smaller 10-acre lakefront parcel on the west side of Star Lake. In 1920, by now married to Della Mary Oelze Voigt, the couple moved to Alturas with son Clifford (from Voigt's previous marriage) and their infant son Edward. In the years that followed, they had two more sons, Richard and John. Above, in this 1943 photograph, Voigt and his wife, Della, are standing beside their 1935 Hudson in front of the home he built. In the 1945 photograph below, the couple stands with their two younger sons, John and Richard. (Both, courtesy of John A. Voigt.)

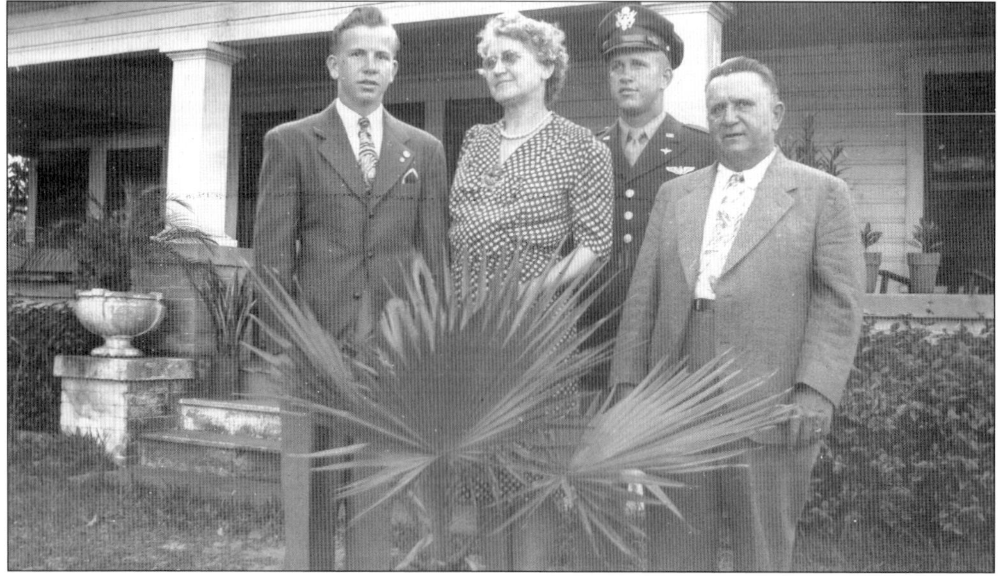

Victor E. Voigt and Alturas Methodist pastor Joseph E. Woodard enjoy a game of shuffleboard in the Voigts' side yard in 1940. Voigt took pride in his shuffleboard court and delighted in sharing the novelty of it with friends and family. He had a natural ability in carpentry and used his skills to build many of the local homes and structures. For a number of years, Voigt's youngest son, John, worked with him and became an accomplished craftsman. (Courtesy of John A. Voigt.)

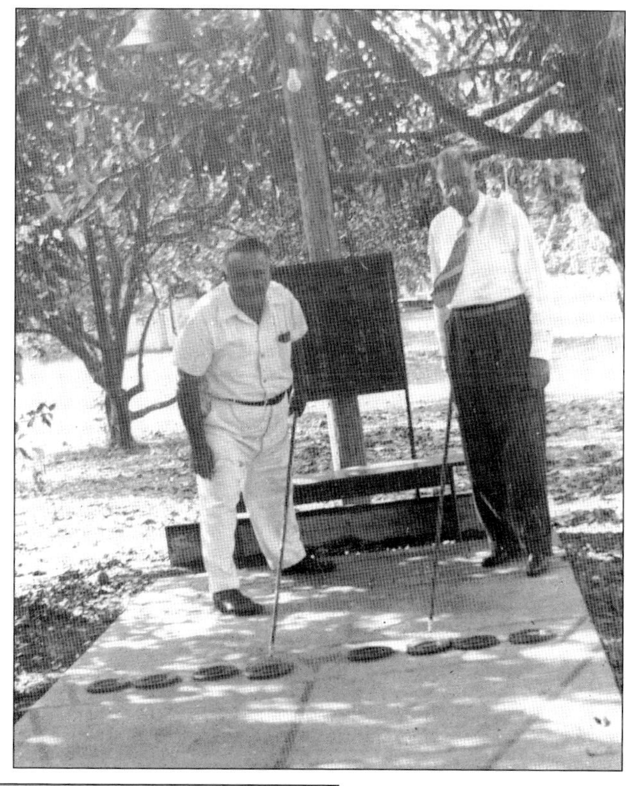

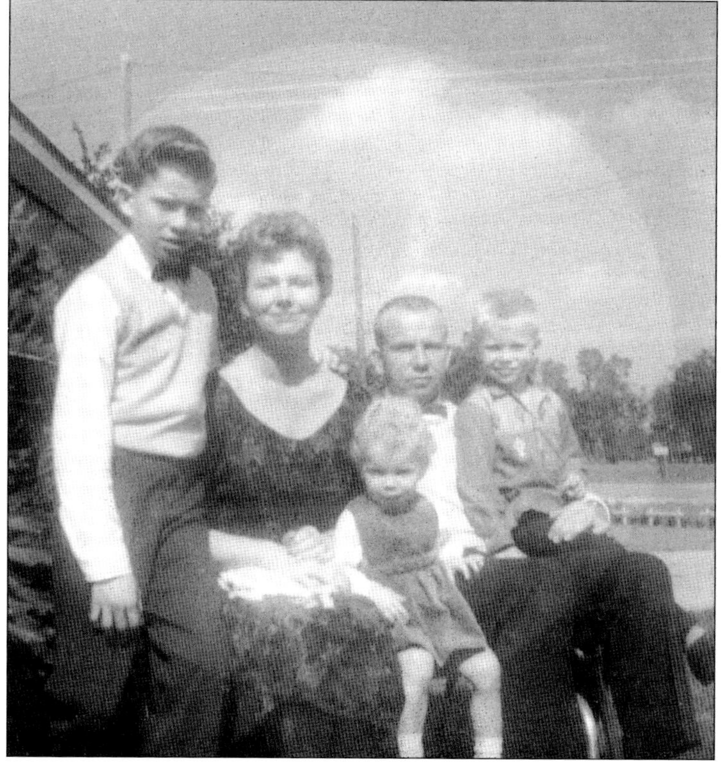

This 1962 photograph shows John Voigt with his family, including his wife, Bessie Forster Voigt, and their children, John Thomas, William Forster, and Mary Christine. The 92-year-old John now lives on part of the Alturas land his father purchased over 100 years ago. John has been married to his second wife, Vida Ray Voigt, for over 45 years. His carpentry skills have been a lifelong source of pleasure for him, and his works have become treasures to his family and friends. (Courtesy of John A. Voigt.)

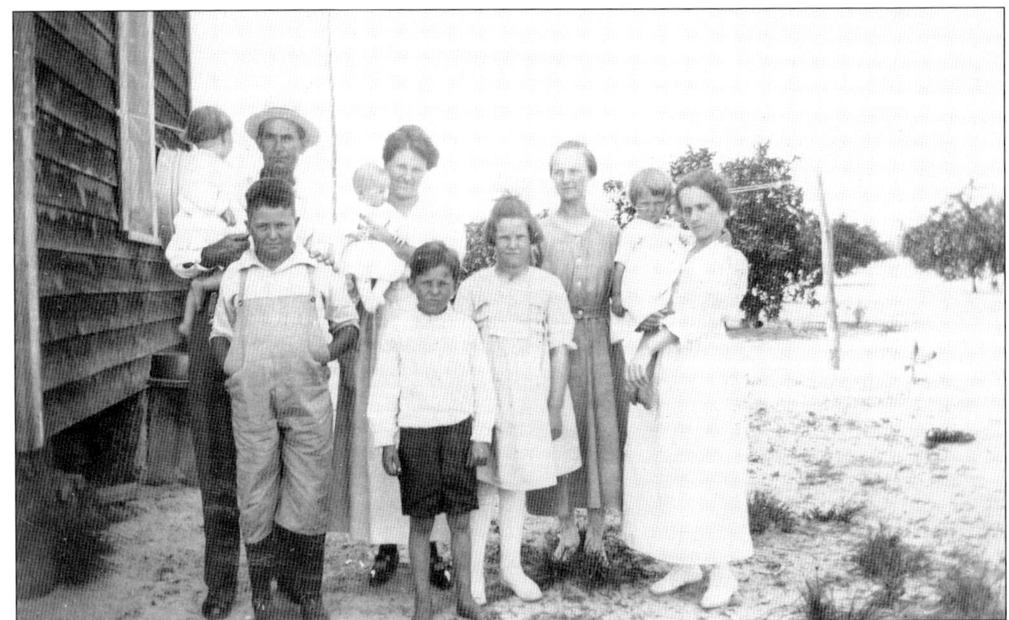

The Rudolph "Rude" A. Voigt family was one of the original settlers in the Alturas community. This 1919 photograph pictured Rude and his wife, Bertha, with all five children. From left to right are Bobby, Carlton, Margarite, Marvin, and Bunk. Also standing with the Voigt family are Ethel Gadau and her daughter Alvena in the arms of Tillie Gadau. (Courtesy of Linda King.)

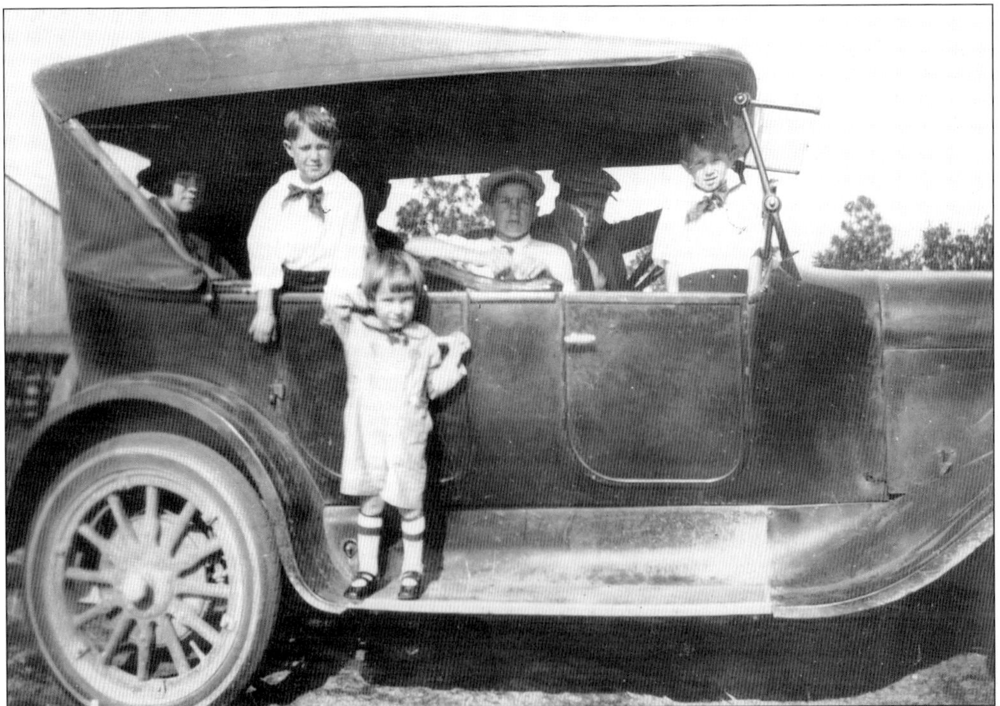

The children of Rudolph A. Voigt are sitting in their 1923 Dodge in this photograph taken in 1925. Pictured are, from left to right, Marguerite, Bob, Verdon, Allen, R.A., and Carldon Voigt. Also pictured is a cousin, Sylva Swartz, standing on the running board. (Courtesy of Karen Kelly.)

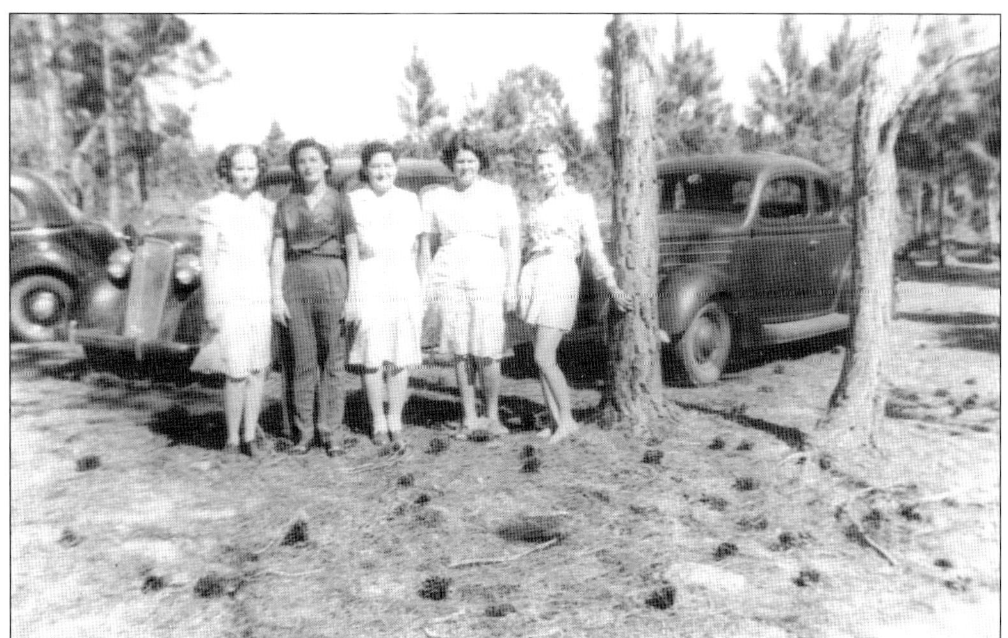

The nearby Pembroke Blueberry Creek, south of Lake Garfield, was a popular place for picnics in 1946. These five lovely sisters-in-law posed for a photograph while picnicking with their husbands. Virginia Sandh married Allen Voigt, Anna Louise McLeroy married Robert "Bob" Voigt; Guynnell Ballentine married Carlton Voigt, Marguerite Voigt married Fred Smith, and Juanita Frost married W.L. "Bunk" Voigt. (Courtesy of Teresa Skeen.)

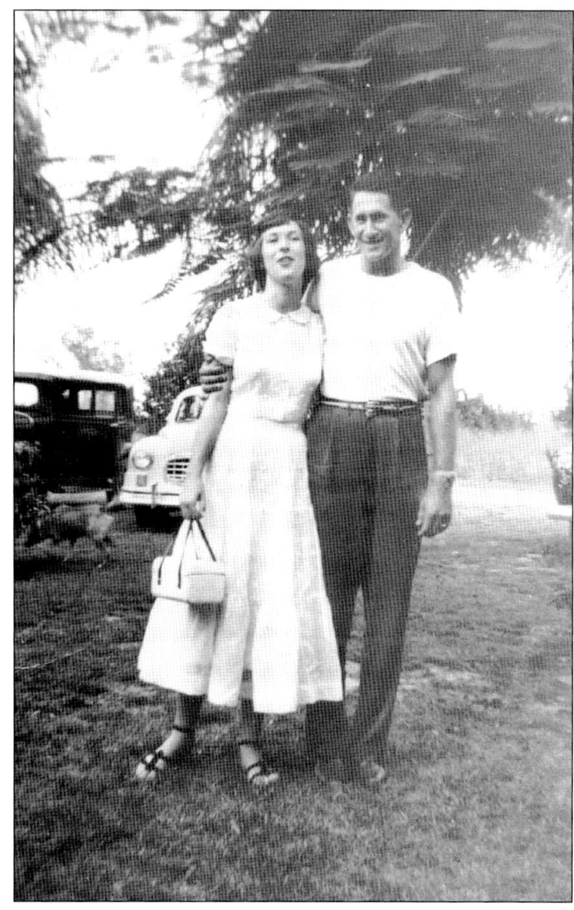

Doris Seng and Marvin Voigt are returning home from their honeymoon in Havana, Cuba, in this September 1950 photograph. Marvin was involved in the citrus industry in Alturas, and Doris opened an upscale dress shop in Bartow, Florida, named Seng's. They had two children, Janelle and Randy. Many years after a divorce, Doris married Isaac Albritton in 1989 after his wife, Nita, passed away. (Courtesy of Teresa Skeen.)

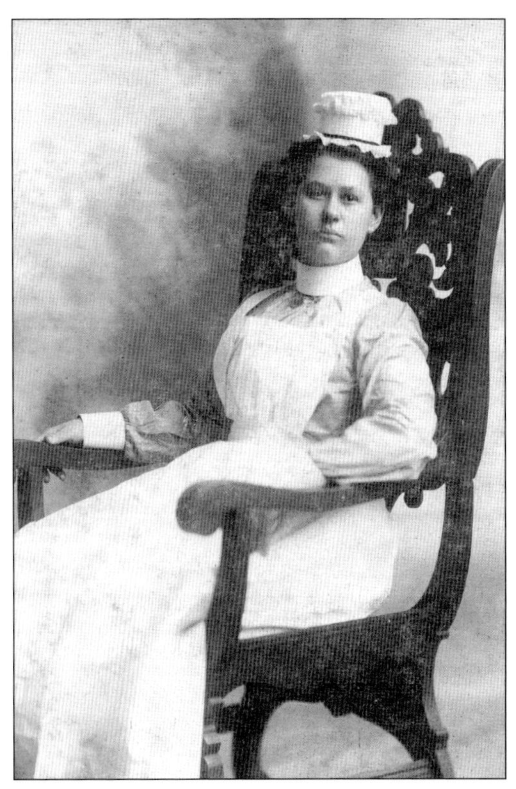

Nurse Nellie Voigt Swartz, Rudolph Voigt's sister, graduated from the Mayfield Institution in 1904. She and husband, Ira Patterson Swartz, moved to Alturas in the 1920s. They built a prefabricated home on the north side of Star Lake, which was ordered from the Sears, Roebuck and Company. An infant girl was left on their doorstep, and they adopted her in 1925. They named her Sylva. The magnolia tree the Swartzes planted in the yard is still there to this day. (Courtesy of Karen Kelly.)

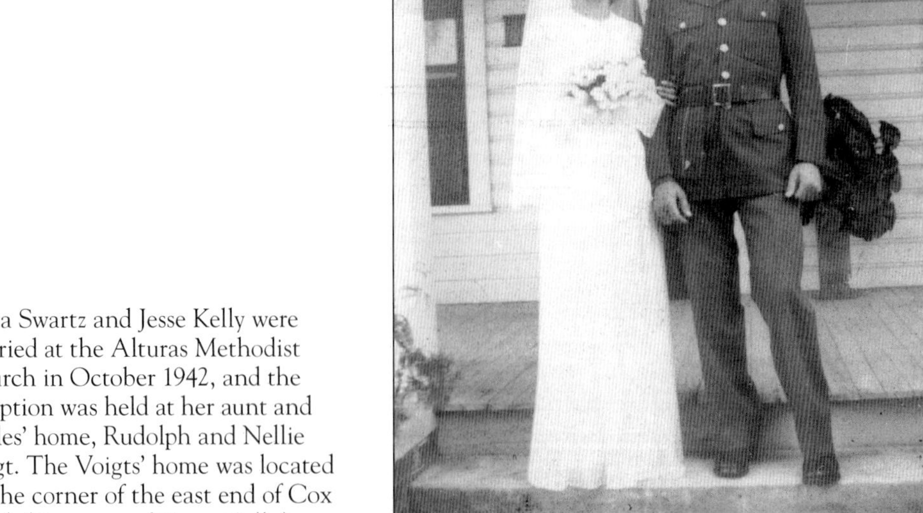

Sylva Swartz and Jesse Kelly were married at the Alturas Methodist Church in October 1942, and the reception was held at her aunt and uncles' home, Rudolph and Nellie Voigt. The Voigts' home was located on the corner of the east end of Cox Road. (Courtesy of Karen Kelly.)

On Christmas morning in 1955, Grandmother Nellie Voigt Swartz, 80 years old, gave these cute outfits to her grandchildren. Wayne Kelly received a military uniform, and Karen Kelly is wearing an Annie Oakley outfit. (Courtesy of Karen Kelly.)

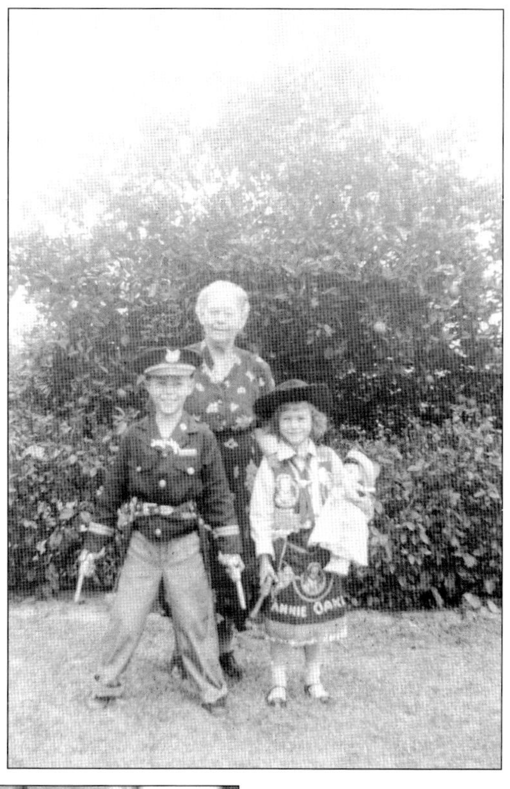

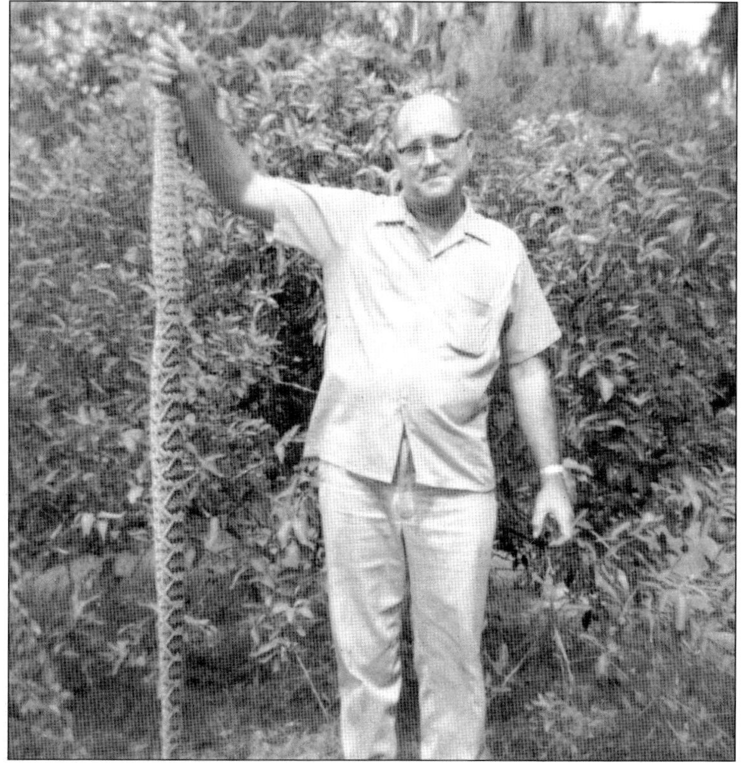

At six feet tall, Bunk Voigt is seen holding up a seven-foot rattlesnake in this 1925 photograph. Rattlesnakes are very venomous and can often be found hiding near palmetto bushes in the hot Florida pastures. Bunk was the youngest son of Rudolph A. and Bertha Voigt and was an Army veteran of World War II. He married Juanita Frost on April 7, 1943, and they had two girls, Cheryl and Teresa. Voigt owned citrus groves in Alturas and was a member of the Alturas Methodist Church. (Courtesy of Teresa Skeen.)

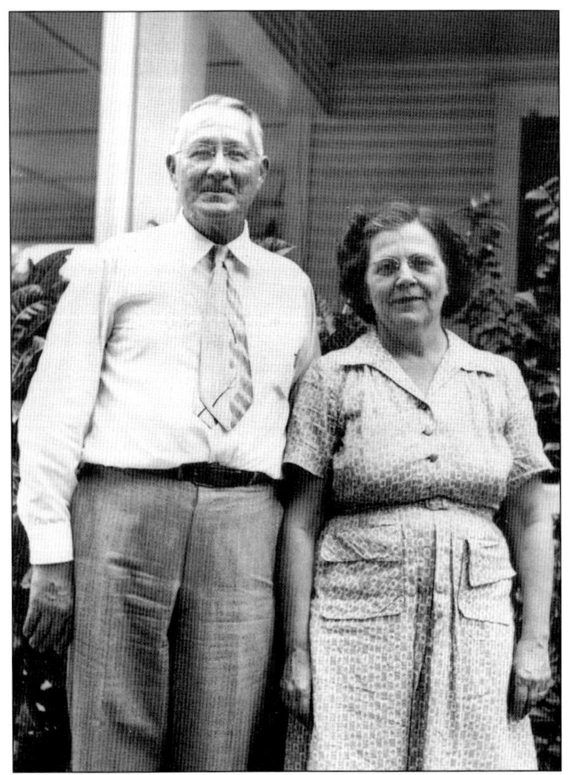

Isbon Jefferson "I.J." Godwin, the youngest of 18 children, and Dorothy Bertha Frances Godwin are standing in front of their Alturas home, which was located across the road from the Alturas Woman's Club. The house was built in 1915 and was already there when the Godwins moved to Alturas from Fort Meade (Breah) in the early 1930s. I.J., along with his two brothers, opened the Southern Fruit Exchange Packing House, whose name was later changed to the Central Fruit Company. Unfortunately, it burned down in the late 1930s. Dorothy was a schoolteacher at Fort Meade Elementary. She graduated from Florida State University when it was an all-girls school. After Dorothy died in 1968, widowed Godwin was invited to move in with his daughter Virginia Godwin Gabriel and her husband, Tommy. His son Jake and his wife, Linda Stringer Gabriel, moved into Godwin's old homeplace. (Courtesy of Mary Nell Gabriel Smith.)

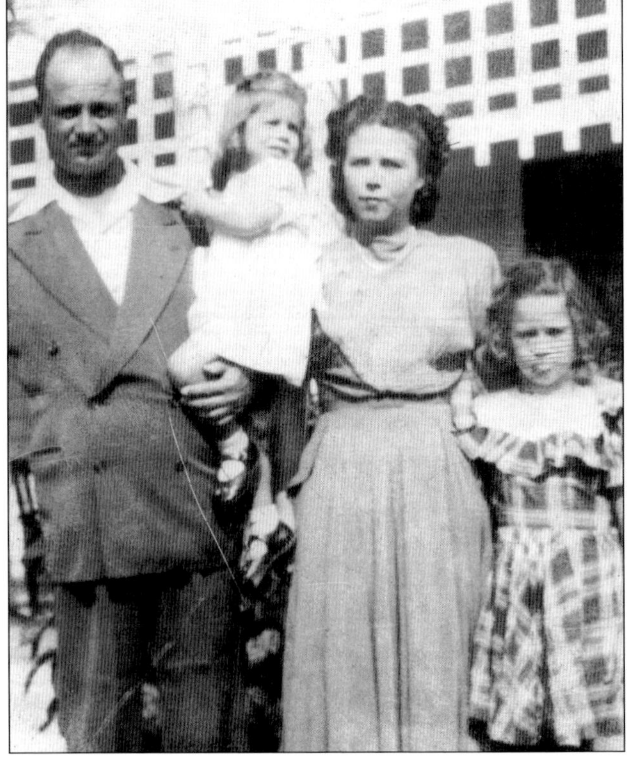

Tommy Gabriel moved from Georgia to Fort Meade, Florida, in the mid-1930s. He and Dorothy Virginia Godwin (known as Virginia) married in 1940. This is a 1948 picture of Gabriel and Virginia with their infant daughter, Dinah Kay, and oldest child, Mary Nell. The middle child, Jake, is not pictured. The family lived in Bartow, Florida, where Tommy sold insurance for Gulf Life and worked at Bartow Ford. They moved to Alturas in 1945 to help Dorothy's father, I.J. Godwin, with his citrus groves. In 1950, Tommy bought I.J.'s company, which was located behind Smith's Texaco Service station, and renamed it Gabriel Grove Service. In 1979, he moved the company one mile north to the Alturas Loop Road. In 1999, Tommy sold his company to Bohde Grove Service. (Courtesy of Mary Nell Gabriel Smith.)

Mary Nell Gabriel and her brother I.J. "Jake" Gabriel Jr. were children of Tommy and Dorothy Virginia Godwin Gabriel. This photograph was taken in 1947 in front of the Godwin homeplace, the children's maternal grandparents. The home was located beside the Alturas Elementary School and across the road from the Alturas Woman's Club. (Courtesy of Mary Nell Gabriel Smith.)

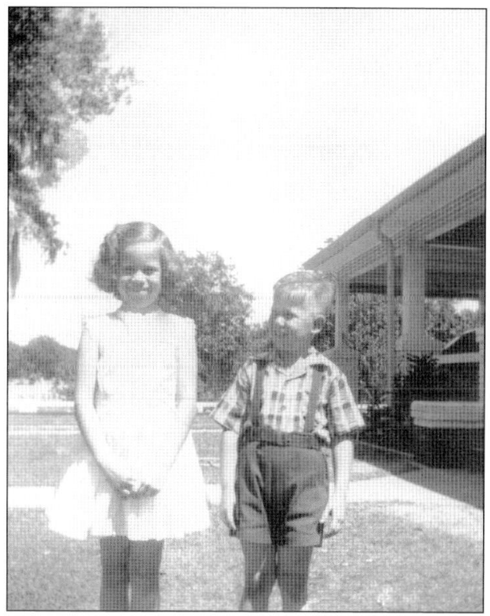

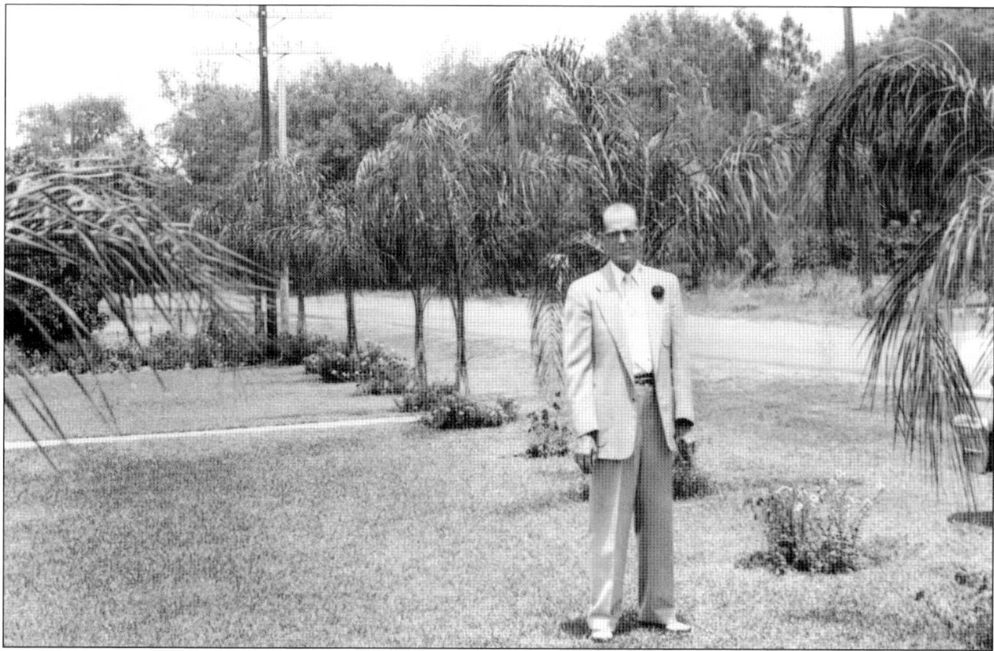

Joe Perdue is standing in front of his Alturas home in the 1960s. He built the home in 1947 and lived there with his wife, Clara, and daughter Wanda Jean. Perdue and his brother Roy moved to Alturas from Georgia in the 1920s, when the boll weevil killed the family's cotton crops. A few years later, their parents, William Henry and Savannah Georgia Anderson, along with several of their 12 siblings, James, Lilly, and Theo, followed them to Alturas. In 1926, the two brothers, as employees of the Come Construction Company, paved the roads in Alturas. Roy became a successful rancher, citrus grower, and one of the founders of the Alturas Packing Company. Roy married Ruth Patton and had one son, John William "J.W." In the early years, Joe Perdue worked for Roy driving a truck hauling fruit. Eventually, he was successful in the citrus industry as well. (Courtesy of Scott Young.)

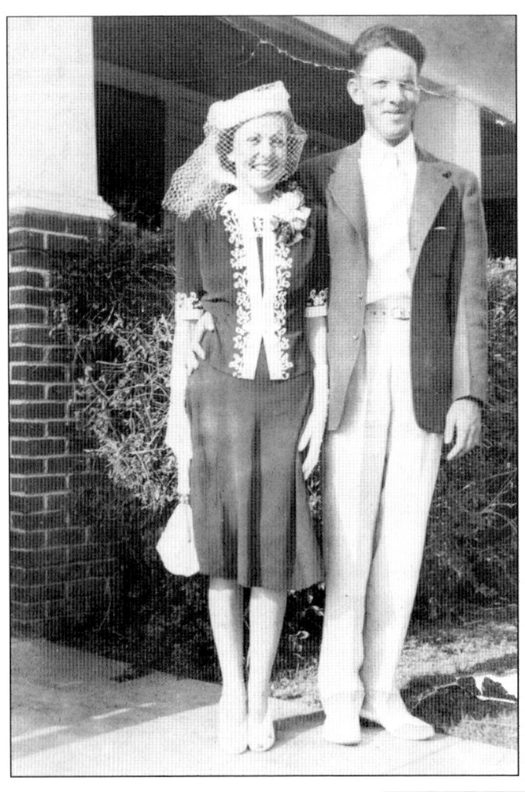

Lawrence Estes moved to Alturas from Haines City in the early 1930s to enter the citrus business. He married Adele Jackson shortly thereafter, and they had one daughter, Diane. Adele tragically died in an automobile accident in 1939. Estes met Inez Ray while stopping to buy a Coke at the Connersville Grocery Store. She was working behind the counter, and it was love at first sight. This photograph was taken on their wedding day in April 1940. The couple raised five daughters: Diane, Gloria, Linda, Rosemary, and Connie. (Courtesy of Rosemary Estes.)

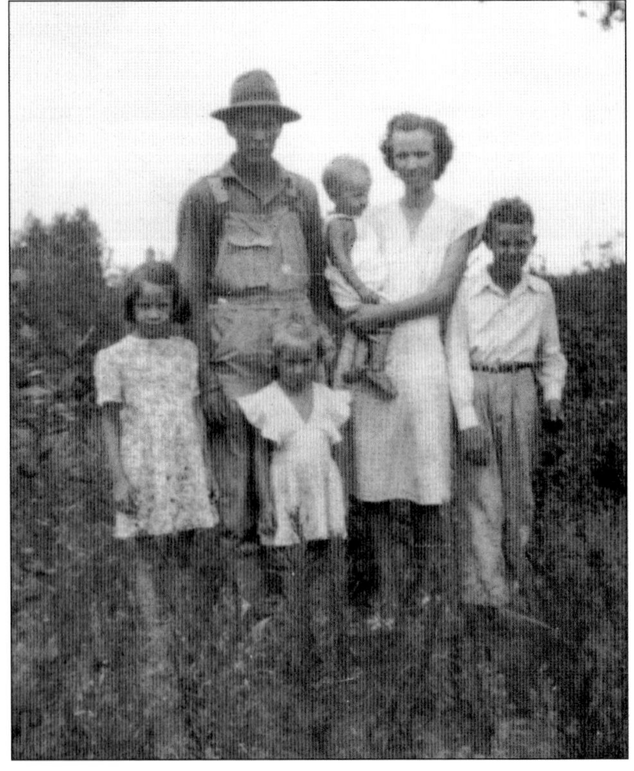

Dudley Sowell and his wife, Elizabeth "Lizzie" Lanier Sowell, moved to Alturas from Alabama with their three children, Arnold, Anise, and Sharon, in the early 1940s, They later had a son, Elon Dudley Sowell Jr., who was born in one of the Murphy's labor homes in Alturas, Florida, in 1947. Flora Lee Young, a nearby neighbor of the Sowells, helped with Elon's delivery. Later in life, Young would tease Elon and tell him that she was the first person to ever see him naked. Lizzie was a homemaker until Dudley died in 1955 at the age of 39. In 1960, she married Otha Watkins and worked at the Bartow Laundry and Dry Cleaners, making as much as 50¢ an hour. She later retired from Alturas Elementary School as a lunchroom lady. (Courtesy of Dudley Elon Sowell Jr.)

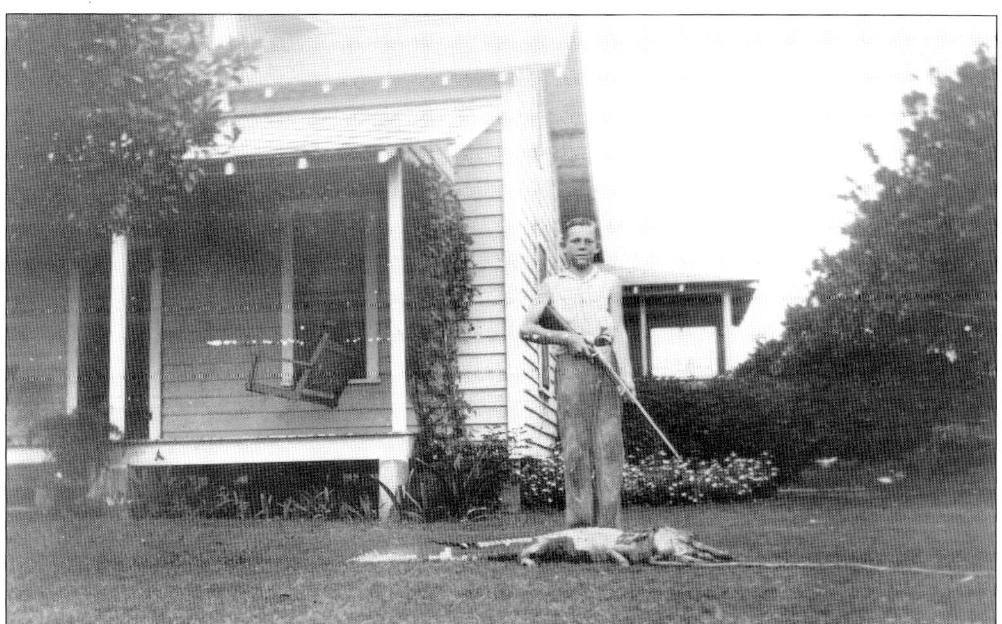

Hunting alligators was a sport in the 1930s that helped supplement meat on the kitchen table and rid the lakes of dangerous predators. Noble Gadau shot a 4.5-foot alligator in Gadau Lake (previously known as Booth Lake) in front of their home. Evidently, based on the photograph, he had to pull the alligator up the hill with a lasso rope. The Gadau house shown in the background was built in 1919. (Courtesy of Linda King.)

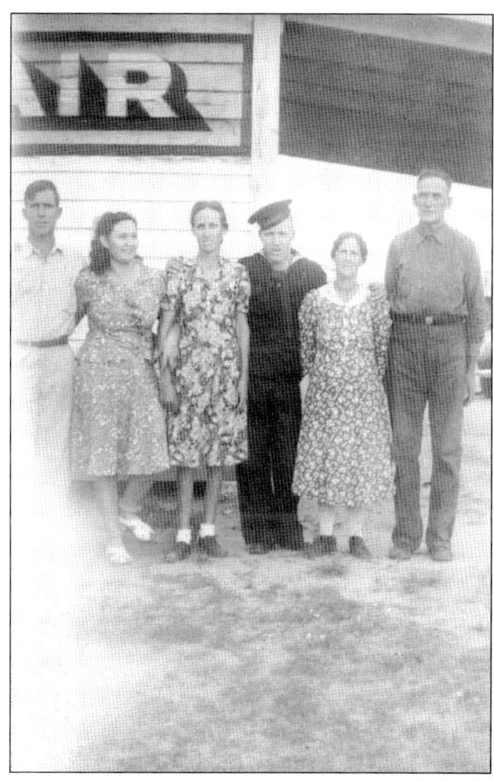

The John King family moved from Atmore, Alabama, in the late 1920s, and bought the home shown in the background. It had previously been a Sinclair store; the residents of Alturas called it Sparky Henderson's store. Note that part of the Sinclair sign is visible. In this 1944 photograph are, from left to right, Jerry Duncan "J.D." King and his wife, Edith Luna King; his sister Odesser King Scarborough; his brother Joseph King, who served in the Navy in World War II; and the King's parents, Rosie Yohn King and the Reverend John King. In addition to J.D., Odesser, and Joseph, the Kings had two more sons, James and Amos. (Courtesy of Diane King Lewellen.)

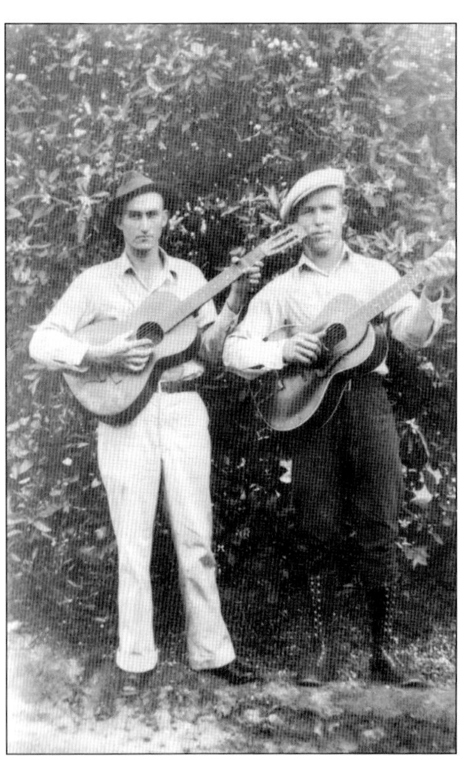

James D. King and Jesse Lee Young, whom everyone called "Shack," were friends and musical buddies as seen in this mid-1930s photograph. (Courtesy of Montez Mercer.)

Floyd Daniel Wiggins and Ila Vera McDuffie Wiggins lived in Lake Garfield and were married on the Polk County Court House steps by Judge Chester M. Wiggins (not related) on March 12, 1943. In the 1952 photograph below, Ronnie and Danny Wiggins, their two oldest children, are sitting on a vintage 1912 car. The couple had four more children, Marvin, Ralph, David, and Carol. Floyd Wiggins spent much of his career working at the Alturas Packing Company as the general manager. (Courtesy of Scott Young.)

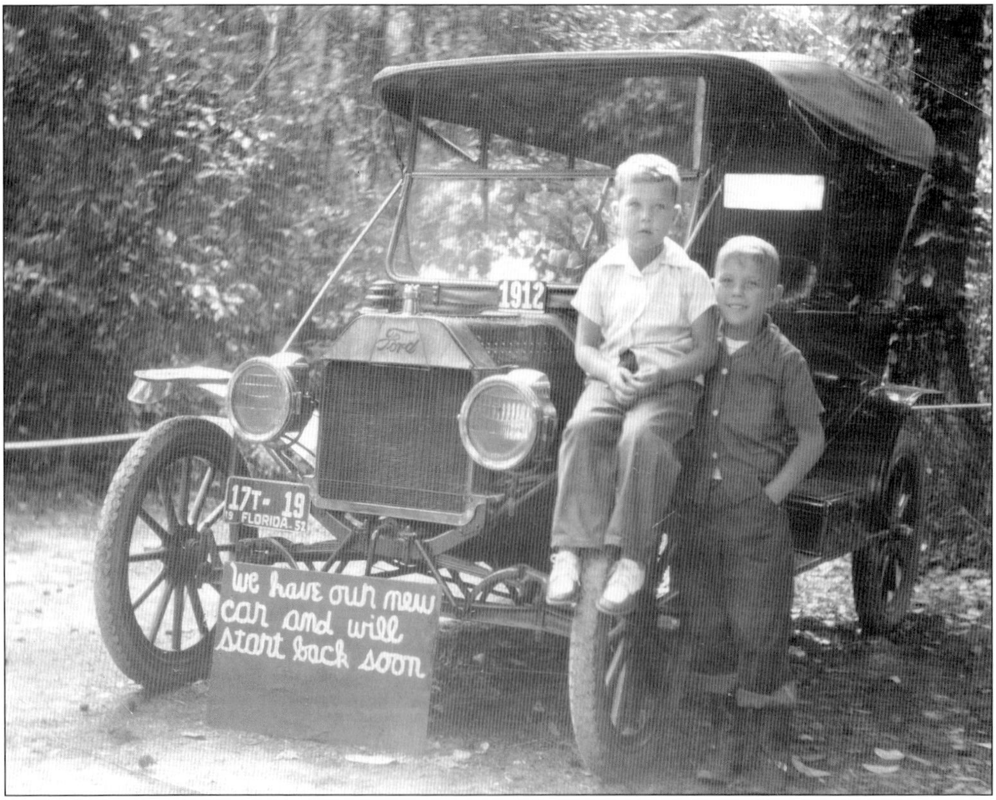

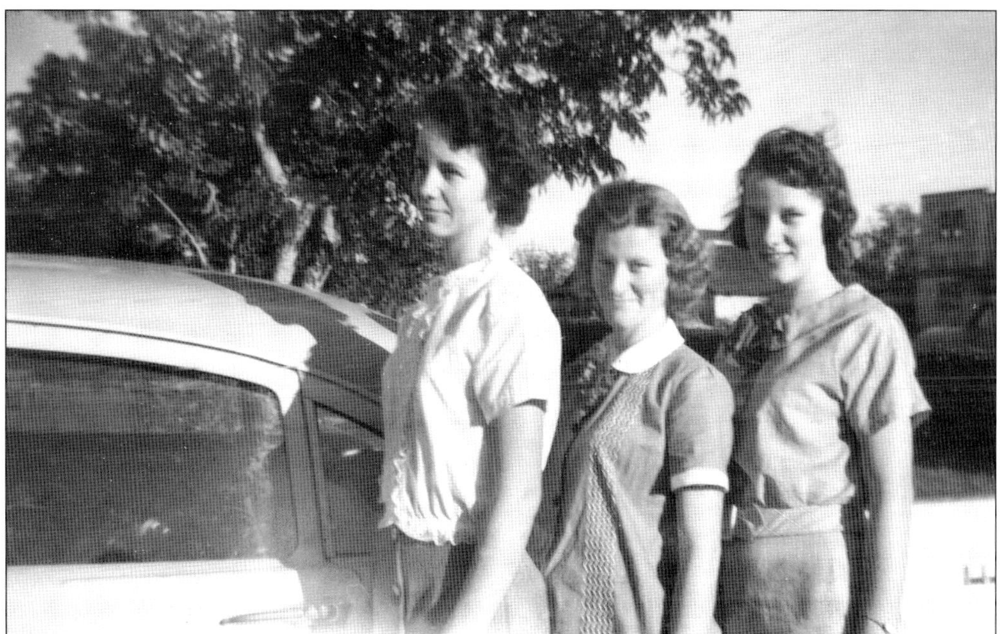

Siblings George Otto Sr., Quince, Luthor, Dan, and Mary Radford moved to Alturas to look for work around 1934. The brothers found jobs clearing land for property owners in the Reynoldsville area. George Sr. married Willie Mae Bennett, and they had four children, Peggy, Lenore, Shirley, and George Jr. The three daughters, pictured here in 1955, formed a gospel trio and were well known for their angelic voices. Most of the Radford families were charter members of the Alturas Assemblies of God Church. (Courtesy of Shirley Skipper.)

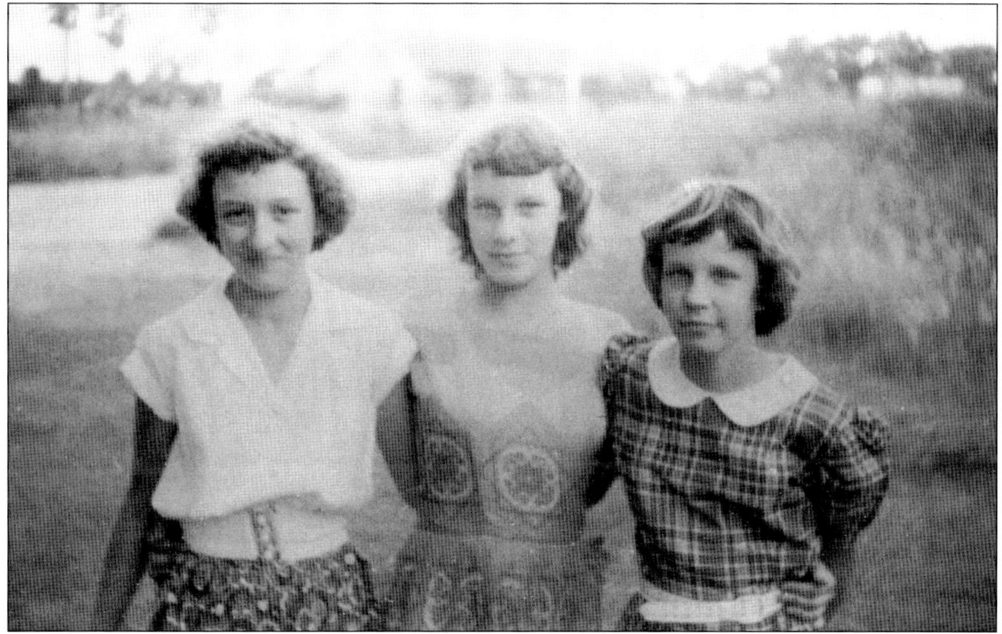

Martha June Watkins, Shirley Radford, and Anis Sowell (left to right), three best friends whose families were Alturas neighbors, are posing for the camera in this 1953 photograph. The picture was taken near the Alturas Depot, seen in the background. (Courtesy of Shirley Skipper.)

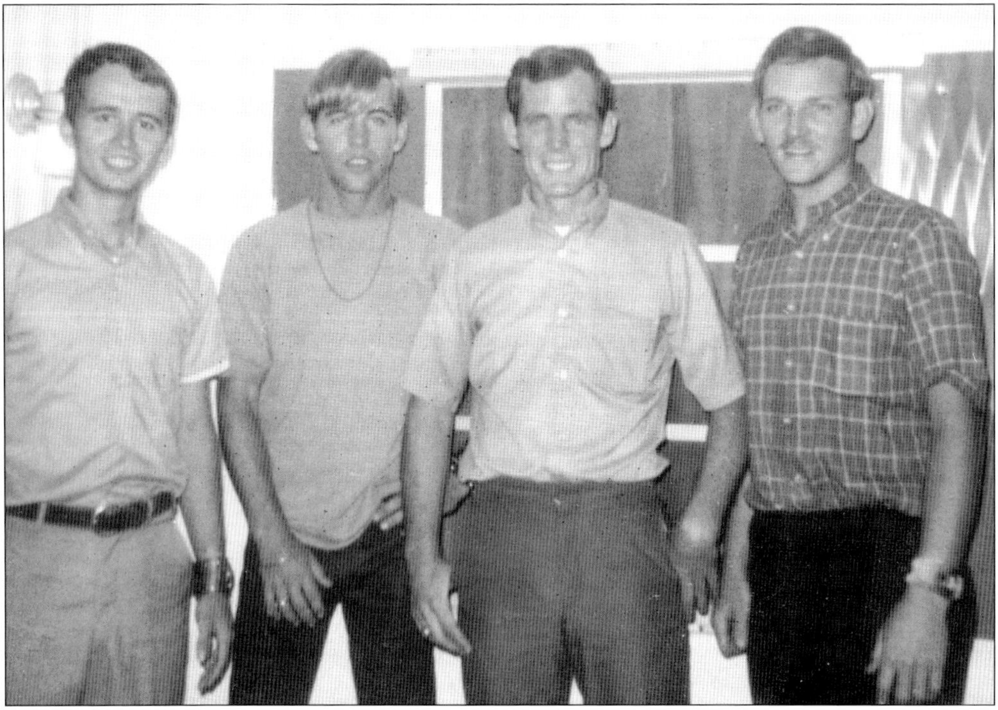

These four Alturas boys, (left to right) Roy Tyson, Wade Mincey, David Sowell, and Robert Werner, joined the Army under the "Buddy Program," which allows friends to enlist and train together. This 1969 picture, taken at Roy Tyson's house on Reynolds Road, was made the day they made the decision to enlist. They were sent to basic training together in Fort Jackson, South Carolina. After basic training, all four were stationed in the Republic of Vietnam during the war; however, they served in different units. Miraculously, all four returned home. Tyson stayed in Vietnam for two years, one month, one week, and five days and was awarded two Bronze Star Medals for valor. Mincey and Sowell served only one term, but Werner remained in the military and retired after 20 years of service. He received the Purple Heart for valor. (Courtesy of Roy Tyson.)

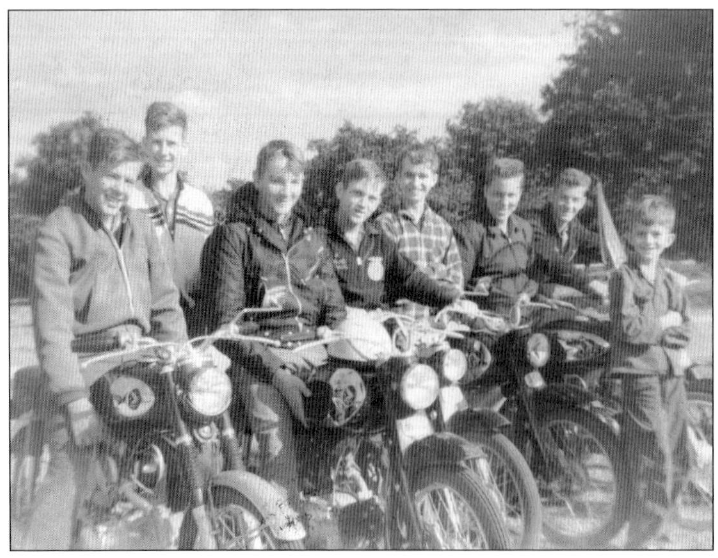

This group of Alturas teenagers rode their Honda motorcycles—some thinking they were the "Leader of the Pack"—around 1964. They were (left to right) Richard Daughtry, Bob Barker, Johnny McKinney, Robert Werner, Roy Tyson, Leon Seger, Harvey Watley, and Roy's younger brother Kenny Tyson. These young men were all 14 or 15 years old except seven-year-old Kenny. (Courtesy of Roy Tyson.)

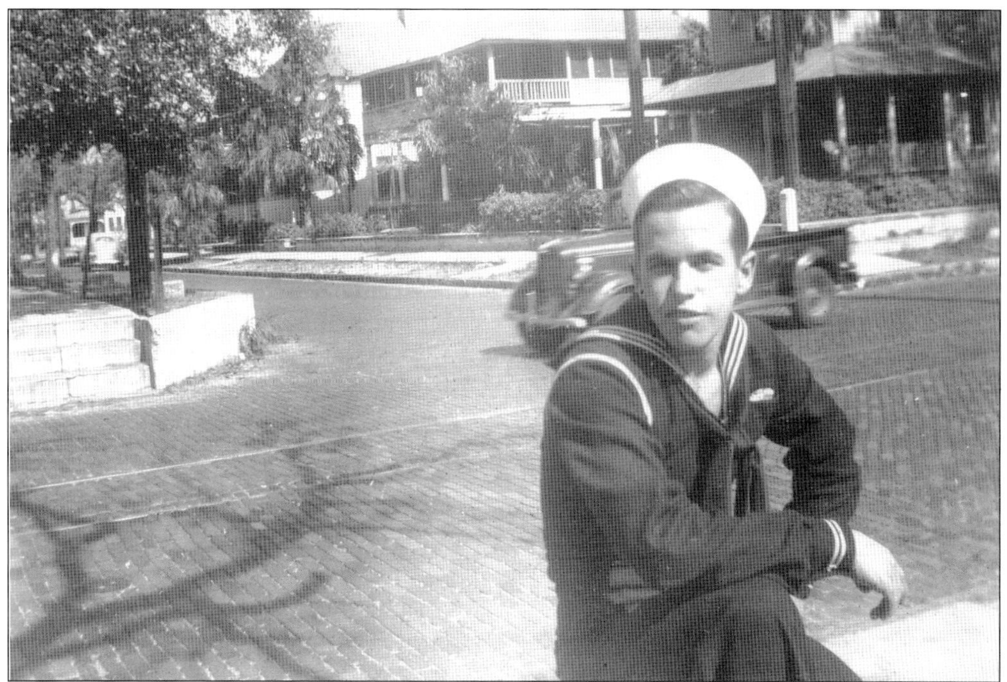

Carlton Wilbur Tyson (above) was a descendant of O.B. and E.B. Tyson, the twin brothers who were the first recorded settlers of Alturas in 1865. He was the son of Wilbur Wesley Tyson and Votie Edna McCall and was born on October 16, 1926. His wife, Hilda Wautelle Kemp (below), was the daughter of Jordan Kinchen Kemp and Annie Mae Pullen, and she was born on November 10, 1924. These two met in Bartow, Florida, after Tyson served his country in the US Navy in World War II. The couple married on May 17, 1946, and resided in Alturas on Reynold's Road. They had three sons, Jimmy Carlton (1947), Roy Jordan (1950), and Kenneth Edwin (1958). Below, Roy (left) and Kenneth (right) are pictured with their mother. (Both, courtesy of Roy Tyson.)

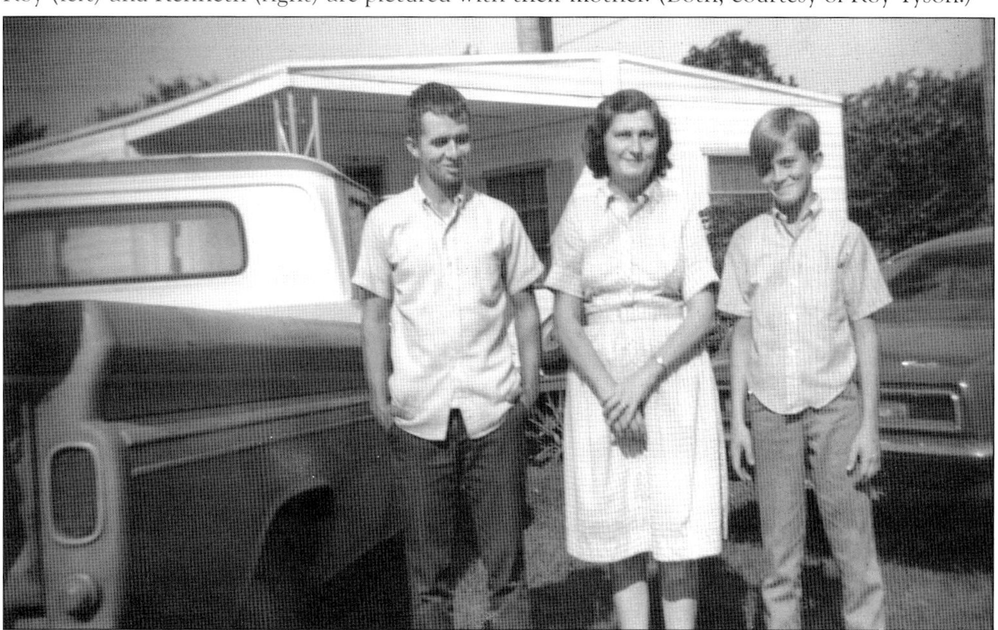

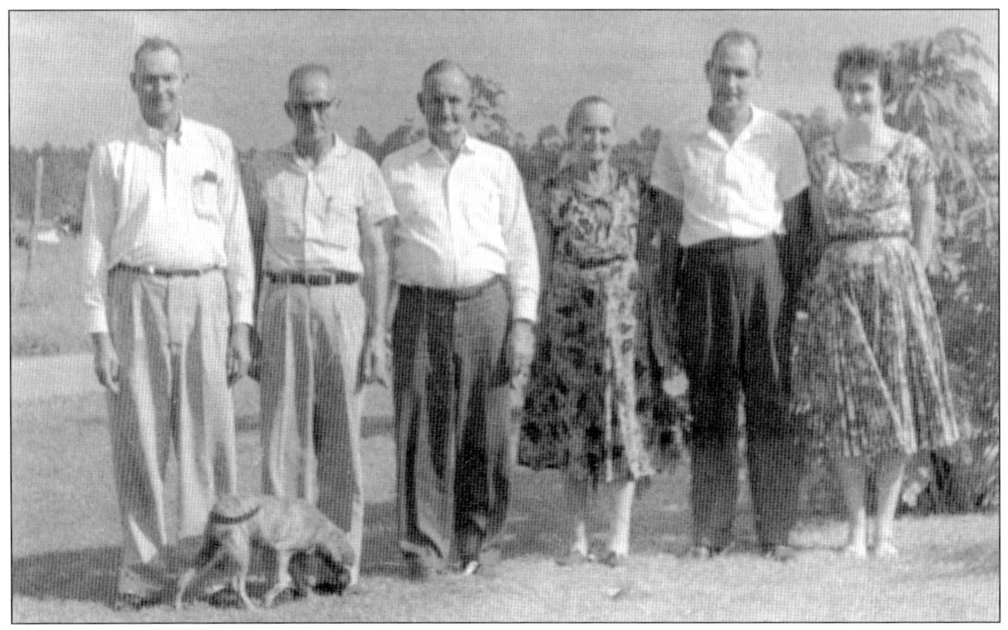

The Young family is pictured here in the 1950s. From left to right are William "Henry," Jesse Lee "Shack," Riley Monroe (father), Mary Elizabeth "Molly" Palmer (mother), Daniel Elijah "Lige," and Lillian Montez Young Mercer. In 1933, brothers Henry and Lige Young left Alabama to work for Wilton Murphy in Alturas, Florida. In 1934, their wives, children, siblings, and parents joined them. Most came by railway to Lake Wales and then made their way to find Henry and Lige. (Courtesy of Montez Y. Mercer.)

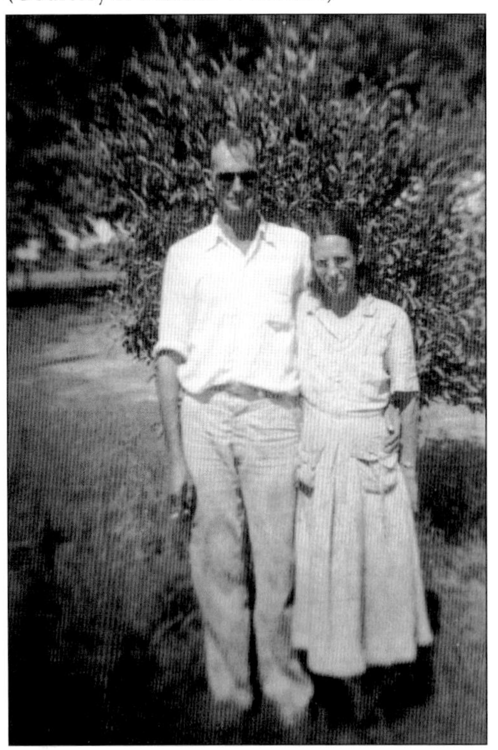

William "Henry" Young and his wife, Flora Lee Peacock Young, are pictured here in this 1940s photograph. In 1934, Flora Lee and her two small children, Evelyn and Leland, joined Young, already residing in Alturas. Henry's life work was in the citrus industry. He ran crews, picked and hauled fruit for the Pasco Packing Company, and owned a few small groves. His wife was often right by his side, working as hard as any man. Their eight children were Evelyn Alpine, Leland Kenneth, Raymurl, Virgil Glynn, James Vaughn, Flora Isaetta, Allen Wayne, and Thailia Doniece. Sadly, Glynn was killed in 1952 when his car collided with a train on Cox Road near Boggy Branch. (Courtesy of Sherry Maberry.)

Henry Young's four oldest children, from left to right, are Raymurl, Glynn (in front), Evelyn, and Leland. They are pictured here in 1938. They lived in Alturas all their lives. Evelyn served as the Alturas postmaster for 33 years, Raymurl was the Alturas Elementary School secretary for 28 years, and Leland started his own citrus company, Peace Valley Enterprise Inc. Glynn passed away at age 16. (Courtesy of Sherry Maberry.)

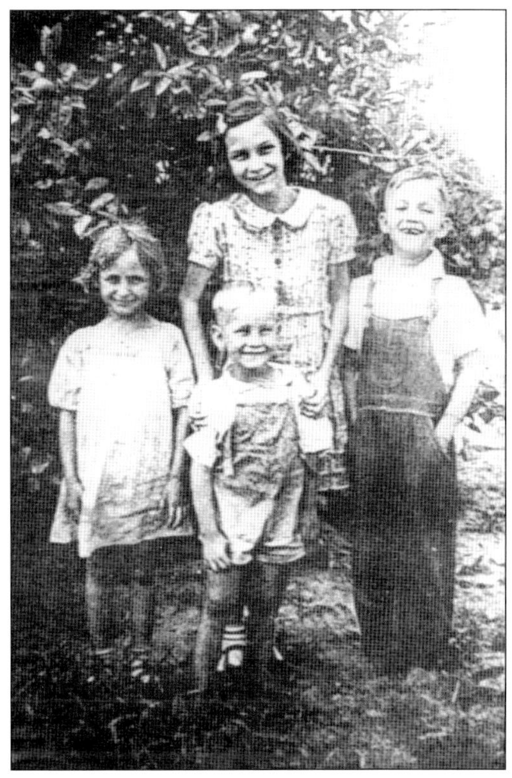

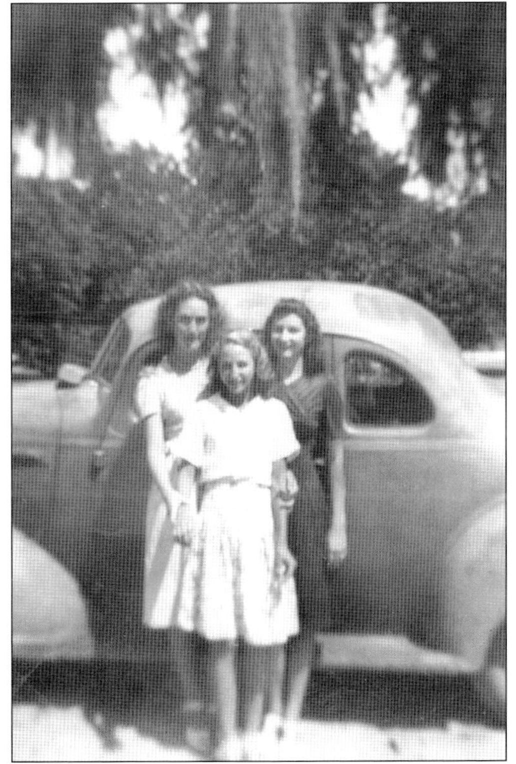

Montez Young Mercer and her two nieces Flora Young and Evelyn Young Adams are pictured from left to right in this 1953 photograph. These Alturas relatives were "thick as thieves." Evelyn married Alturas cowboy Corbet Adams in 1949. (His parents were Samuel Paul and Shadie Adams, Alturas grove owners.) After a divorce, she married Merlin R. Hielscher in 1954. Flora married Harold Graddy in 1959; she later married George Conley in 1992. Montez married Edwin E. Mercer in 1947. (Courtesy of Sherry Maberry.)

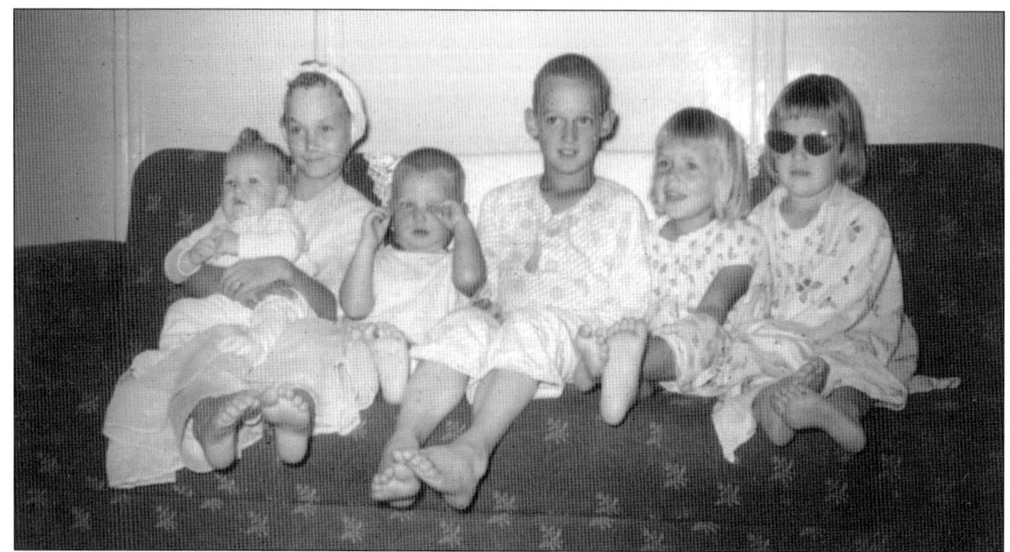

Edwin Eugene Mercer and Lillian Montez Young, daughter of Riley and Molly Palmer Young, Alturas residents, married on June 6, 1947. As an Air Force officer, Edwin took his family with him on location. He served in World War II, Korea, and Vietnam. After retiring from the military in 1968, the Mercers returned home to Alturas and bought the old Ed Grass store/house. The Mercers' six children are pictured here in 1958. From left to right are Carolyn, Glenda, Jerald, Duane, Alice, and Rebecca. (Courtesy of Montez Y. Mercer.)

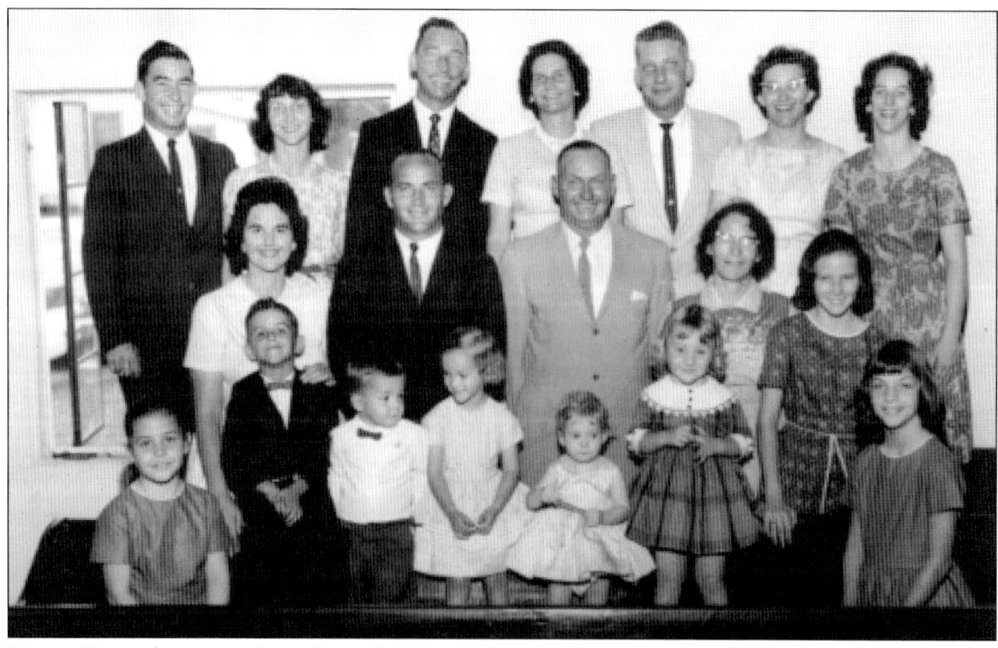

Henry Young beams with pride as the patriarch of his large family in this 1964 Alturas Baptist Homecoming photograph. Pictured are, from left to right, (first row) Vicki Hielscher, Scott Young, Kevin Hielscher, Lisa Young, Janan Graddy, Leanne Hielscher, and Sherry Hielscher; (second row) Wanda Perdue Young, Leland Young, Henry Young, Flora Lee Peacock Young, and Dee Hielscher; (third row) Carl Hielscher, Raymurl Young Hielscher, Merlin Hielscher, Evelyn Young Hielscher, Harold Graddy, Flora Young Graddy, and Doniece Young. (Courtesy of Scott Young.)

Robert and Annie Lee Smith Peacock traveled from Alturas, Florida, around 1935. This 1973 photograph shows five generations of Annie Lee Peacock's lineage, all of whom resided in Alturas, Florida, for most of their lives. Pictured are, from left to right, infant Richard Sowell, Dee Hielscher Sowell, Evelyn Young Hielscher, Flora Lee Peacock Young, and Annie Lee Smith Peacock. Annie Lee was born in 1896 and had a twin brother, Vernon Lee Smith. (Courtesy of Sherry Maberry.)

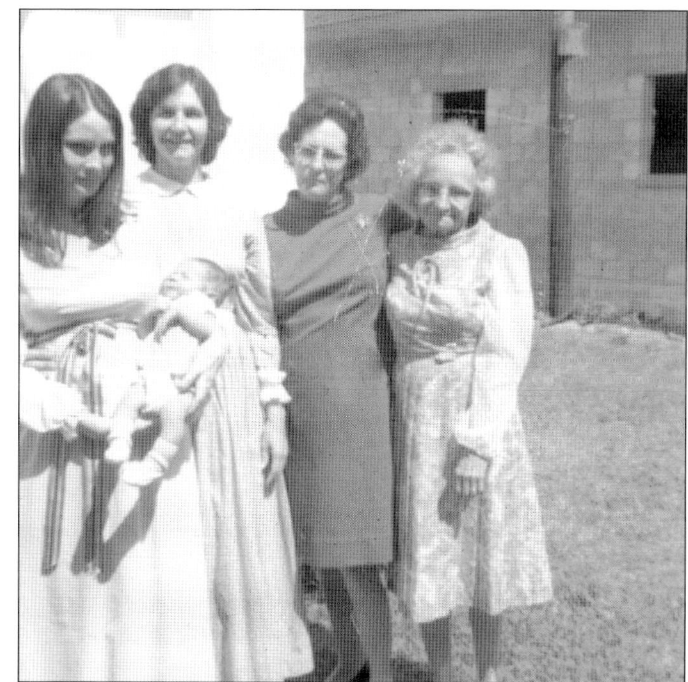

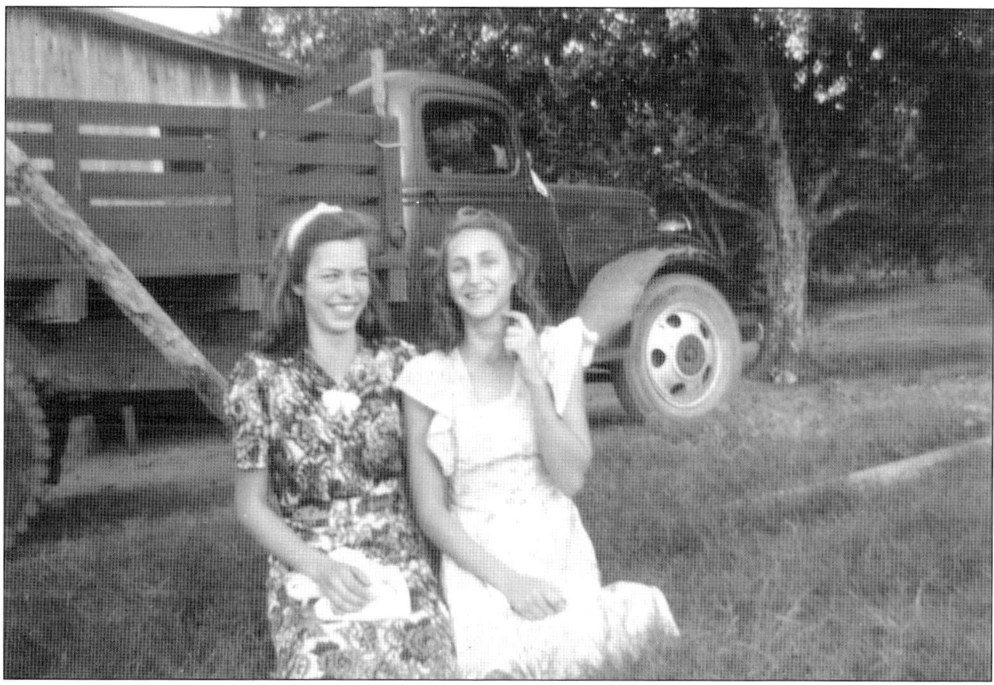

Annette Sowell and Raymurl Young were daughters of Alturas farmers and grove workers. Sowell's parents were Claude and Anna Sowell, who moved from Alabama to Alturas in 1946. Her siblings were Olin, Charles, Nadine, Fay and Ray (twins), and Robert. Sowell married Jeff Best and had two children, Wayne and Howard. Young's parents were Henry and Flora Lee Young (previously mentioned on page 39). Note the farm truck in the background used as grove or ranching equipment. (Courtesy of Sherry Maberry.)

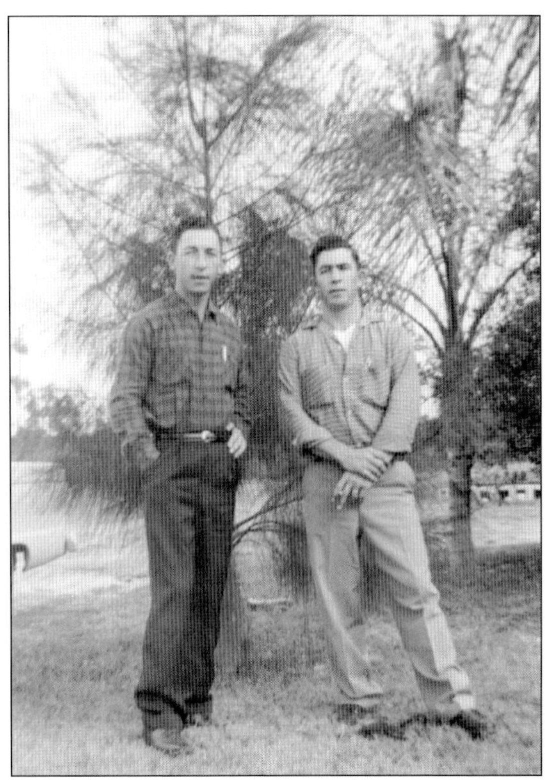

Two handsome boys from Frostproof, Florida, Merlin and Carl Hielscher (left), were invited to a revival at the Lake Buffum Baptist Church, near Alturas in 1949. They met two girls there, Raymurl Young and Merle McCullough, and gave them a ride home. Carl was smitten with Raymurl, and when Merlin saw her sister Evelyn at their Alturas home, it was love at first site. Carl married Raymurl in 1950 and had three children, Vicki, Leanne, and Kevin. Merlin married Evelyn in 1954 (below). They had one child, Sherry. Evelyn had a daughter, Dee, from a previous marriage. The Hielschers made their homes in Alturas for a lifetime. Carl opened Creative Landscape Inc., Raymurl was the secretary at Alturas Elementary School for 28 years, Merlin was a fruit broker, and Evelyn was the Alturas postmaster for 33 years. All four were charter members of the Alturas Baptist Church and involved in the Alturas Elementary School PTA. (Both, courtesy of Sherry Maberry.)

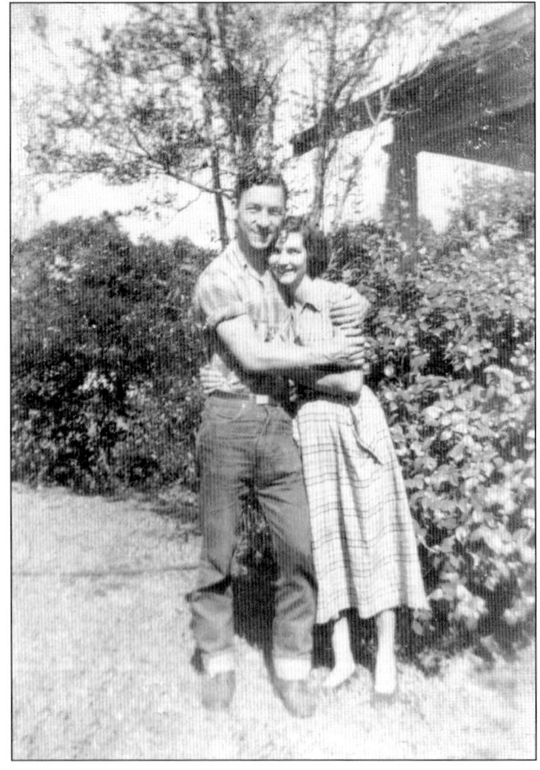

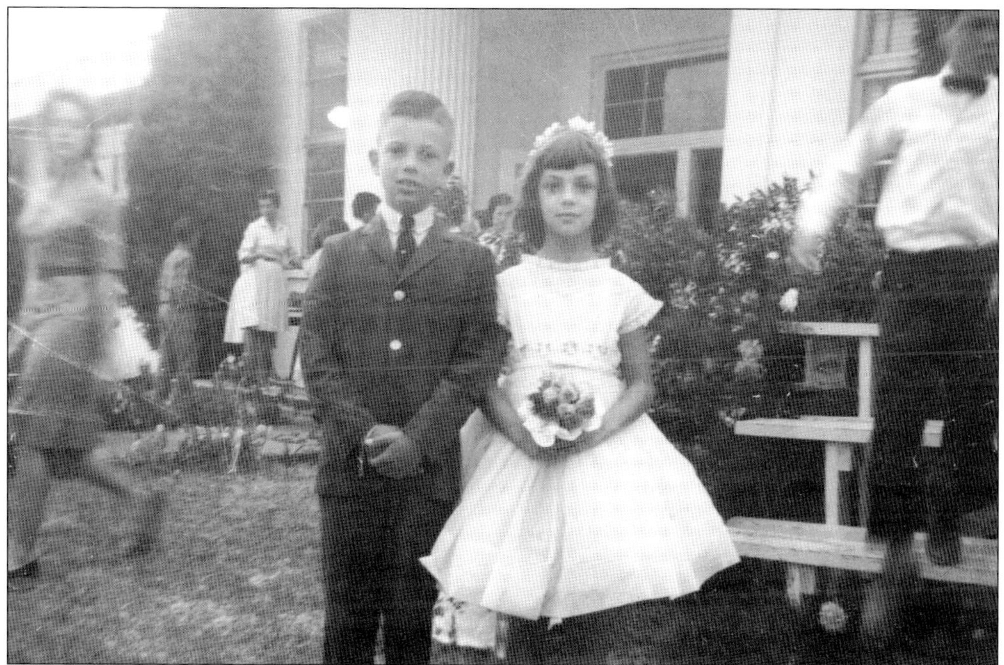

In 1963, John Emory Register and Sherry Hielscher were in the May Day royal court at Alturas Elementary School. Register's grandfather, Benjamin Brookes Register Sr., known as "Papi," was a true entrepreneur. He owned the old sawmill with partner Strother Booth on the Lake Wales/Alturas road, built a grocery store, and ran the Alturas Post Office for 16 years from that location as the third postmaster. He was a citrus grower and started the Alturas Water Works Company. Papi's sons, Emory and Brookes Jr., continued the family businesses. (Courtesy of Sherry Maberry.)

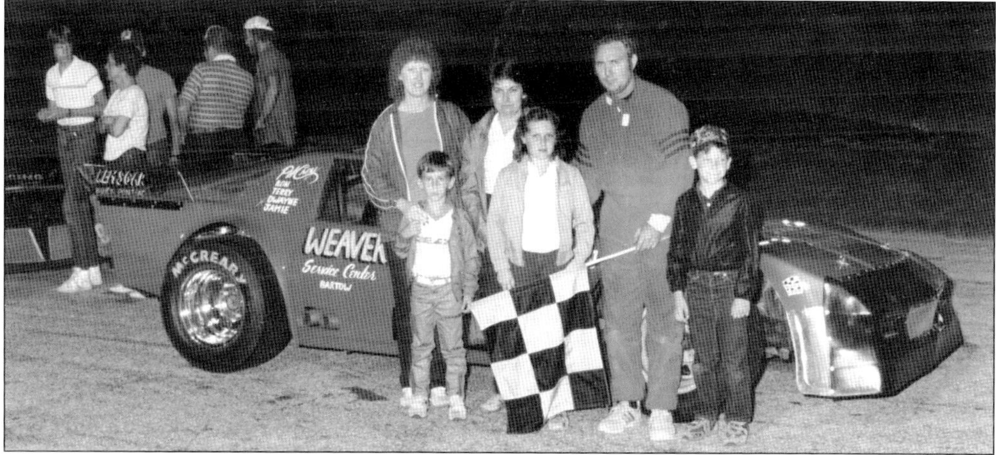

In 1979, David King won first place at a stockcar race on the Auburndale Speedway. Those pictured with him are sister Eva King Massey; her son Kevin Massey; David's wife, Patsy King; and their daughter Dana King. David and his brother Eddie King started racing in 1971, which was a perfect sport for this family of car mechanics. In 1989, Eddie won the Florida Champion Stockcar Race, and David came in second place. Their parents were Amos and Betty King, and they had six children, Eddie, David, Shelia, Rita, Eva, and Reba. Their grandparents, John King and Rosie Yohn King, arrived in Alturas from Alabama in the late 1920s. Rev. John King was the first pastor of the Alturas Assemblies of God Church, which was established in 1937. (Courtesy of David King.)

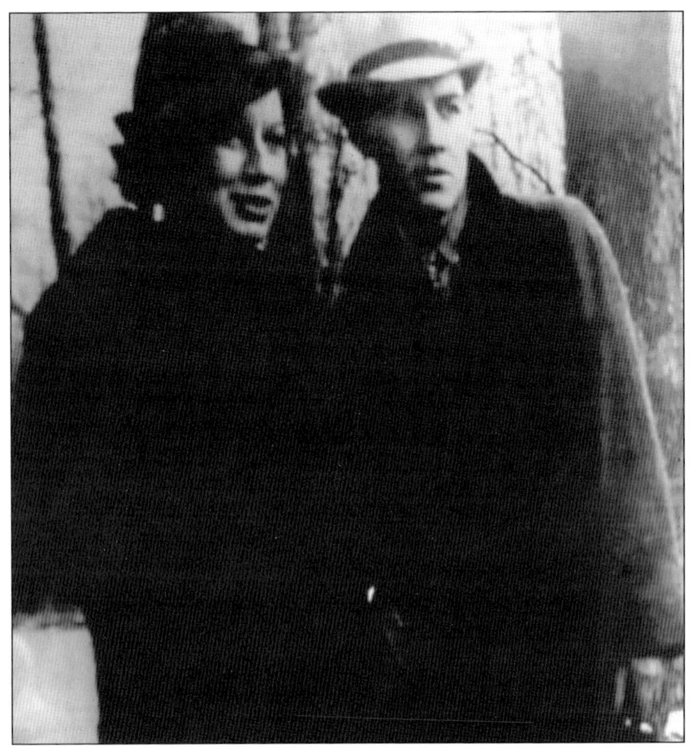

Engineer Hubert Beechler Hurley and his wife, Agnes Margaret Malloy, moved to Alturas from Pennsylvania in 1947. Rust Engineering brought Hurley to central Florida to build the Bonnie Mine, located in Mulberry. They lived in the Methodist parsonage while contractor Victor Voigt and his crew workers John A. Voigt, Russell Stevens, and Wendel Rothrock built their home on Star Lake. Hurley assisted them when possible. The Hurleys raised five children: Heather, Robin, Jon, Hubie, and Kim. In the 1950s, Hurley built a cottage next door for his parents, Edward and Anna Bouvier Hurley. (Courtesy of Sherry Maberry.)

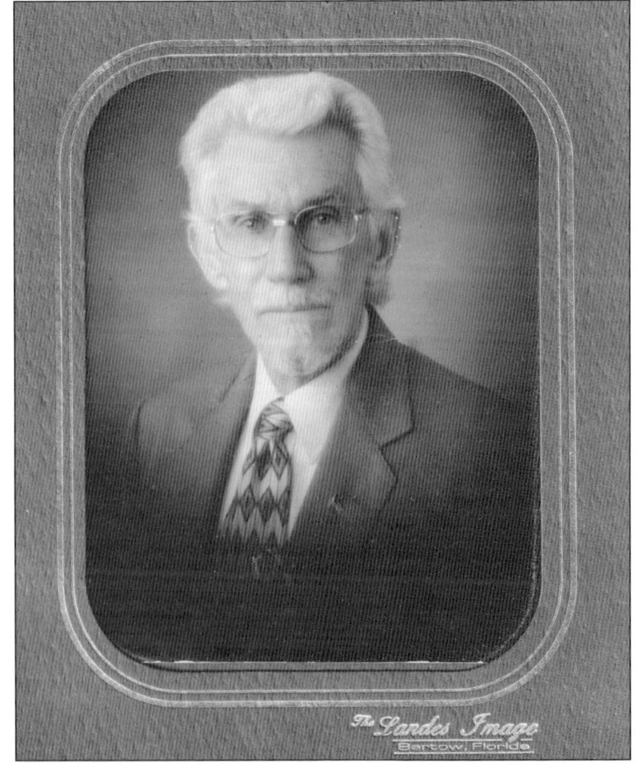

Since 1956, Jack T. Edmund was perhaps Polk County's most famous criminal defense lawyer. At Edmund's funeral, friend and adversary Jerry Hill, the state attorney, talked about Edmund's clients. He said, "Most of them are free today . . . and a FEW are innocent." Edmund moved to Alturas in 1971 and resided there until his death in 2002. He was a North Carolina native and a true Southern gentleman. Edmund was a fighter pilot in World War II and during the Korean War. He married Mary Jane Hopping, and they had four children, Marianne, Malcolm, Andrew, and Bruce. (Courtesy of Andrew Edmund.)

Patsy Garner married Paul Ayers of Wahneta, Florida, on April 19, 1970, at the Alturas Baptist Church. Patsy's parents, J.D. Garner (retired from Armour Mines) and Katie Lee Smith met in Alturas in the early 1930s and married in 1934. They had eight children, Terrell, Betty Jo, David, Jack Charles, Sarah, Mary, and Patsy. Patsy's maternal grandfather, Frank Smith, moved from Georgia to settle in Alturas in the early 1920s. (Courtesy of Sherry Maberry.)

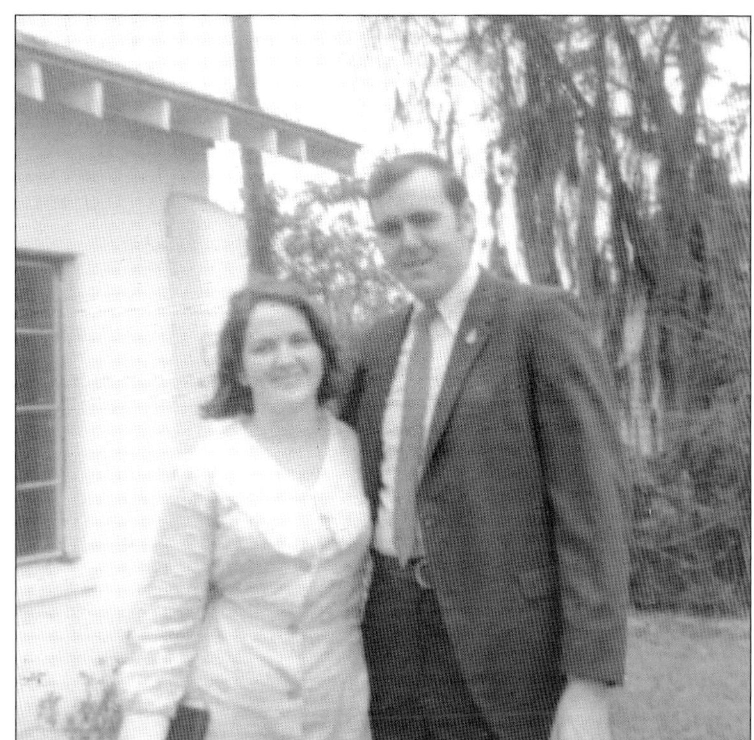

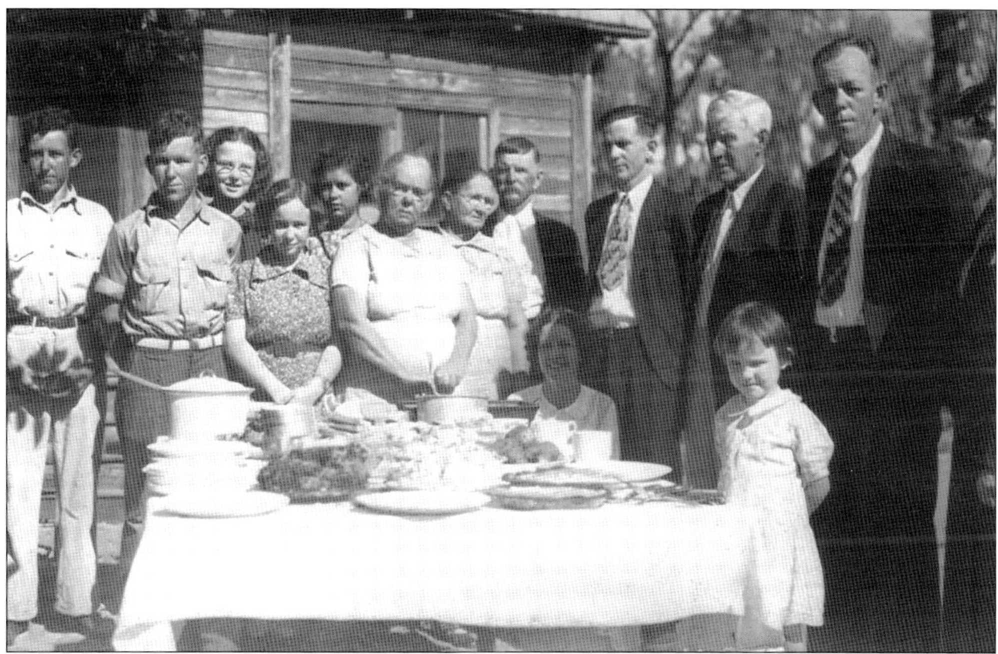

This was a typical family dinner for William Noah and Frances Adeline Mobley Waters at their homestead on Lake Erin in the Lake Garfield tract around 1936. From left to right are Sam Lusk Waters, Harold Waters, unidentified, Shorty Waters, Lucey Waters, Frances Adeline "Addie" Mobley Waters, unidentified woman and man, Aron Rice, Minnie Waters Rice (kneeling), William Noah "Will" Waters, unidentified child, and Lee and Molly Waters. (Courtesy of Ned Waters.)

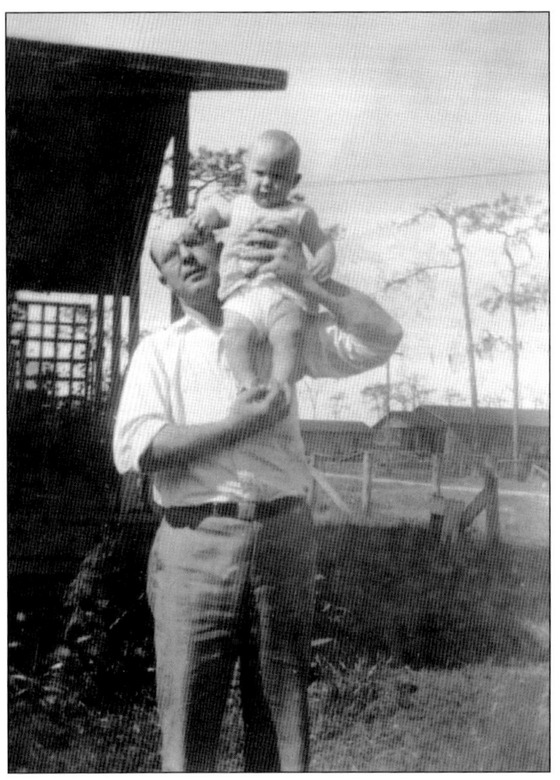

Junius Warren "J.W." Huff and family came to Lake Garfield in 1930 to work for the Roux Crate and Lumber Company as its master mechanic in charge of maintenance for the sawmill. In this photograph from 1930, he is holding his infant son Pat. Huff moved to Lake Garfield from the Griffin sawmill in Holopaw, Florida, when that mill closed because it had harvested all the available timber in the area. (Courtesy of W. Patrick Huff.)

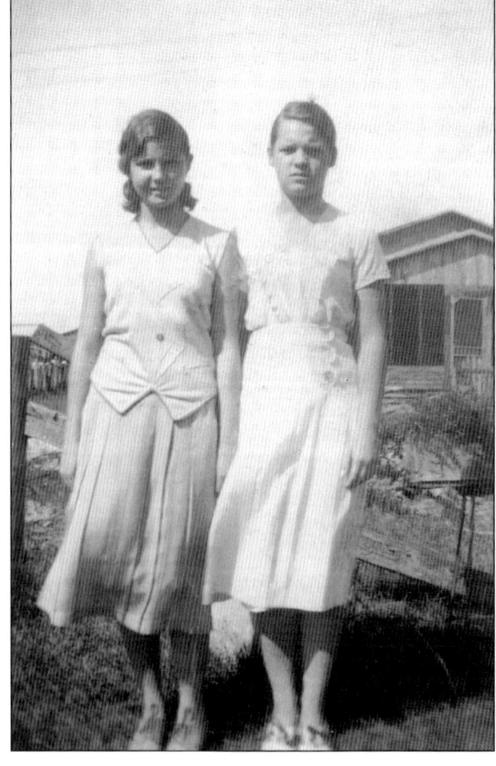

Zara Catherine Huff and Mary Jo Huff, daughters of Junius Warren "J.W." Huff, are standing in front of their residence in Lake Garfield in 1930. The J.W. Huff family included his wife, Mae Belle Robinson Huff, and their infant son Warren Patrick "Pat" Huff. His two teenage daughters (right) were children from Huff's previous marriage to Mamie Tisdale. The family lived in a company house across the road from the commissary, which was the Roux Crate and Lumber Company's store, and it was the center of activity for the community. The commissary sold groceries and dry goods and had a soda fountain as well as an office for the sawmill doctor, Dr. W.G. Gilchrist. (Courtesy of W. Patrick Huff.)

Mae Belle Huff and her infant son Warren Patrick and stepdaughter Zara Catherine Huff are pictured near their home in Lake Garfield in 1930. Zara married Jack E. Frankenburger of Lake Garfield. They raised four children, Patrick "Pat," James Warren Frankenburger, William Michael Frankenburger, Jack Eneix Frankenburger Jr., and Lyda Catherine Frankenburger. (Courtesy of W. Patrick Huff.)

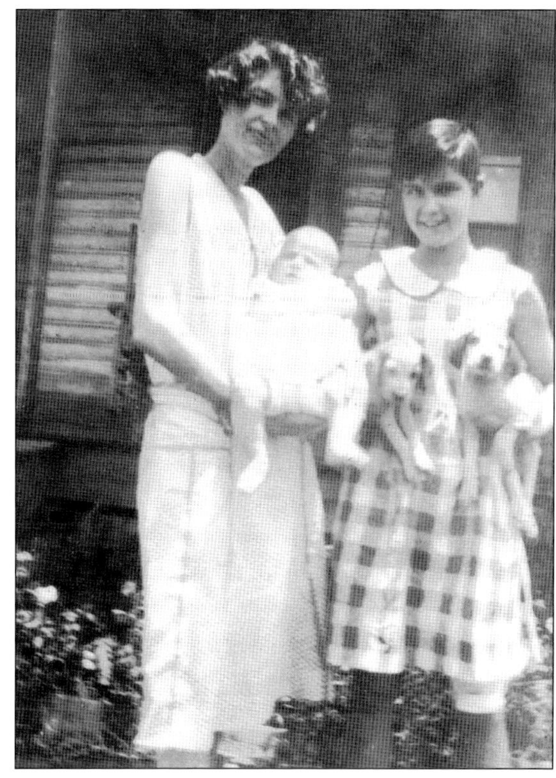

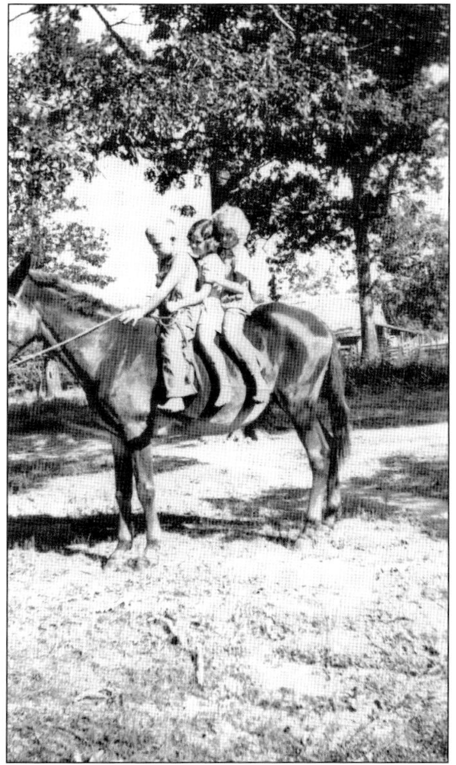

Warren Patrick Huff is taking his two cousins visiting from Mobile, Alabama, for a horse ride in 1934. The "city" cousins enjoyed vacationing in rural Lake Garfield where the climate, lakes, and rural nature of the area encouraged children to play outside. (Courtesy of W. Patrick Huff.)

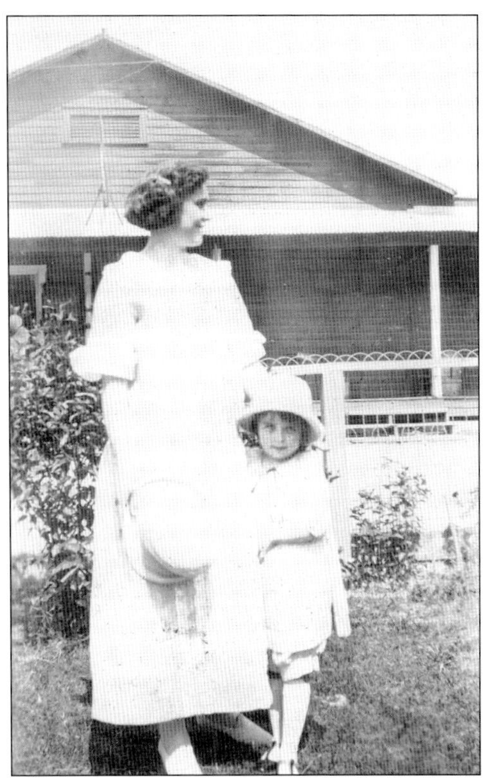

Early residents of Lake Garfield, Birdie Beach and daughter Mariella Beach are standing in front of one of the Roux Crate and Lumber Company's shotgun style homes in 1934. Some homes had nice large porches, which made the hot, muggy Florida weather bearable before air-conditioning was invented. Beach had two other children, William and Albert A. Beach, a famous songwriter. (Courtesy of Christine and Keith Miller.)

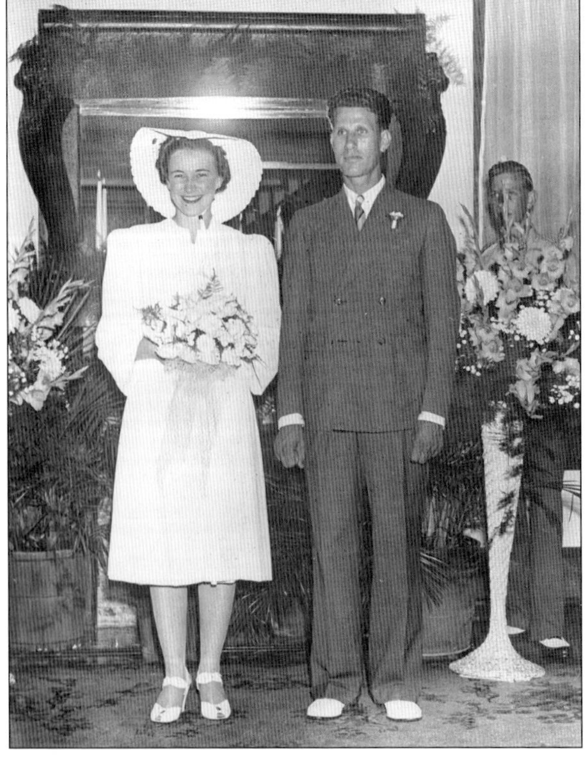

Louis and Mildred Stenger are pictured here on their wedding day on June 12, 1940. They had two daughters, Jacqueline and Barbara. The couple resided in Lake Garfield near the homestead where his father, John George Stenger Sr., settled when he came to that area in 1912. Stenger was a citrus grower and avid aviation aficionado. (Courtesy of Jackie Stenger Stoltz.)

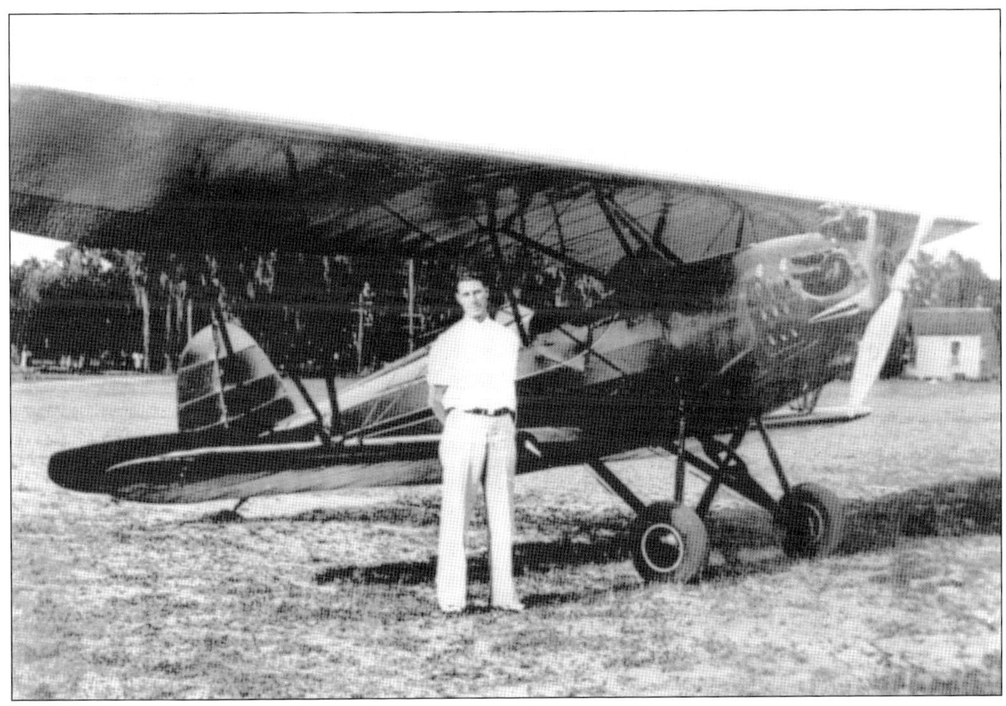

In 1934, Louis Stenger, Lake Garfield pioneer aviator, stands proudly beside his Kinner Bird aircraft. The Bird was capable of carrying the pilot and three people. The Raymond Aircraft Company in Lakeland, Florida, was the local distributor for the Bird. The Stenger family were ground breakers in aviation's infancy. Stenger was an instructor in the US Army Air Force for the aviation training program during World War II. An interesting fact regarding Stenger: His pilot license was signed by Orville Wright. (Courtesy of Harry Stenger.)

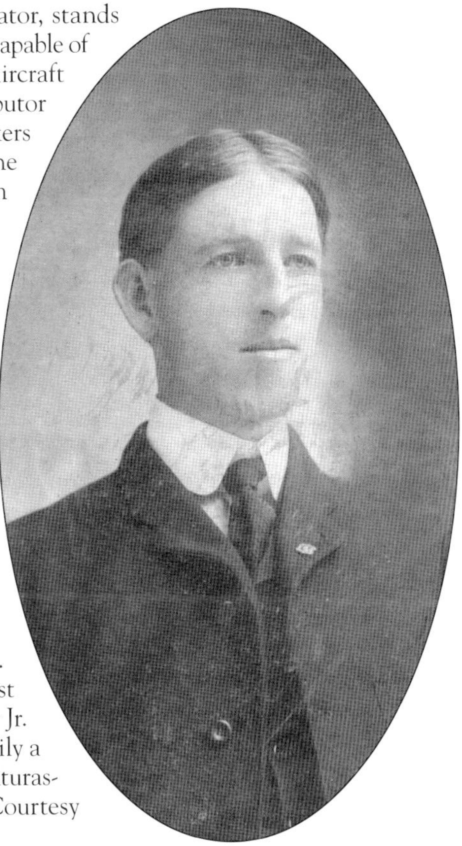

William Greene Frankenburger moved to Lake Garfield in 1923 from Morgantown, West Virginia. He settled on 100-acre plot with his wife, Lyda Frost Frankenburger and sons William G. Frankenburger Jr. and Jack Eneix Frankenburger. William was primarily a citrus grower and became the vice president of the Alturas-Lake Garfield Citrus Cooperative in the 1930s. (Courtesy of Cathy Curtis.)

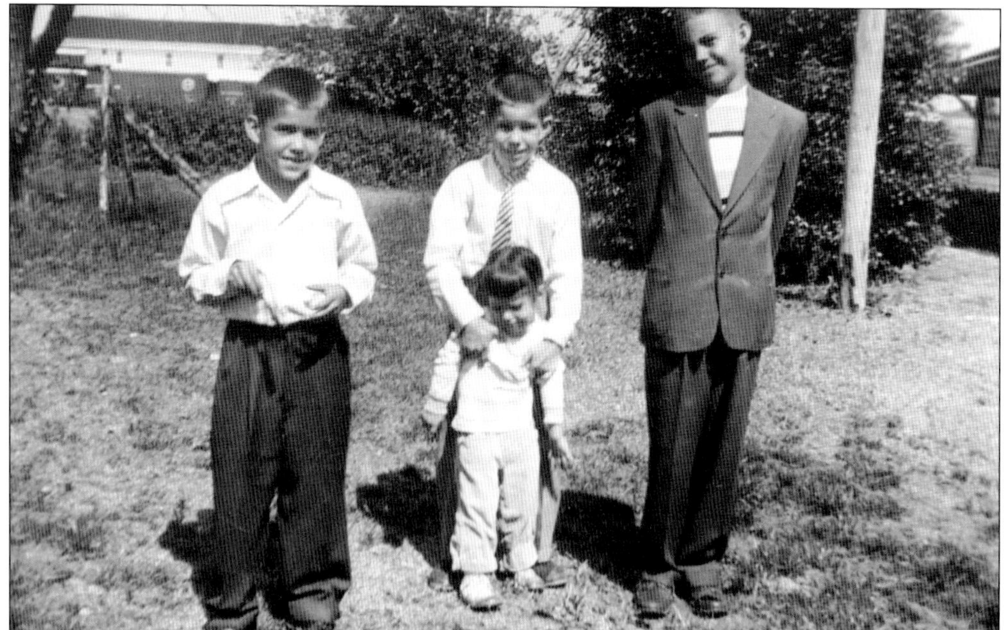

In 1955, Patrick James Warren Frankenburger, William Michael Frankenburger, Jack Eneix Frankenburger Jr., and Lyda Catherine Frankenburger are playing in the yard of the original homestead of their grandparents, William G. and Lyda Frankenburger, who established ownership in 1923. Generational ownership was passed down to son Jack and his wife, Zara Huff Frankenburger, who maintained the groves, pastures, and store. The business presently remains active under the stewardship of Michael Frankenburger, Cathy Frankenburger Curtis, and her husband, Raymond Curtis. The homestead is proudly approaching its centennial, having survived the wrath of Mother Nature's hurricanes and freezes. Visible in the background of this photograph are the Lake Garfield Packing House and the Seaboard Air Line railroad cars. (Courtesy of Cathy Curtis.)

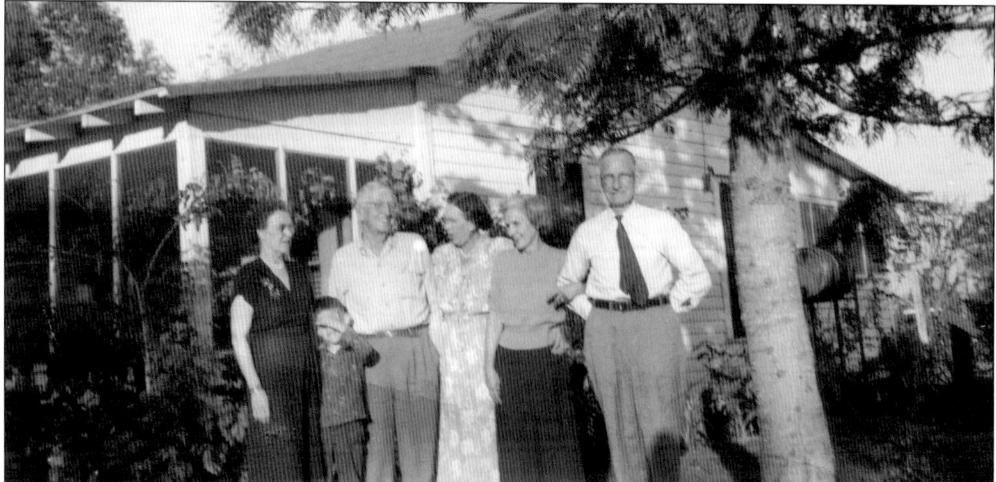

Early Lake Garfield settler William G. Frankenburger was a citrus grower and cattle rancher for more than 35 years. In this 1952 photograph are, from left to right, friend Nell Hostetler, grandson Jack Frankenburger Jr., W.G. Frankenburger, wife Lyda Frankenburger, sister-in-law Betty Frankenburger, and brother Frank Frankenburger. Note that this home is built in the Cracker-style architecture popular in Florida during this era. (Courtesy of Cathy Curtis.)

Three

The Businesses and Agriculture

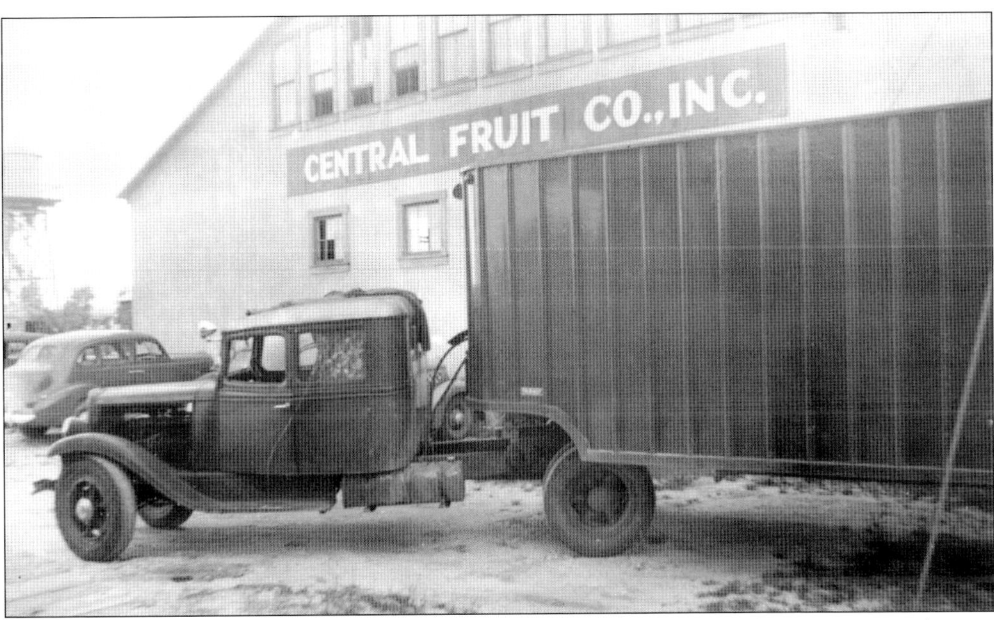

The three packing houses in Alturas and the one in Lake Garfield were the communities biggest assets. However, none are in existence today. In Alturas, the Alturas Packing Company (Blue Goose) was built in 1921–1922. Then came the Alturas Citrus Fruit Packing Company, also known as Turnbull and Gadau (Tug and Grunt), built in the mid-1920s. The Southern Fruit Exchange Packing House was later named the Central Fruit Company, pictured here. This company was located beside the Alturas Train Depot and burned in the late 1930s. The only packing house in Lake Garfield was built 1915. (Courtesy of Linda Smith.)

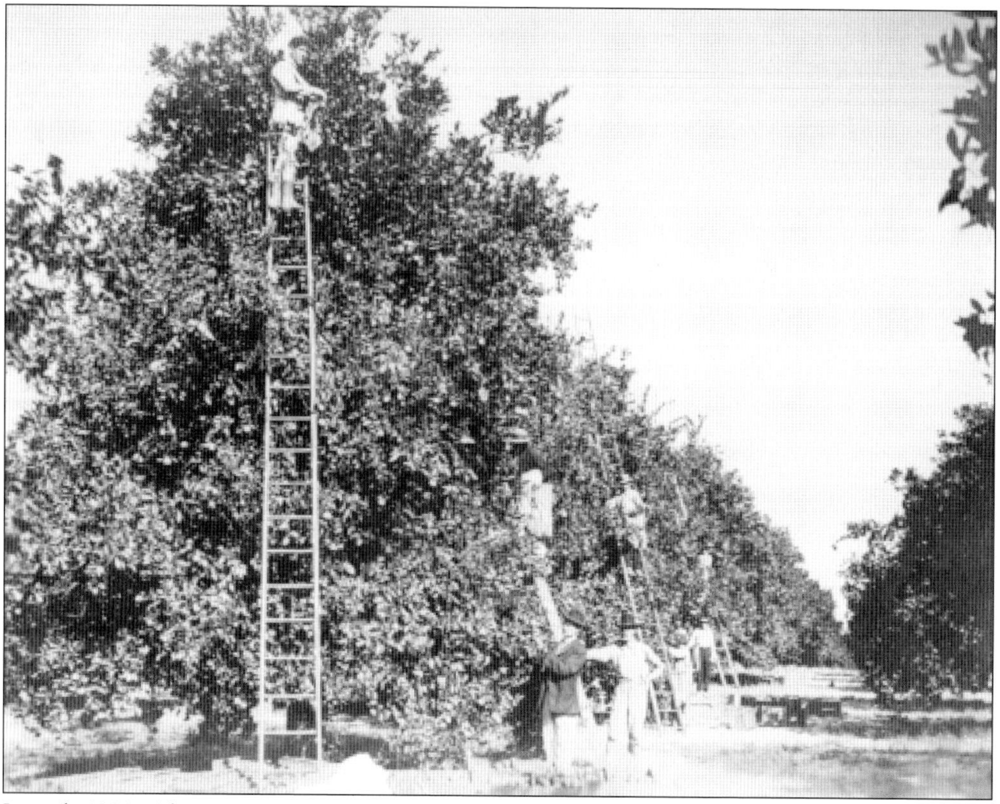

In early-1920s Alturas, Josey Kreps's orange grove included these tall seedling trees. Fruit pickers climbed 22-foot wooden "seedling" ladders to reach the fruit. They used large canvas bags, harnessed over their shoulders, to carry the fruit safely to the ground and place it into the wooden crates for hauling. Workers were paid according to the number of crates they harvested and were truly rewarded for the fruit of their labors. (Courtesy of Scott Young.)

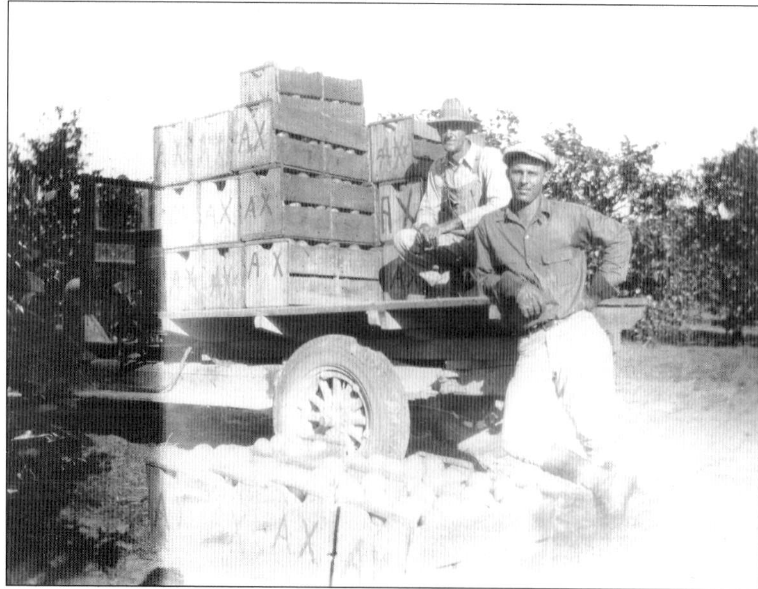

A 1928 Chevrolet truck was used to haul the crates of oranges to a local packing house in Alturas. Pictured are W.N. Gadau (left) and Harold Rothrock (right). Rothrock was a family friend who helped Gadau in various capacities, from harvesting citrus to the construction of new homes. (Courtesy of Linda Smith.)

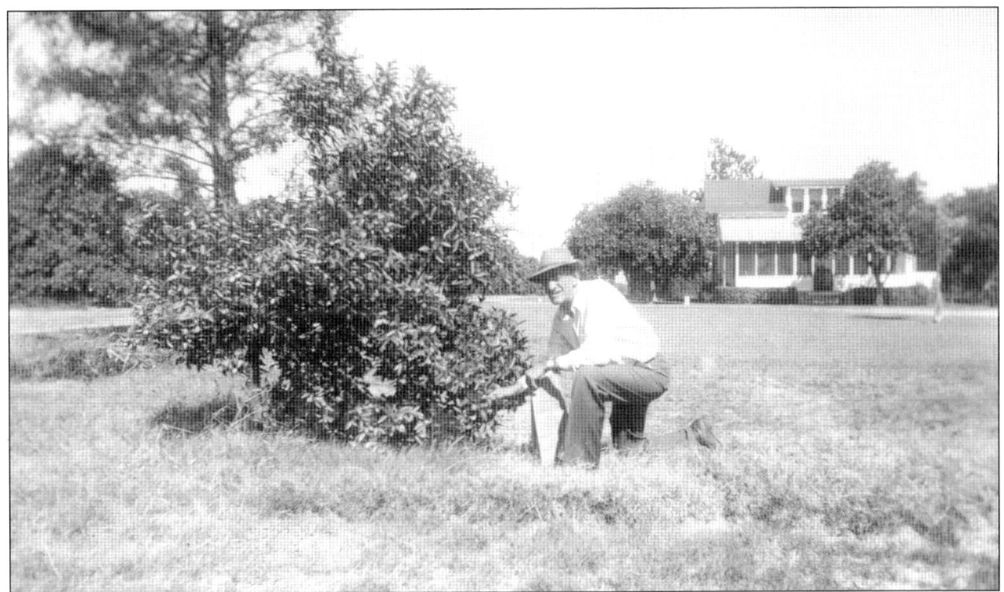

Wesley N. Gadau relocated to Alturas from Marseilles, Illinois, in 1914 to establish a citrus business. He is pictured picking kumquats in February 1947. Built in 1916, the Gadau home, pictured here, was located on the Old Lake Wales Road. Gadau and his wife, Ethel, and their two children, Alvena and Noble, lived there until the mid-1950s. They then moved to "up town" Alturas. Their 1916 home burned in the mid-1970s. (Courtesy of Linda Smith.)

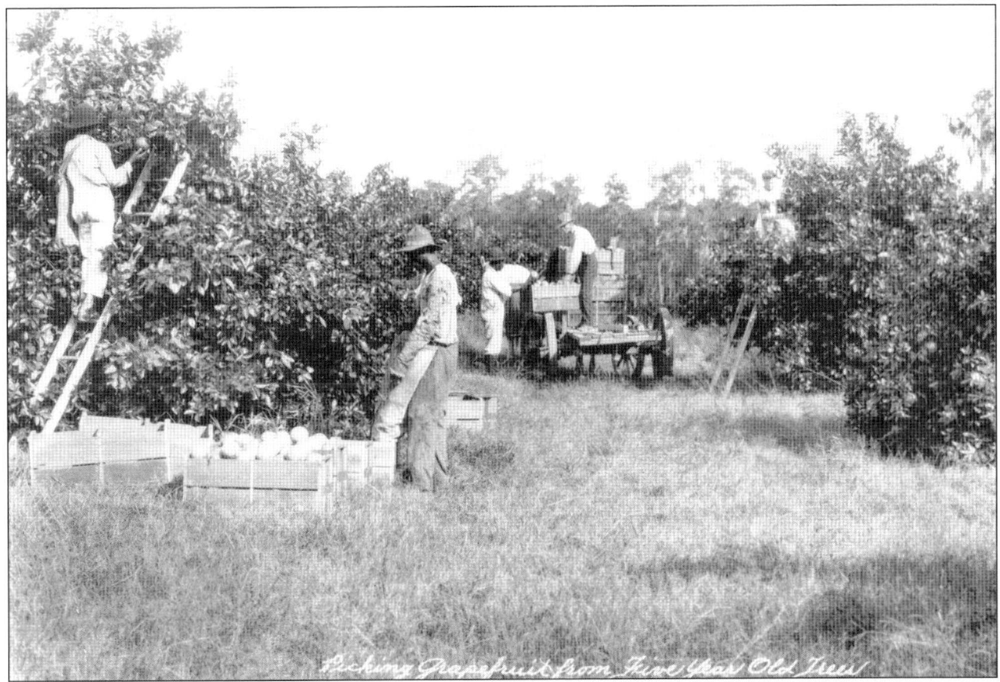

Around 1920, near Alturas and Lake Garfield, a five-year-old grapefruit grove is being harvested by fruit pickers using ladders and canvas pick sacks to get fruit from the tree to the field crates. Mules (pre-automotive power) are pulling a wagon loaded with this season's yield. (Courtesy of Scott Young.)

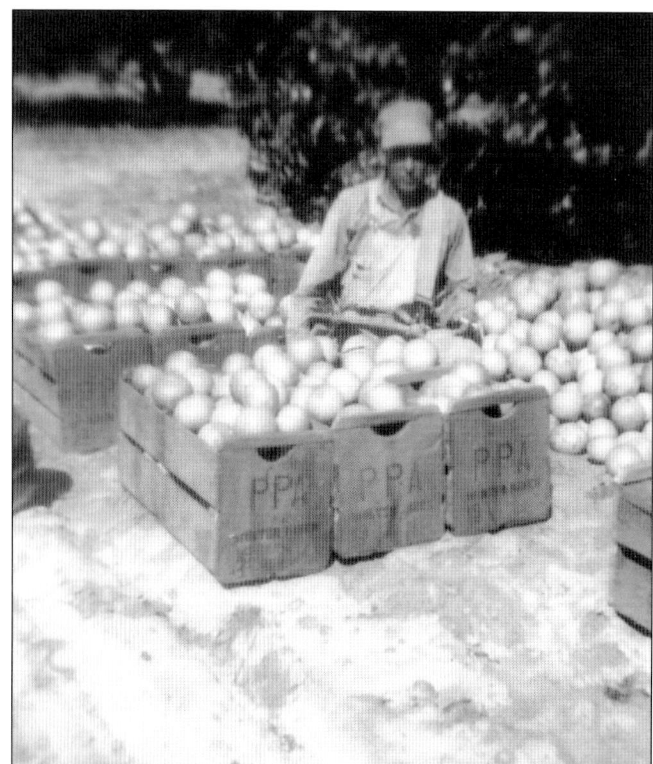

Thirty-one-year-old Dudley Sowell is posing for a rare photograph while picking fruit in an Alturas orange grove. Sowell worked as a grove laborer in the citrus industry, first for Wilton Murphy and then for Roy Perdue at the Perdue Groves and Ranch Company. (Courtesy of Sharon Sowell Dixon.)

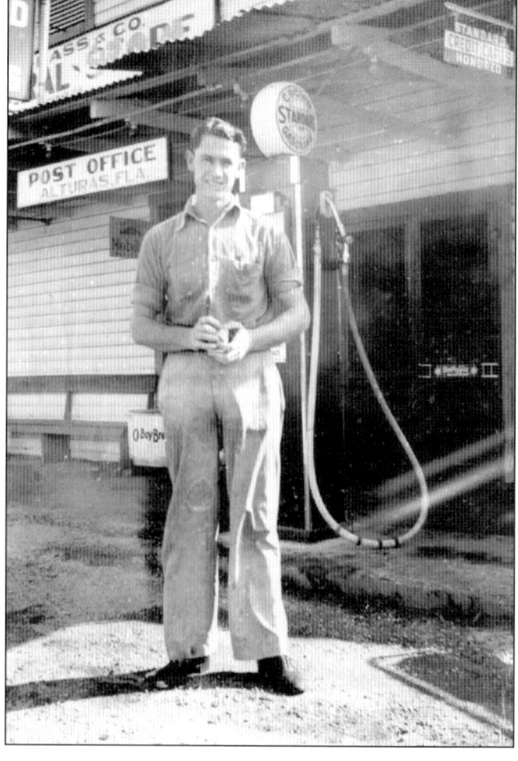

"Uncle Buck" Luna is standing next to a gas pump at the Ed Grass & Company General Store in Alturas. In 1926, the store was so busy on a Saturday morning that five clerks had a difficult time serving all the customers. Also, the post office was in the store at that time, and Ed Grass was the fourth postmaster. Note the signs on the building. (Courtesy of Montez Mercer.)

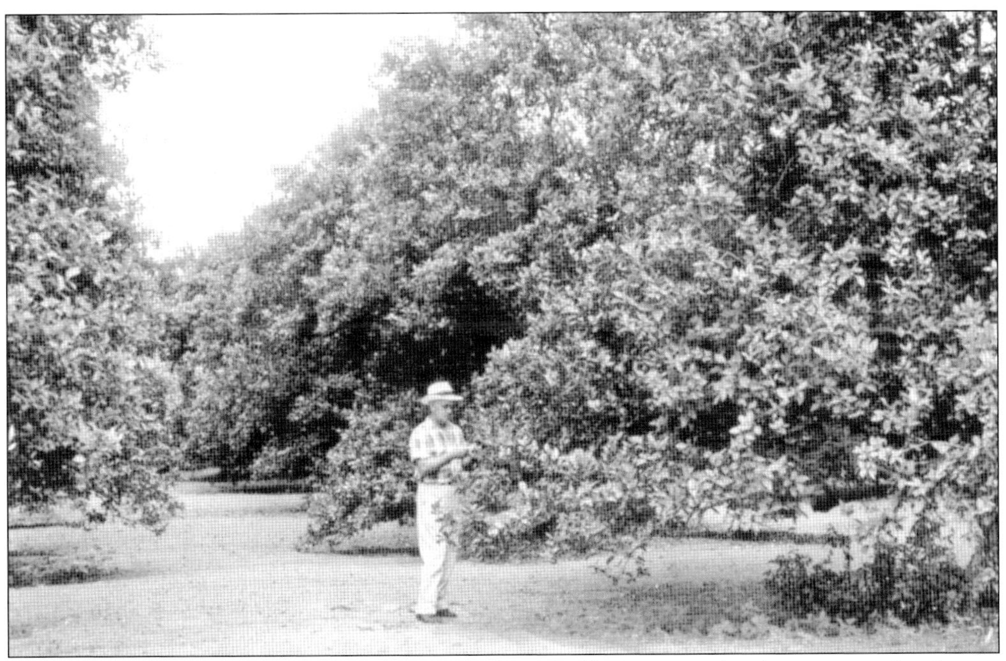

Lawrence Estes (pictured) and his brother Robert (Polk County school superintendent) were active in a local agriculture business known as the Estes Plantation. Lawrence was known for contributing to the emerging technology of the citrus industry. For several years, he worked with the University of Florida's Citrus Experiment Station in Lake Alfred, Florida (University of Florida Citrus Research and Education Center). Lawrence often drove through his groves with one of his dogs sitting beside him. This routine included a stop at the Alturas store for ice cream for both driver and passenger. This photograph was taken in 1955. (Courtesy of Connie Estes Meeks.)

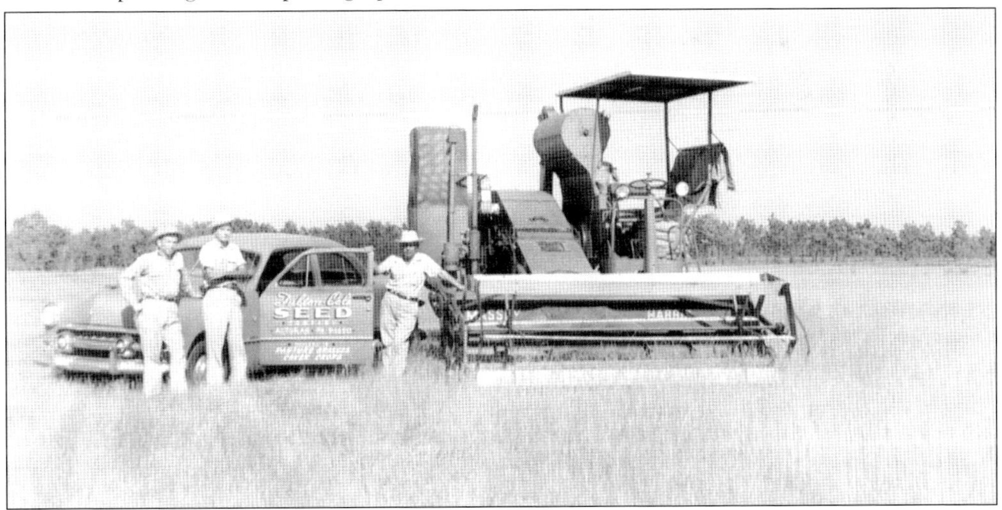

Warren Clay "W.C." Fulton and Gene Cole started the Fulton Cole Seed Company in the early 1950s. Their business was located on Packing House Road in Alturas but later moved to a building on Oak Avenue. Their grass seed company was well-known. In this photograph, W.C. "Skeet" Fulton Jr., Gene Cole, and Serge Cole are in front of a large combine used to harvest the grass seeds. Commodities included Argentina Bahia, rye, millet, and other grass varieties. (Courtesy of Jan Fulton Crawford.)

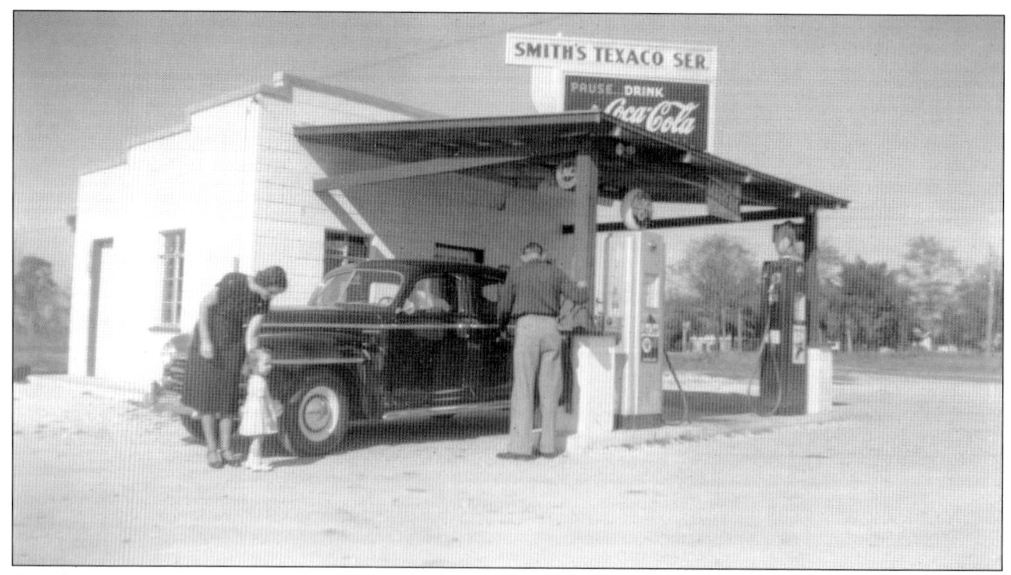

Smith's Texaco service station was one of the first businesses opened by Douglas Smith following his discharge from the Army at the conclusion of World War II. This 1948 photograph shows the small gas station Smith built in central Alturas. He later added onto the building, and it became a self-service grocery and the local post office. The building is now a nursery/day-care center in Alturas. Pictured are, from left to right, Alvena Smith, 18-month-old daughter Linda, and Doug Smith. (Courtesy of Linda Smith.)

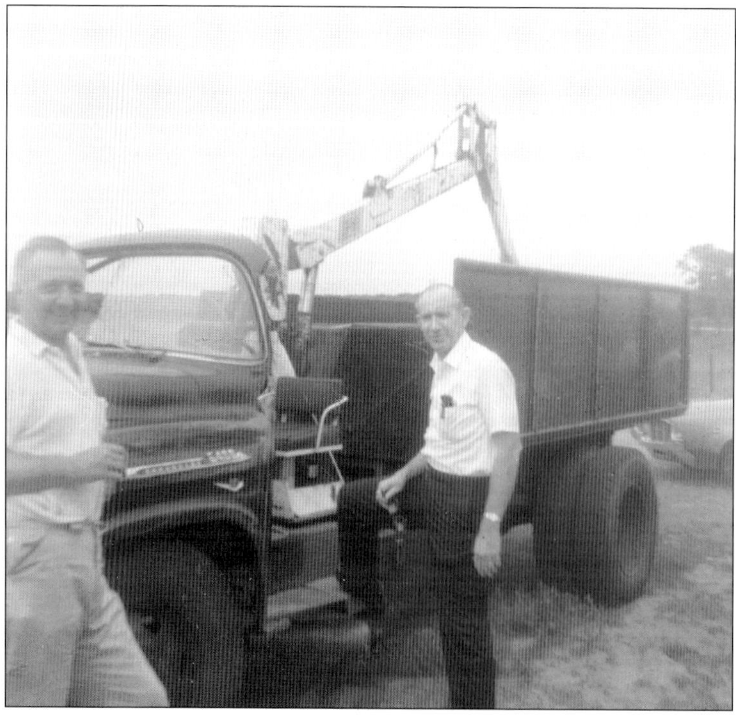

Monte Tillis (left) and Douglas Smith (right) inspect one of the new Lightning Loaders by Petersen Industries of Lake Wales around 1960. The device eliminated the need for two men to heave 90-pound boxes of oranges over the side of a truck. Smith arrived in Alturas in the mid-1930s. He left Georgia to drive a truck for the Perdue Groves and Ranch Company. Smith married Alvena Gadau, W.N. Gadau's daughter. (Courtesy of Linda King.)

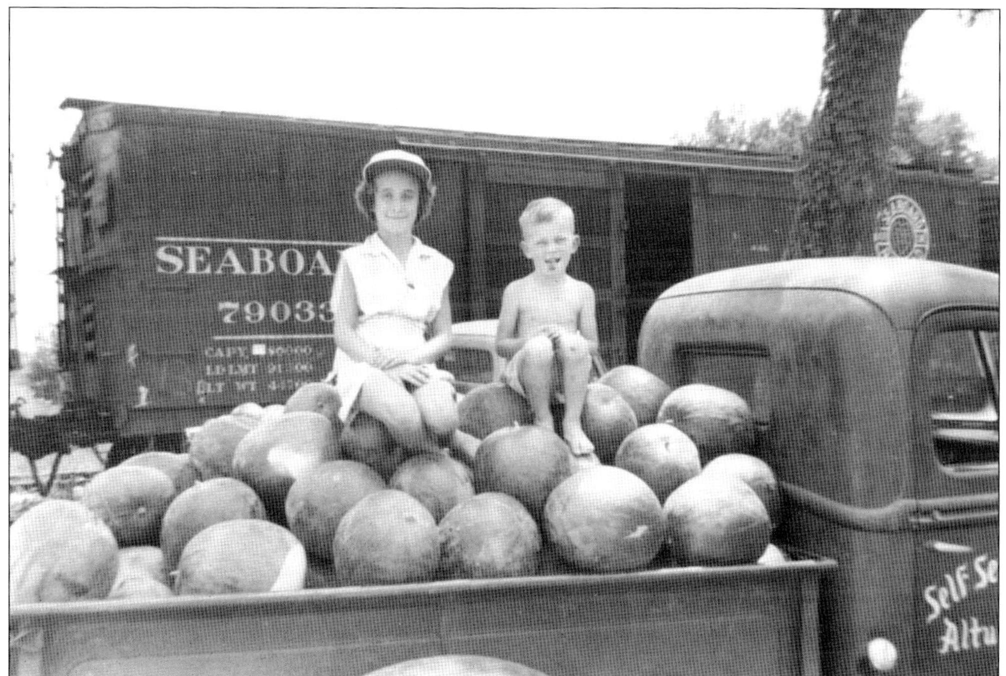

In the 1960s, Douglas Smith grew watermelons as a money-making crop. He followed in the footsteps of an early Alturas resident, a George Knauff, who, in 1914, grew a melon six feet wide in circumference, three feet long, and weighing 64.5 pounds—and got his name in the *Tampa Tribune*. Smith's children, Linda and Leland, are sitting on a load of watermelons ready to be put on the railcars behind them. The truck was from Smith's Texaco self-service station. (Courtesy of Linda Smith.)

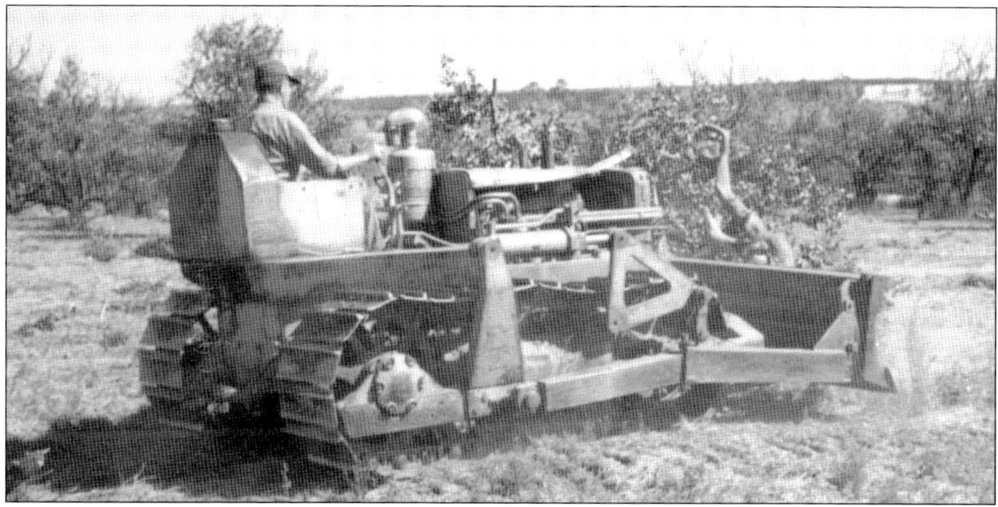

In the early 1960s, Florida's citrus industry faced the devastating threat of burrowing nematodes, a micro insect that could kill trees. The initial find was east of Alturas in the Lawrence Estes grove. Trees were removed to help prevent the spread of this disease. Large barriers were plowed, and the ground was treated with dichlorodiphenyltrichloroethane, commonly known as DDT (insecticide). The bulldozer in the photograph is pushing up dying trees before the barrier was plowed. (Courtesy of Scott Young.)

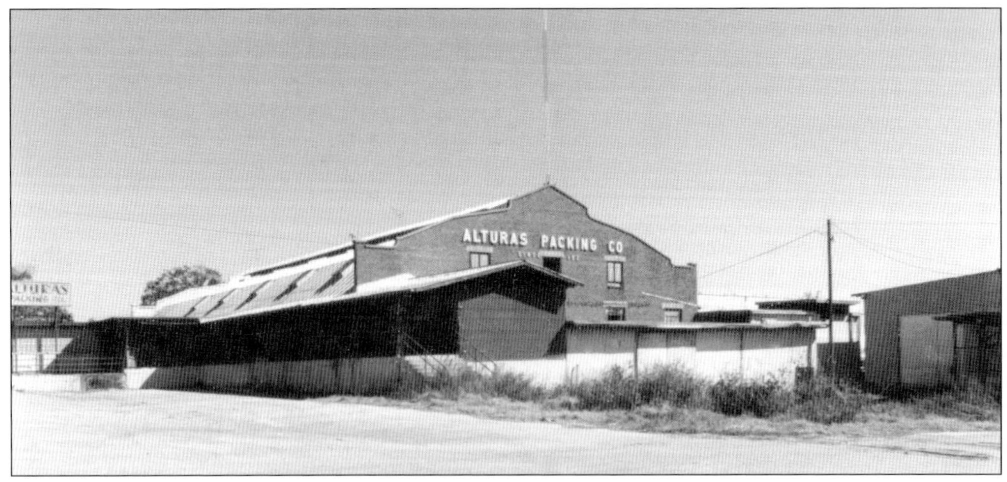

The Alturas Packing Company was established in 1928. This medium-sized packing house could handle 45,000 cartons of fruit a week during the harvest season. Once one of the first citrus packing companies in America, it now sits abandoned, as do many in central Florida. According to the company's general manager, Floyd Wiggins, in the 1970s and 1980s, "high labor cost and overhead, and the freeze made it more profitable to ship out to other packing companies than to do it ourselves." Therefore, the industry was taken over by larger packing companies. It stopped packing fruit in March 1981 and permanently closed in 1983. (Courtesy of Sherry Maberry.)

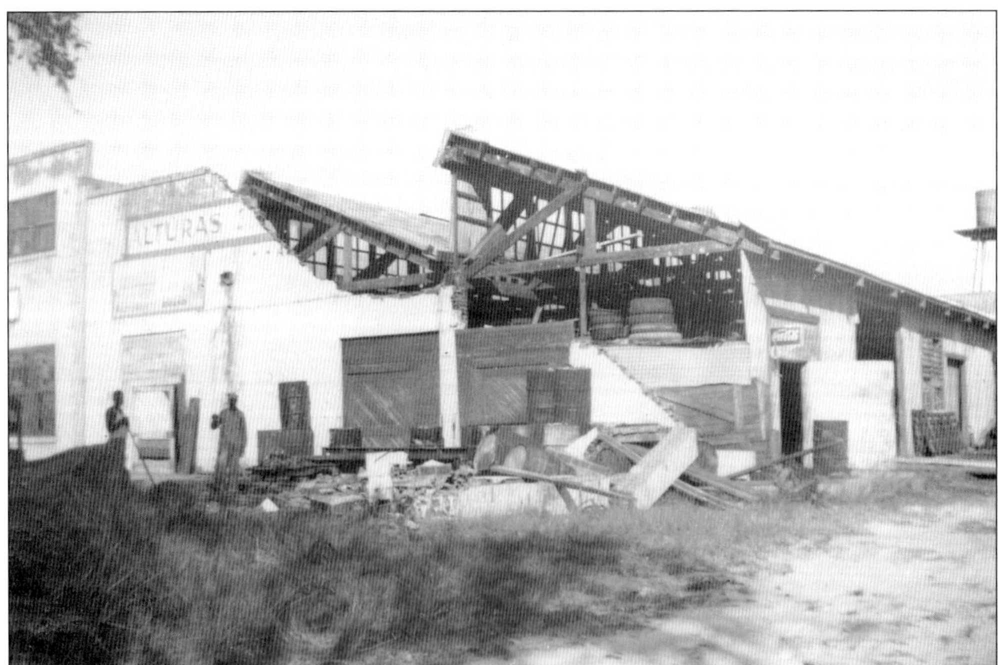

Alturas was hit hard by the 1944 Cuba–Florida hurricane, a category four storm. Though the hurricane weakened before striking Florida, it struck before crops were picked, causing significant citrus crop loss. Buildings were also damaged, as seen in this photograph of the Alturas Citrus Fruit Packing Company. Many men were away due to World War II, and repairs were slow due to the lack of manpower. (Courtesy of Linda King.)

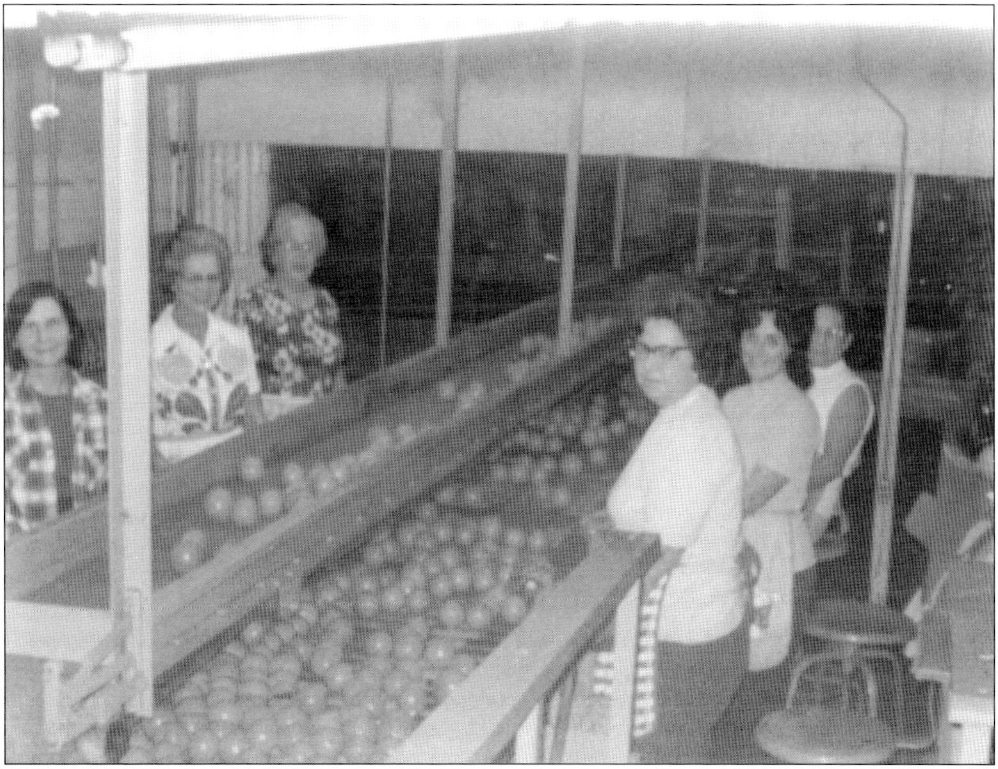

These women are "grading" fruit at one of the packing houses in Alturas or Lake Garfield. They would remove the bad fruit, called culls, before it reached the packing boxes to be shipped out. Much of this work was seasonal. Those pictured are, from left to right, Evelyn Hielscher, two unidentified, Doris Peacock, unidentified, and Flora Lee Young. (Courtesy of Sherry Maberry.)

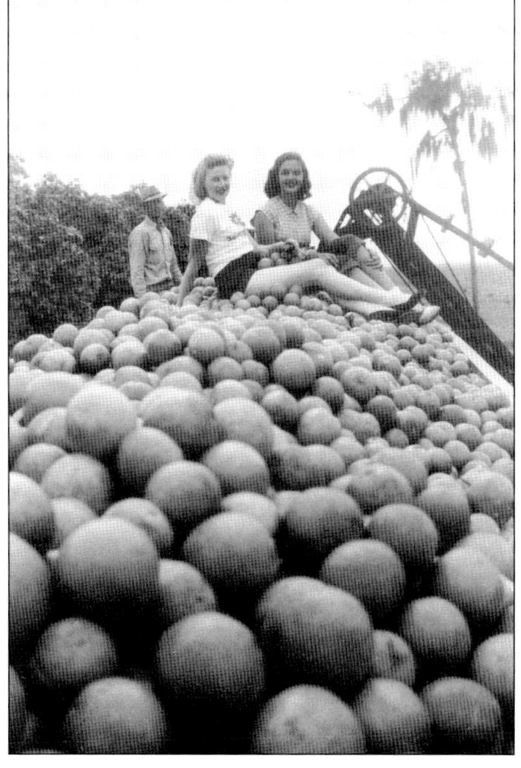

This 1940s picture shows a loading machine that lifted the picked oranges onto a conveyer belt to an open-topped trailer. This was an integral piece of equipment because each crate of oranges weighed 90 pounds (two bushels). The beauties sitting on top of the fruit are Wanda Perdue (right) and Doris Gustine (left), a cousin visiting from Fort Lauderdale, Florida. Joe Perdue, an Alturas fruit grower and Wanda's father, looks on proudly. (Courtesy of Scott Young.)

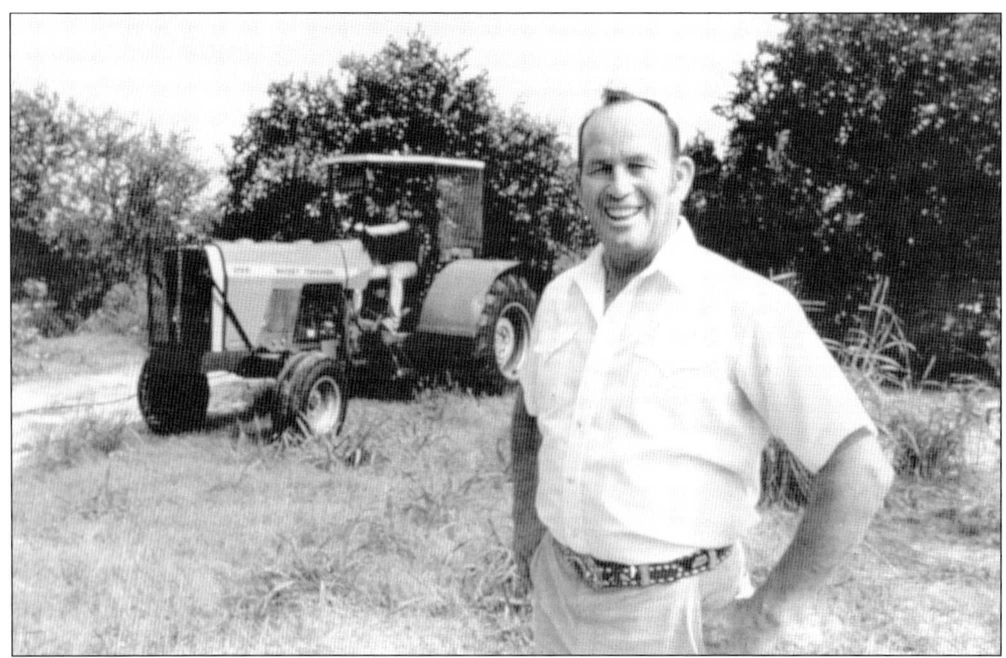

Leland Young (pictured above in 1986) founded Peace Valley Enterprise in 1972 with his wife, Wanda Perdue Young. The Youngs' children, Scott and Lisa, played an integral role in the success of this Alturas grove care company. In the 1980s, Young designed and marketed micro emitters (irrigation) under the name of Nu-Jet Inc. The large, working barn (below) that he built by hand for the headquarters of his business became a much-used venue for many important events such as political and social functions, Muscular Dystrophy fundraisers, Rotary Club meetings, wild game dinners, class reunions. Even Miss USA celebrations (1984 and 1985) were held in the barn. And all functions were free of charge. (Both, courtesy of Scott Young.)

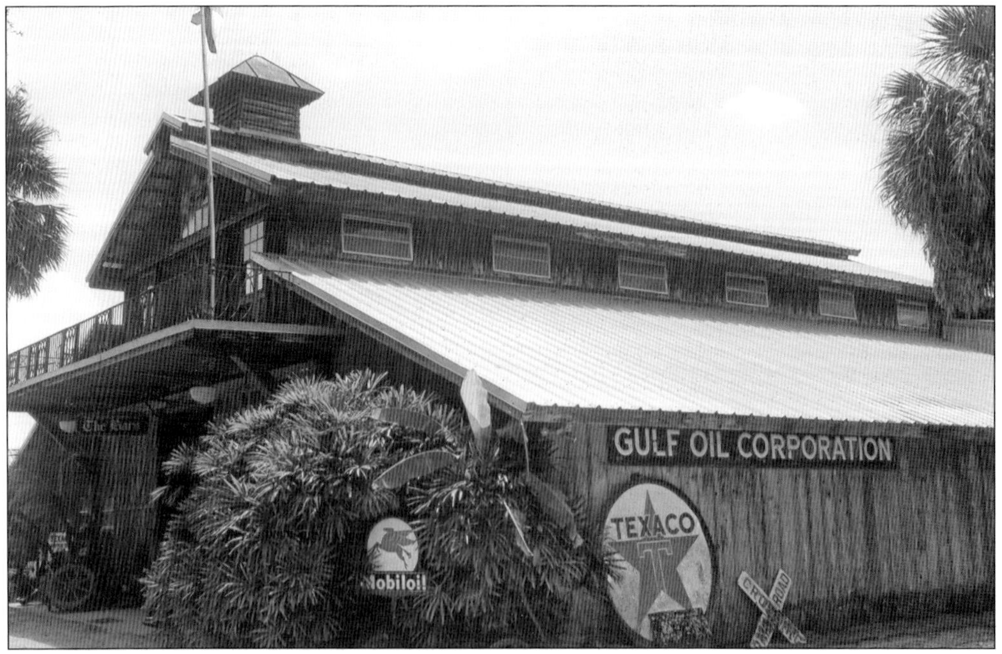

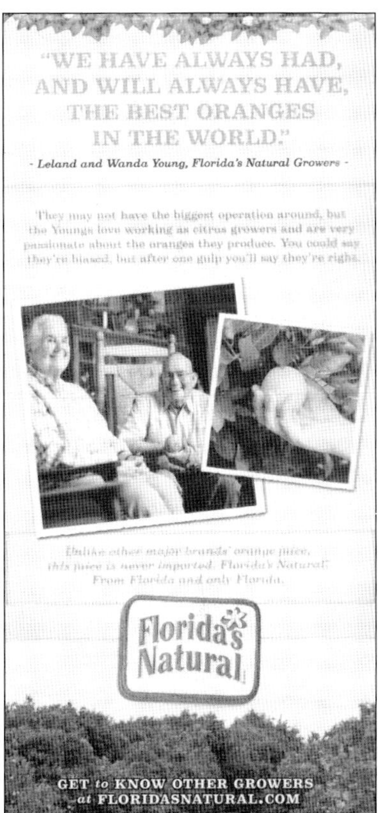

As members of the Haines City Citrus Growers, Alturas residents Wanda and Leland Young were featured on a Florida's Natural orange juice carton in 2012. Their picture and the following quote were placed on the carton: "They may not have the biggest operation around, but the Youngs love working as citrus growers and are very passionate about the oranges they produce. You could say they're biased, but after one gulp you'll say they're right." The orange juice cartons were sold in grocery stores throughout the country. (Courtesy of Scott Young.)

Edwin Mercer bought the old Ed Grass general store and homeplace in the late 1960s. Here, he is grilling beside his home in Alturas. Across the road, seen in the background, was Langford's General Store, owned and operated by Bud Langford and his sons, Mike and Joe. This store was originally built by sawmill owner Brookes Register Sr. in the 1930s. Register opened it as a general store and post office and served as the third postmaster. Later, sons Emory and Brookes Jr. ran the store. (Courtesy of Montez Y. Mercer.)

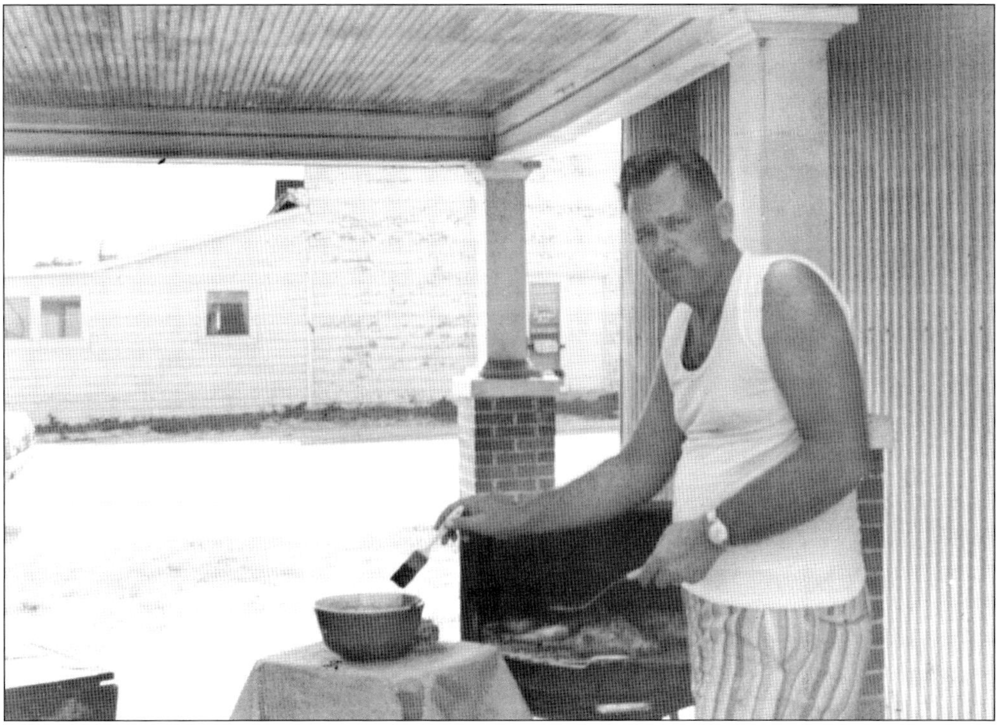

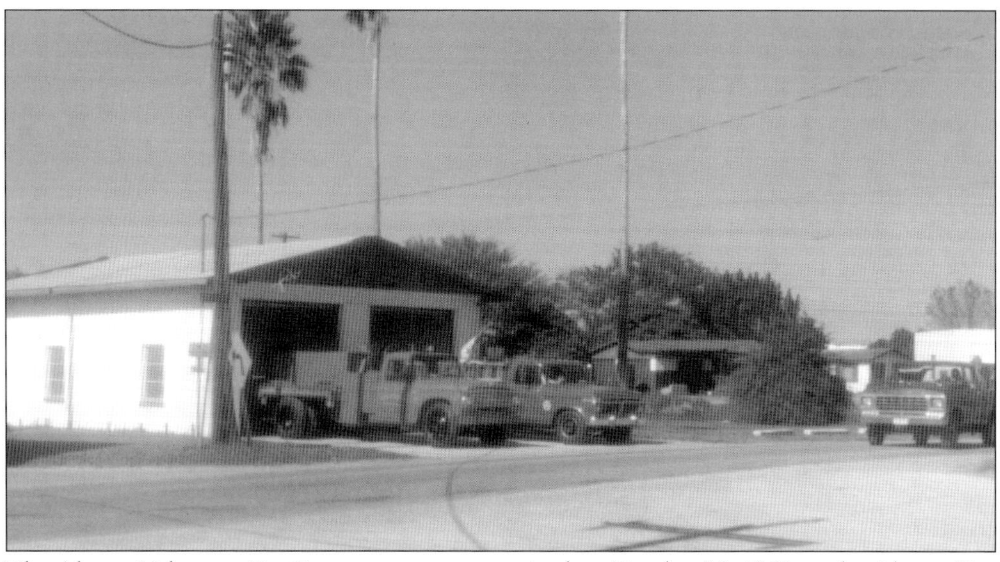

The Alturas Volunteer Fire Department was organized on October 28, 1960, as the Alturas Fire Station Association Inc. However, as early as the 1950s, the men in the community were given an old fire truck by Polk County, which they used to put out fires. Two of those memorable fires were the Isaac Albritton and the Fulton Ray homes. Local volunteers would rush to the scene when the siren sounded on the old fire truck. Some citrus owners would bring extra water from their grove trucks, which they used to water their groves. Lawrence Estes and Jesse Kelly were among the first fire chiefs, and Loy Locke was the last chief before the department closed in the 2008s. In the 1980s, the fire department became a combination department, where one paid county fireman would man the station during the day and the community volunteers served during the evening hours. (Courtesy of Sherry Maberry.)

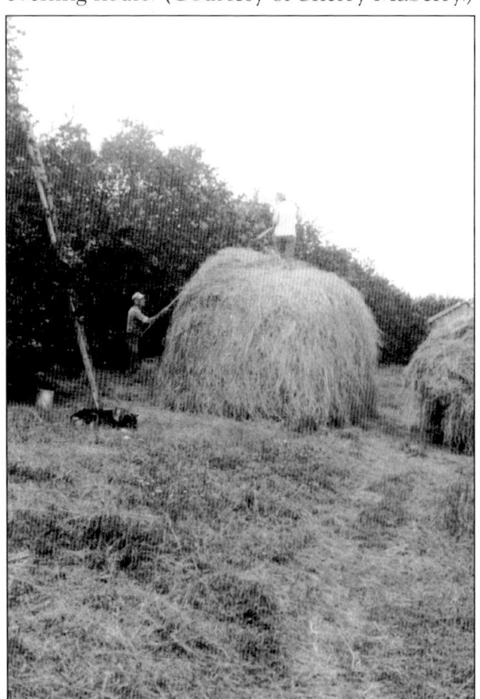

Siblings Adolph Wojteczko and Mary Wojteczko Werner worked on this large haystack at their homestead, established in 1910 on Snell Road in Alturas. This 1960s photograph is a good example of the hard work required when one family owns different agricultural ventures, as many in Alturas and Lake Garfield did. The Wojteczkos had cattle and citrus groves. Note the ladder lying against the tree waiting for someone to pick the fruit. (Courtesy of Mary Lou Young.)

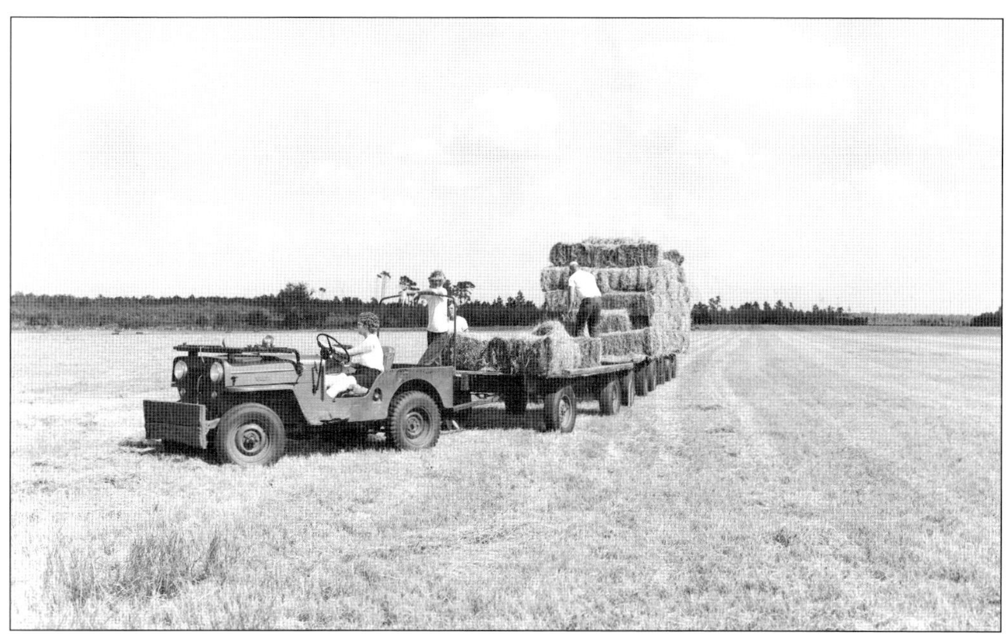

In 1964, Milton "Buster" and Betty Jean Bryan, along with their children, Mitty, Bobby, Beverly, Raymond, and David, moved from Largo, Florida, to their 1,776-acre ranch in Alturas. The ranch included 450 head of Angus cattle and 100 Angus bulls. The previous name of the ranch was Knollwood Angus Ranch, but Bryan renamed it the Circle Cross Ranch. In this 1967 photograph, Betty Jean is driving the 1950s jeep while Buster, Mitty, and Bobby load hay. Around 1975, they added poultry and raised 32,000 chickens, producing approximately 28,000 eggs a day. (Courtesy of Bobby Bryan.)

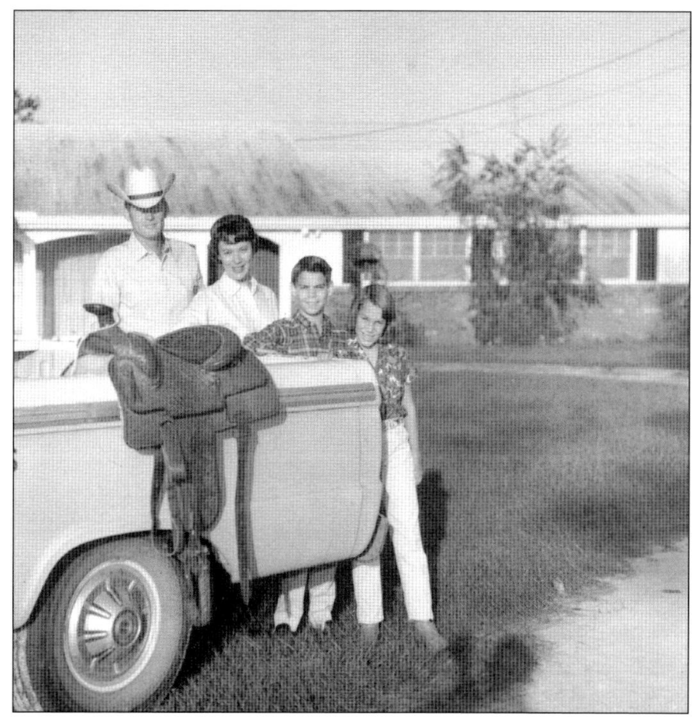

Jack Booream settled in Alturas after serving in the US Navy during the Korean War. He owned the Two Bits Horse Ranch in Alturas, where he raised and trained Thoroughbred quarter horses. The most famous was a horse named Bandos Pete. He and his wife, Nancy, and their children, Johnny and Janet, worked the ranch as a family. Jack served as the director of the American Quarter Horse Association and the Florida Quarter Horse Association. This is a 1969 family Christmas card picture. (Courtesy of Sherry Maberry.)

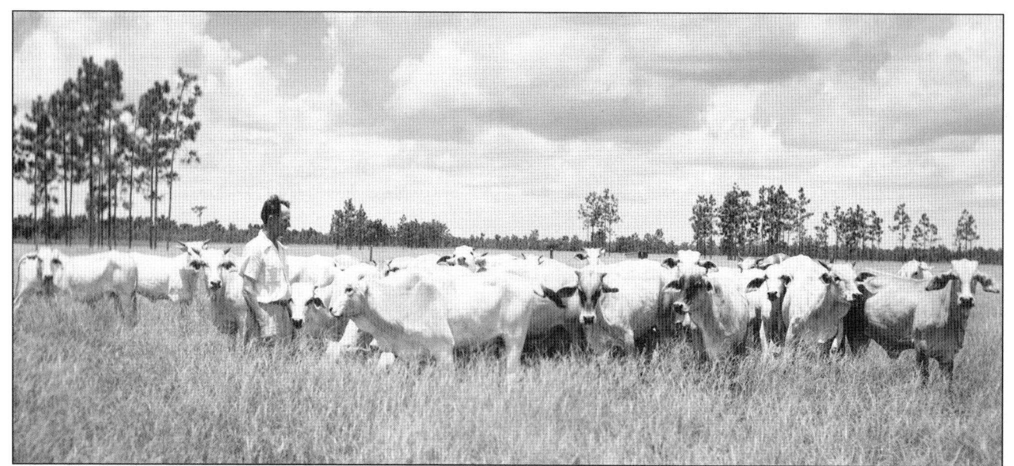

William H. Perdue and his wife, Savannah Anderson, brought their sons, Roy and Joe, to Alturas from Georgia in the early 1920s. Roy Perdue worked at the Blue Goose packing house, where he met his wife, Ruth Patton, daughter of well-known community leaders John and Maude Patton. After the couple married, Roy bought many groves and opened the Perdue Grove and Ranch Company. The couple had one son, John William, who helped in the family business. Later, Perdue invested in the cattle business as well. In this early 1950s photograph, Roy (above) inspects his herd of purebred Brahma cattle. Below, in April 1962, Lanny Johnson (left) and Roy (right) inspect a Valencia orange grove near the Perdues' office, located south of Packing House Road. This Valencia grove was lush and healthy until a rare Florida freeze killed the crop that same year. (Both, courtesy of Scott Young.)

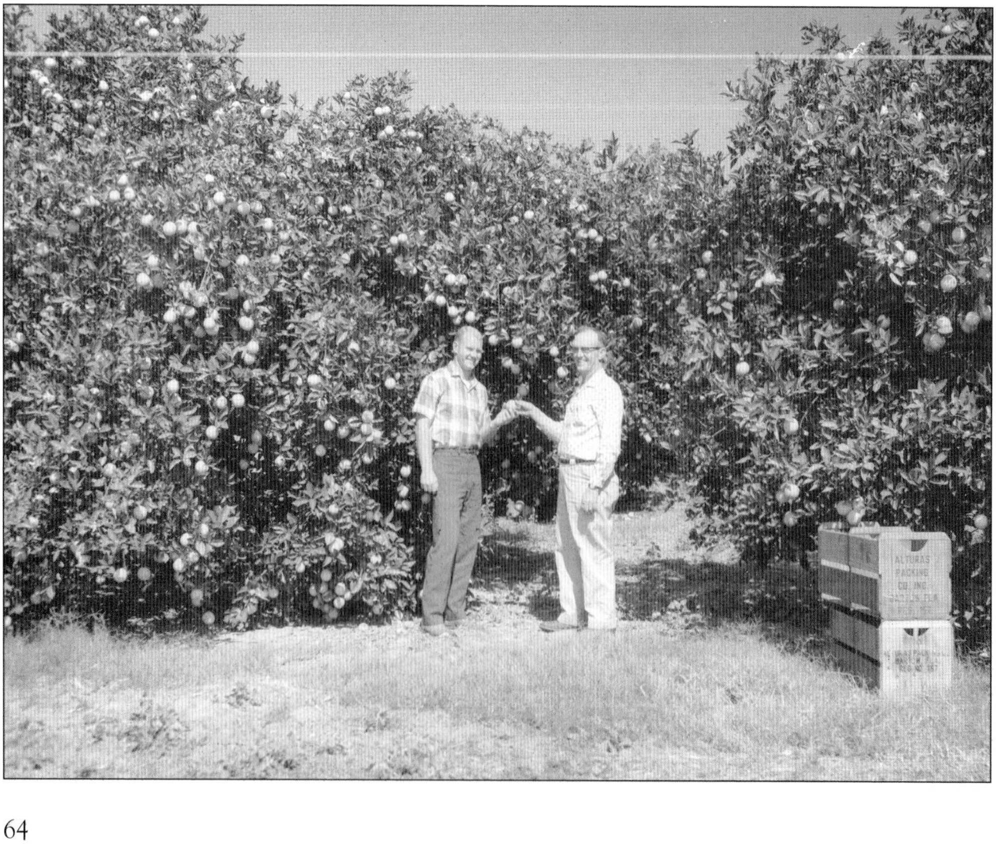

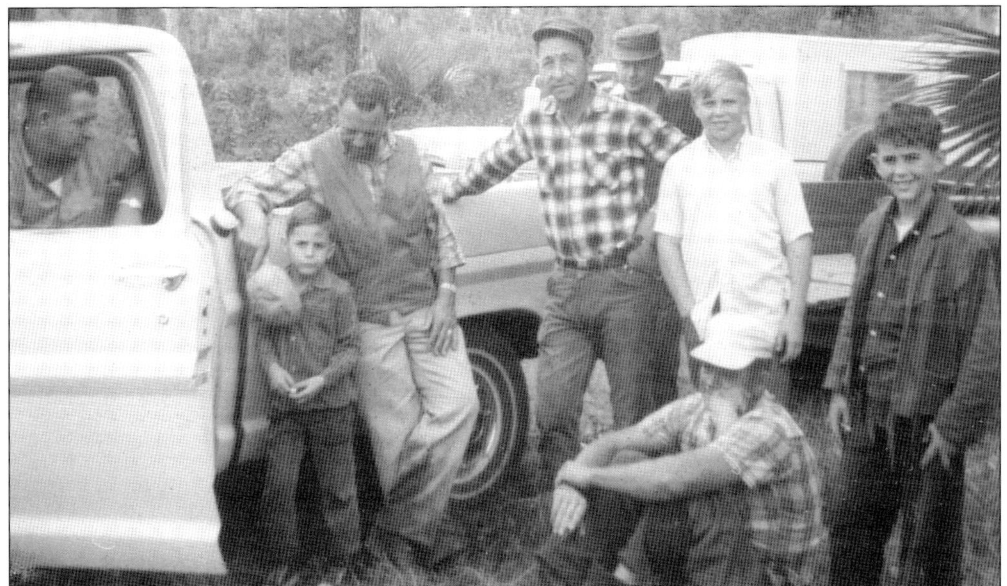

Pictured from left to right in 1968 are Dick Willis, Kevin Hielscher, Isaac Albritton, Merlin Hielscher, Carl Biebricher, Bill Voigt, Scott Young, and an unidentified man (sitting). The Florida Everglades hunting trips were considered a rite of passage for many a young Alturas boy. In 1977, grove and cattle owner Isaac Albritton (after years of affiliation with the Alturas Packing Company), formed Tri-Britton Citrus and Cattle Caretaking Company of Alturas with his sons, Nick and Dale, and their spouses, Nita, Phyllis, and Carolyn. This business venture is still thriving today under the leadership of Albritton's son Dale and grandchildren Jeff Albritton and Sabrena Albritton Smothers. (Courtesy of Scott Young.)

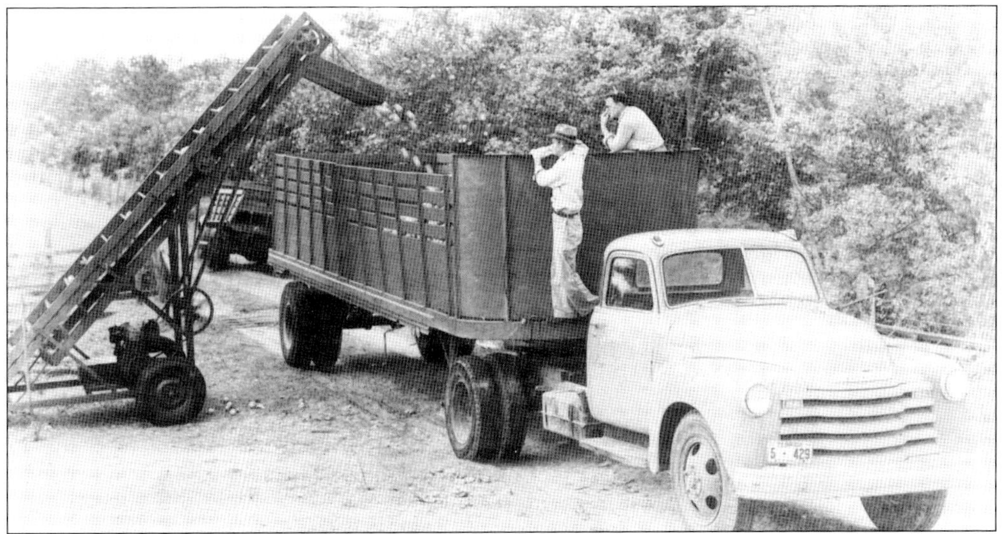

Two unidentified Alturas men look down on a standard citrus harvesting operation in 1968 before the invention of hydraulic loaders. Oranges were fed from the tailgate of a truck into a Rube Goldberg–like contraption that consisted of a series of paddles sending the citrus "escalator style" into the waiting semitrucks. The Wiggins truck was owned by the Wiggins Packing House, located in nearby Bartow, Florida. Note that Florida car tags were numbered by population, and Polk County was No. 5. (Courtesy of Scott Young.)

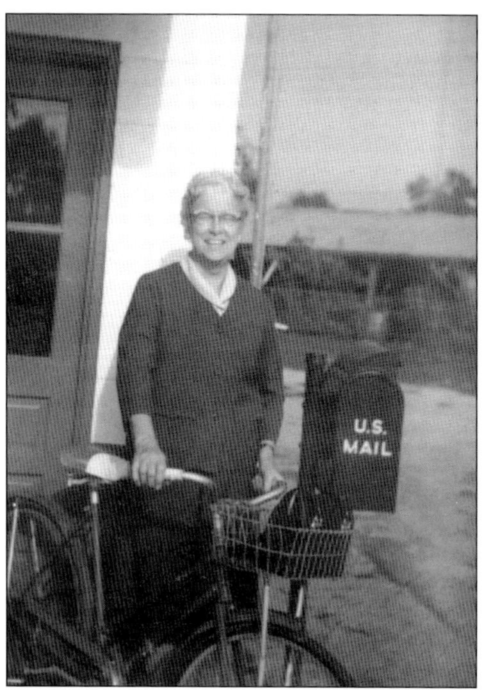

Grace Davis became the first female postmaster in Alturas in the 1960s. She and her husband, George, were local residents. Grace was very efficient and always wore her uniform proudly. It those years, all residents had a post office mailbox, and they all had letter combinations to open them. The post office was a local gathering place for the small community. Other postmasters were George G. Seiler (1911), Benjamin H. James, Brookes Register Sr., Brookes Register Jr., Ed Grass, Douglas Smith, Grace Davis, Evelyn Hielscher, and Brenda Aust (the last postmaster for the area). (Courtesy of Sherry Maberry.)

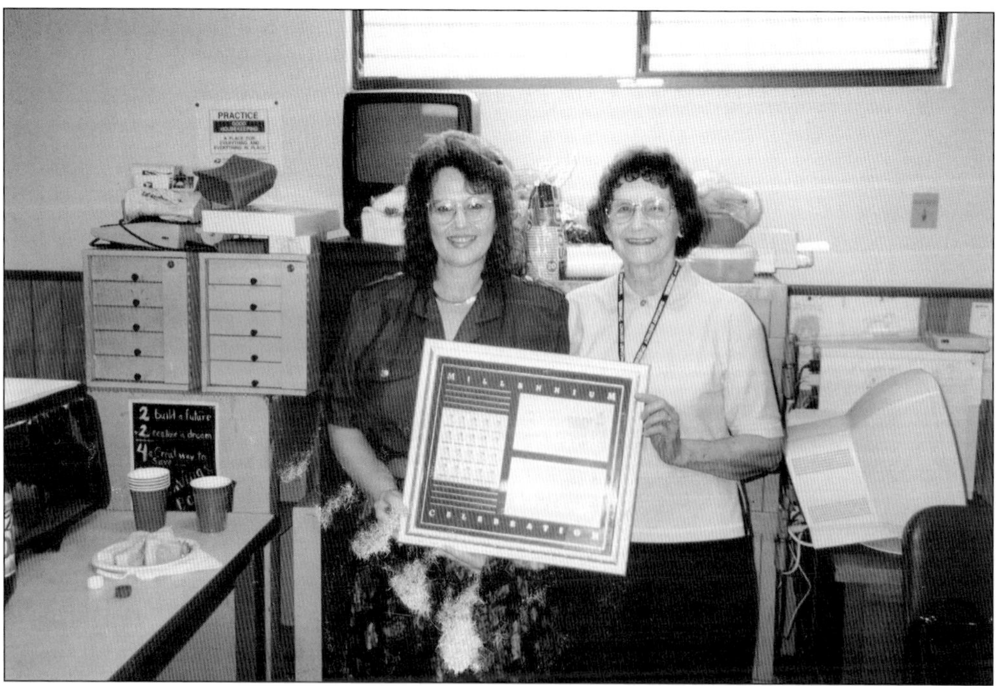

Alturas postmaster Evelyn Hielscher (right) served for 33 years in the US Postal Service. In 1989, she won the first place National Award as the most energy-efficient Class C (small) post office. She was honored during a recognition ceremony in Washington, DC, and was presented an award by the postmaster general at the time. In this photograph, Brenda Aust (left, who later became the Alturas postmaster) and Hielscher are holding the Millennium Celebration plaque showing the first stamps of the 21st century. (Courtesy of Sherry Maberry.)

SOUTH FLORIDA DIVISION--VALRICO SUB-DIVISION--VALRICO AND ALCOMA

SOUTHWARD THIRD CLASS		SECOND CLASS	FIRST CLASS		Distance from Richmond	Station Numbers	Distance from Valrico		TIME TABLE No. 10 April 29, 1951			Distance from Alcoma	CAPACITY TRACKS Siding	CAPACITY TRACKS Other	NORTHWARD FIRST CLASS		SECOND CLASS	THIRD CLASS	
467	481	387	257	321											258	322	380	468	482
Local Freight	Local Freight	Red Ball Freight	Local Passenger	Local Passenger											Local Passenger	Local Passenger	The Marketer	Local Freight	Local Freight
Daily	Ex. Sun.	Ex. Sat.	Daily	Daily											Daily	Daily	Ex. Sun.	Daily	Ex. Sun.
A. M.	A. M.	P. M.	P. M.	A. M.					STATIONS						A. M.	P. M.	P. M.	P. M.	P. M.
5.00		10.30	f 2.17	f 8.25	832.5	Z 833	0.0	NP LV	VALRICO	4.9	AR	51.7	85		f10.31	f 6.05	10.00	12.35	
5.15		10.45	f 2.25	s 8.32	837.4	Z 837	4.9	NP	DURANT	6.9	Y	46.8		180	f10.23	s 5.58	9.40	12.20	
5.32		11.00		f 8.40	844.3 834.2	Z 844 V 834	11.8	NP	WELCOME	1.6	Y	39.9		40		f 5.50	9.10	12.01	
5.36		11.05		f 8.42	835.8	V 836 VC836	13.4	NP	EDISON	3.1	Y	38.3		126		f 5.47	9.05	11.50	
5.45					838.9	V 839	16.5	P	NICHOLS	2.0		35.2	90	Yard				11.15	
5.50					840.9	V 841	18.5	NOP	IM & C JCT.	1.4	Y X IMC	33.2	90	Yard				10.55	
6.15					842.3	V 842	19.9	NP	MULBERRY	0.7	X ACL	31.8		5 S				10.50	
					843.0	V 843 VH852	20.6	P	SOUTH MULBERRY	2.5	Y	31.1							
6.40					845.5	V 846	23.1	P	RIDGEWOOD	5.3	Y	28.6	90	Spur				10.30	
7.10					850.8	V 851	28.4	NP	BARTOW	0.3	Y X ACL X ACL	23.3	90	82				10.00	
7.20					851.1	V 851	28.7	P	PEMBROKE JCT	2.0		23.0		Spur N 35				9.45	
7.30					853.1	V 852	30.7	P	CONNERS	2.3	Y	21.0	90	Spur				9.35	
7.40					855.4	V 855	33.0	P	LAKE GARFIELD	3.2		18.7		10 S 18				9.30	
8.00					858.6	V 859	36.2	DP	ALTURAS	4.9		15.5		67				9.15	
8.30	7.00				863.5	V 864	41.1	N	WEST LAKE WALES	3.9	X SAL O Y	10.6		Yard				9.00	1.00
	8.50				867.4	V 867	45.0	NP	LAKE WALES	6.7	X ACL	6.7		Yard					12.4[illegible]
	9.25				874.1	V 874	51.7	AR	ALCOMA		LV	0.0		5 N					9.30
A. M.	A. M.	P. M.	P. M.	A. M.					EASTERN STANDARD TIME						A. M.	P. M.	P. M.	A. M.	A. M.
Daily	Ex. Sun.	Ex. Sat.	Daily	Daily											Daily	Daily	Ex. Sun.	Daily	Ex. Sun.
467	481	387	257	321											258	322	380	468	482

(Rule 72) All northward trains are superior to trains of the same class in opposite direction.
No. 482 WAIT AT ALCOMA INDEFINITELY FOR No. 481.
THE TIME OF TRAINS AT WELCOME APPLIES AS FOLLOWS:
NORTHWARD TRAINS AT SOUTH CROSSOVER.
SOUTHWARD TRAINS AT NORTH CROSSOVER.

THE TIME OF TRAINS AT EDISON APPLIES AS FOLLOWS:
NORTHWARD TRAINS AT JUNCTION SWITCH.
SOUTHWARD TRAINS AT NORTH CROSSOVER.
Special instructions pages 13 and 14.

The 1951 Seaboard Airline employees timetable was for the governance of trains on the Valrico Subdivision of the South Florida Division. Note the station names on the timetable of Lake Garfield, Alturas, West Lake Wales, Lake Wales, and Alcoma, this line's terminus. (Courtesy of Scott Young.)

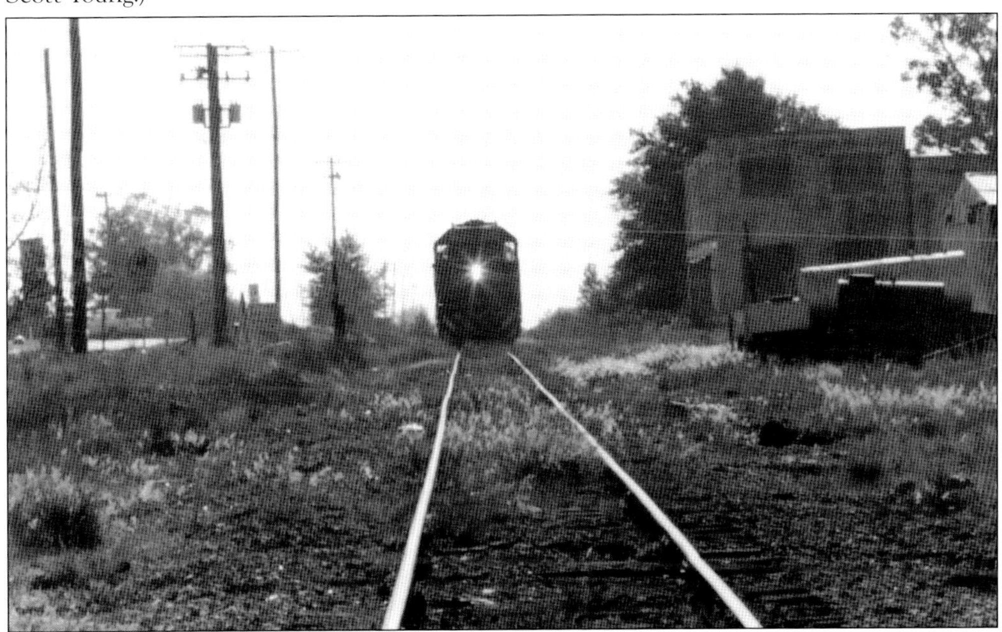

The last train to ever go through Alturas was in 1983. This photograph shows the train as it approaches the old Alturas Citrus Fruit Packing Company at the only crossroad in the township. The packing house, shown at right, burned down in 2017. Although no longer used by passing trains, the railroad tracks continued to be useful, by becoming a harbor for retired train cars. Alturas was quite the railroad town when it was founded in 1911. However, this last train marked the end of an era. (Courtesy of Scott Young.)

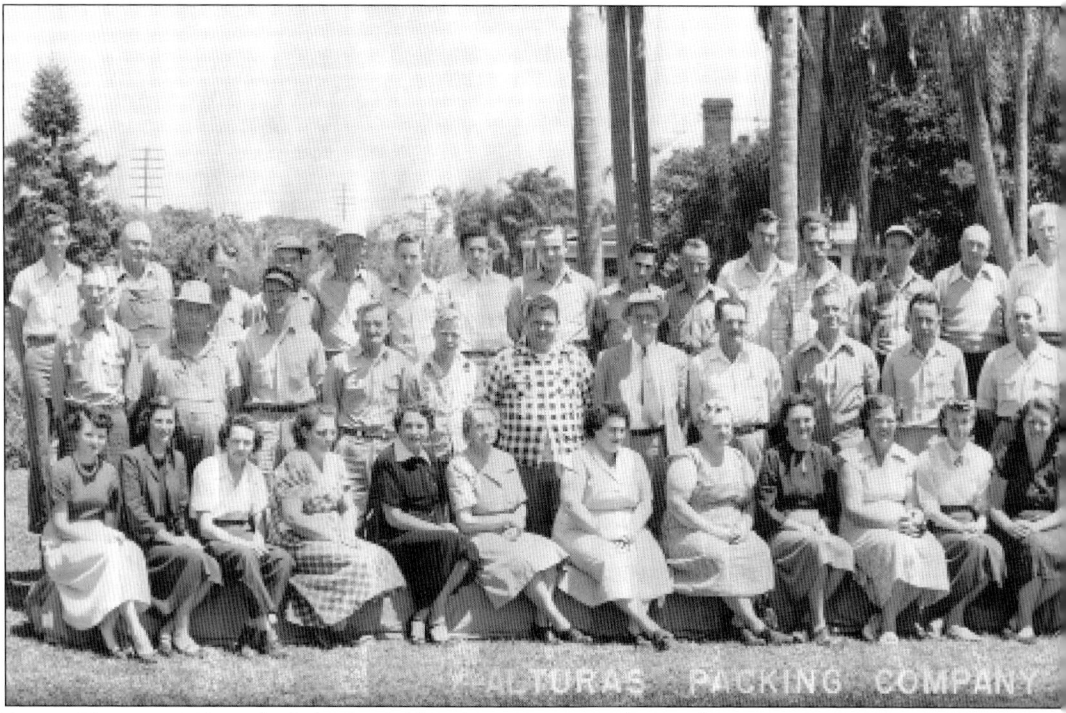

Pictured here in 1955 are the Lake Garfield Packing House employees. (Courtesy of Kevin Hielscher.)

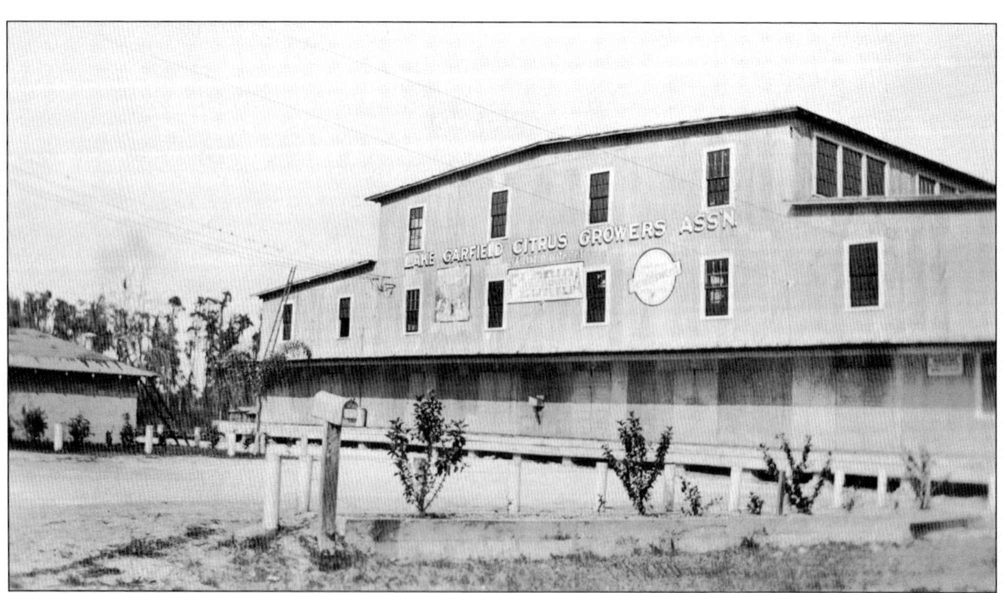

The Lake Garfield Citrus Growers Association, incorporated in February 1914 by George R. Johnson, A.H. Sloan and T.T. Hatton, built the Lake Garfield Packing House in 1915 on Eighty Foot Road near the railroad crossing. The association growers began producing the Queen Orange variety that had been discovered in the area around 1900. The orange was sweet and juicy and was found to be resistant to cold weather. (Courtesy of Florida Southern College.)

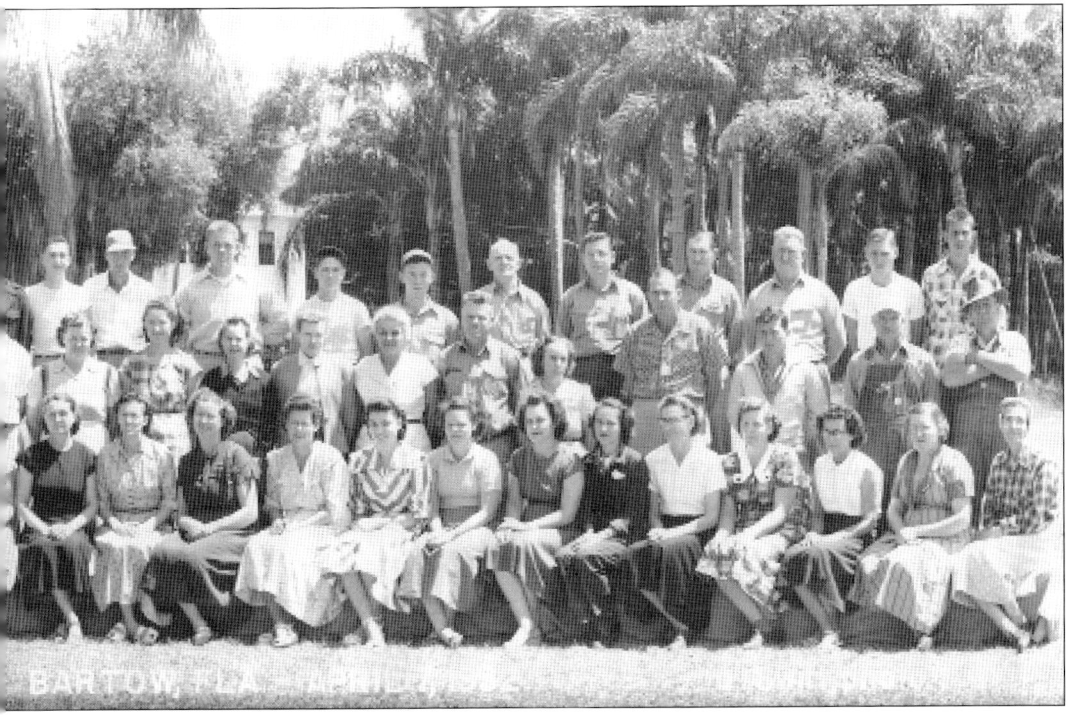

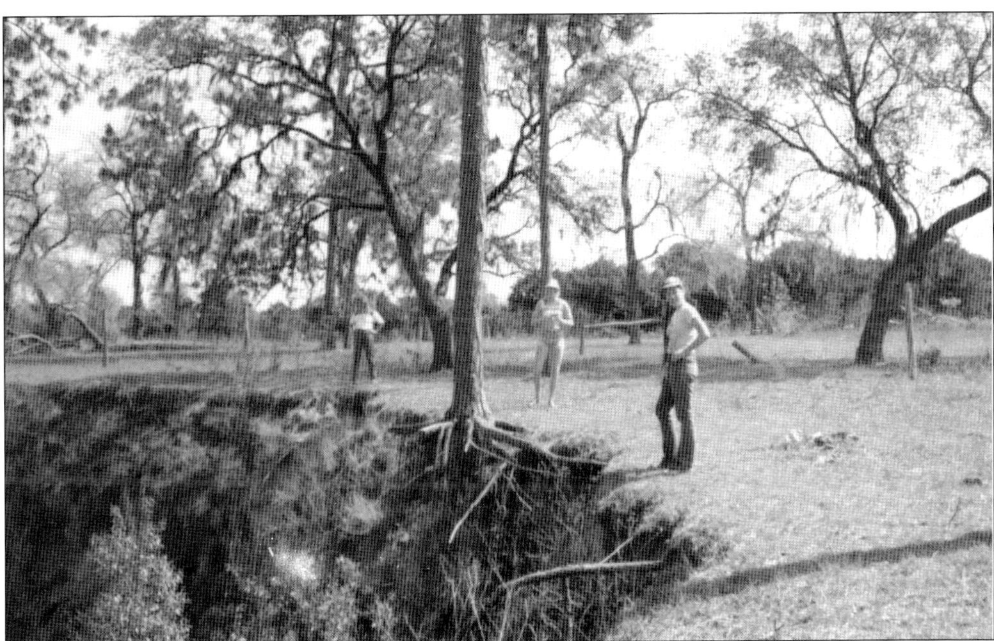

In 1979, sightseers gawk at a gigantic sinkhole that opened in a pasture near District Line Road, located south of Lake Garfield. The tops of pine trees were swallowed whole by Mother Nature, a phenomenon as viable as the chasm itself. (Courtesy of Scott Young.)

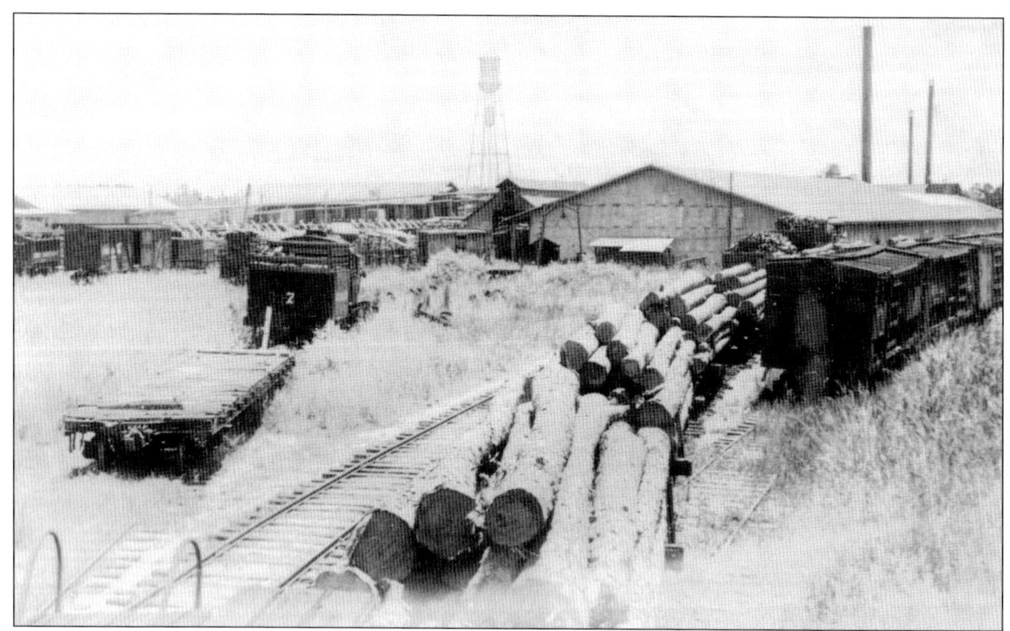

In the 1920s, the Roux family bought the Lake Garfield sawmill, started in 1915, and changed the name to the Roux Crate and Lumber Company. Locomotives hauled lumber to the sawmill to produce crates for shipping fruit. It also milled lumber used to build the Davis Causeway in Tampa. Lumber was shipped to South Africa to shore up gold mines because the hard pine was termite resistant. Sawmill employees, who lived in company homes, were paid with tokens called babbitts. When Pres. Theodore Roosevelt declared babbitts illegal, Col. Edwin T. Roux threw the tokens in Surveyors Lake near his home in Alturas. The sawmill helped grow a bustling community, which gave rise to the other business opportunities such as the commissary, cannery, general store, nursery, churches, and schools. The sawmill closed in 1942 due to the lack of material. In later years, it was converted into a cannery, first for citrus and then for beans to feed World War II soldiers. (Both, courtesy of Cathy Curtis.)

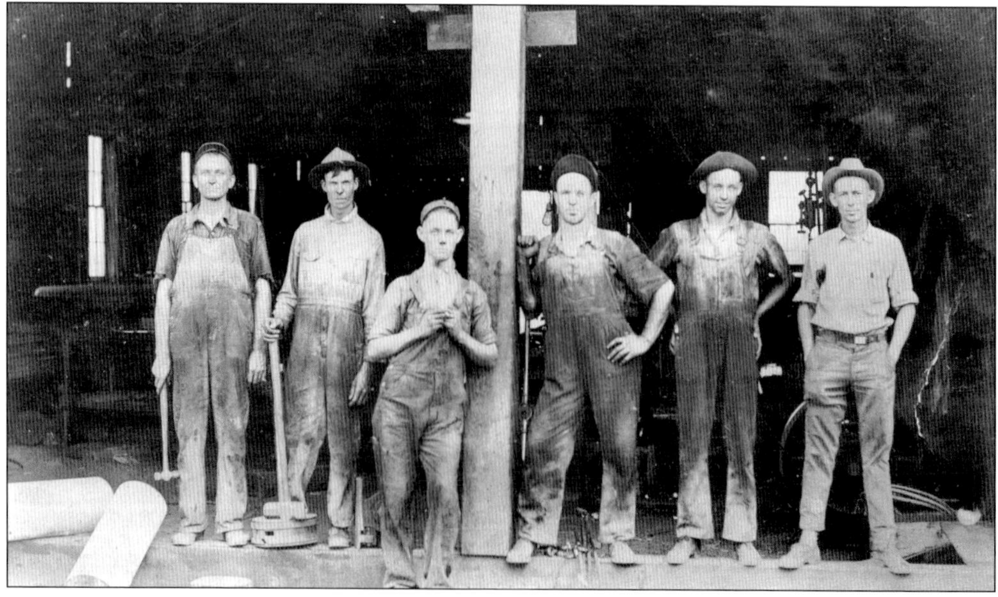

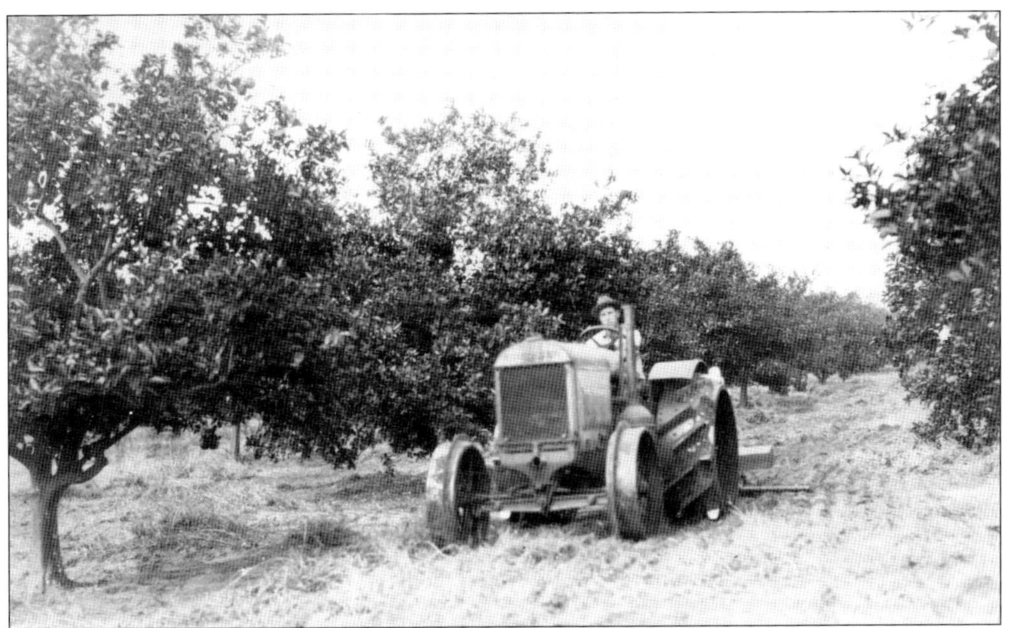

The Stenger patriarch John George Stenger Sr. and his wife, Olga, relocated to Lake Garfield from Cincinnati in 1912. They immediately began clearing the land to plant citrus. They harvested lumber off the land to begin construction of their home. This photograph, from around 1915, depicts their son Louis Stenger working in the family orange grove with their steel wheeled tractor. (Courtesy of Jackie Stenger Stoltz.)

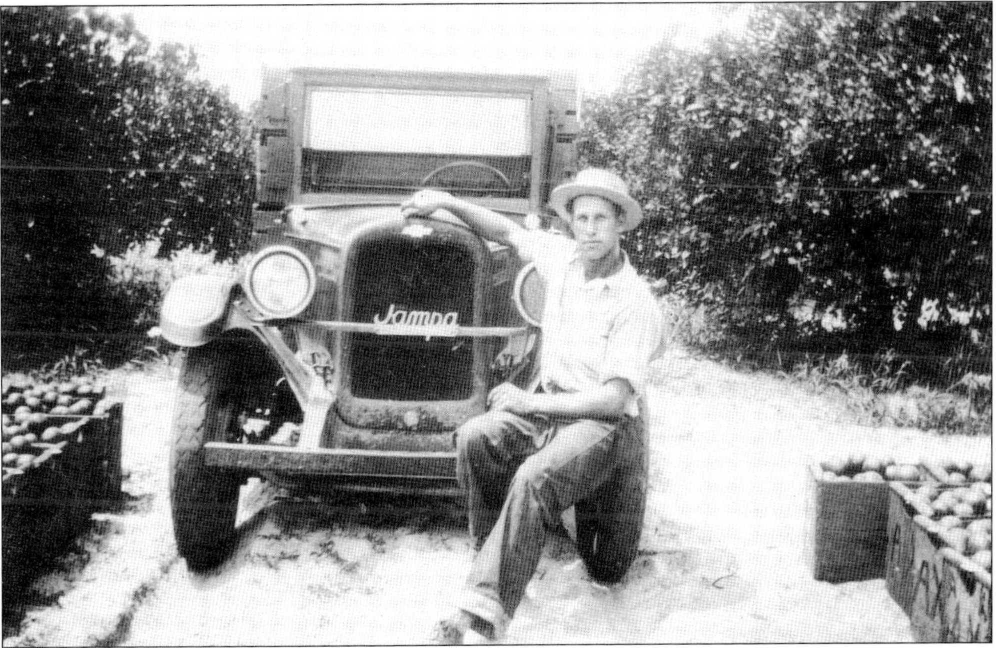

Lake Garfield's pioneer Louis Stenger relaxes on a Chevrolet truck loaded with produce harvested from the parallel rows of orange trees in 1924. Beautiful fruit in Alturas Exchange field crates await their turn to be taken to the Lake Garfield Packing House and eventually shipped to consumers in the north. (Courtesy of Scott Young.)

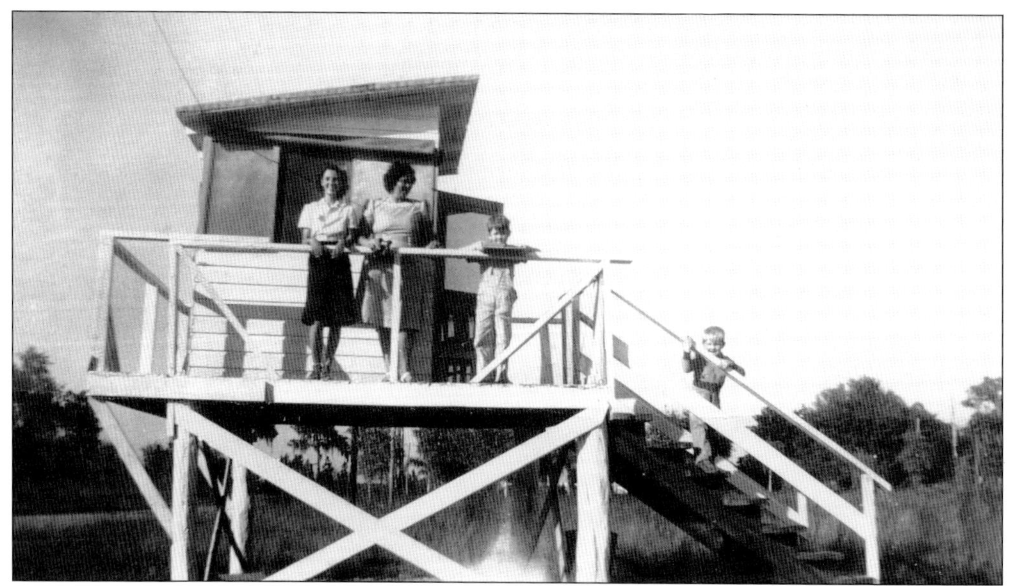

Alturas residents would watch for World War II enemy airplanes from the Civil Defense Plane Spotting Tower (known locally as the Listening Post), located at the main crossroad in the heart of Alturas. Patriotic citizens, like the ones seen here in 1943, served their country by manning the tower 24 hours a day. Women would take two-hour shifts during the day, and the men would take the night watch. Those identified are Sylva Swartz, far left, and John Voigt, far right. (Courtesy of Leanne Hielscher Mitchell.)

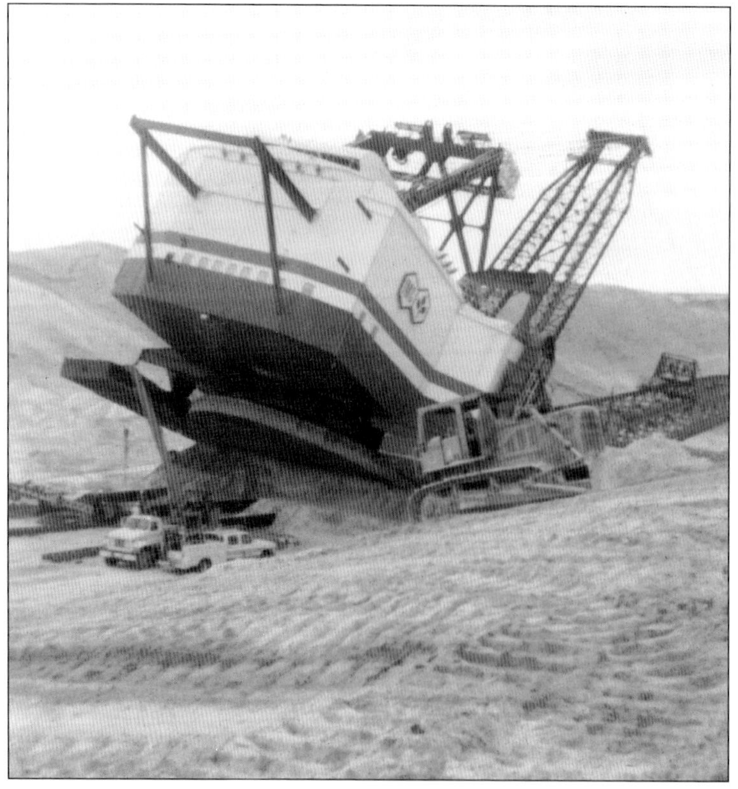

The International Mineral and Chemical Company (IMC) dragline excavated phosphate from the Lake Garfield vicinity beginning in 1968. This dragline toppled into a huge pit in the late 1970s. The incident was referred to as "Ace in the Hole" by Lake Garfield residents who were secretly pleased since the dragline was digging up their beloved community. Note how small the trucks look compared with the IMC dragline, whom many referred to as the "Bigger Digger." (Courtesy of Cathy Curtis.)

William G. Frankenburger and his wife, Lyda Frankenburger, were entrepreneurs in the beginning years of the Lake Garfield settlement. Not only did they profit from the citrus industry and cattle ranching, but they also opened one of the first general stores in the Lake Garfield tract in the late 1930s or early 1940s, pictured right. It had two gas pumps, a kerosene tank, and a hydraulic car lift. The store was managed in the beginning by John and Ann Stanley, who lived in one of houses on the Frankenburger property. Later, the store was managed by Ruby Goff and her mother and was known to the locals as Goff's Groceries. The store closed in the late 1960s. (Courtesy of Cathy Curtis.)

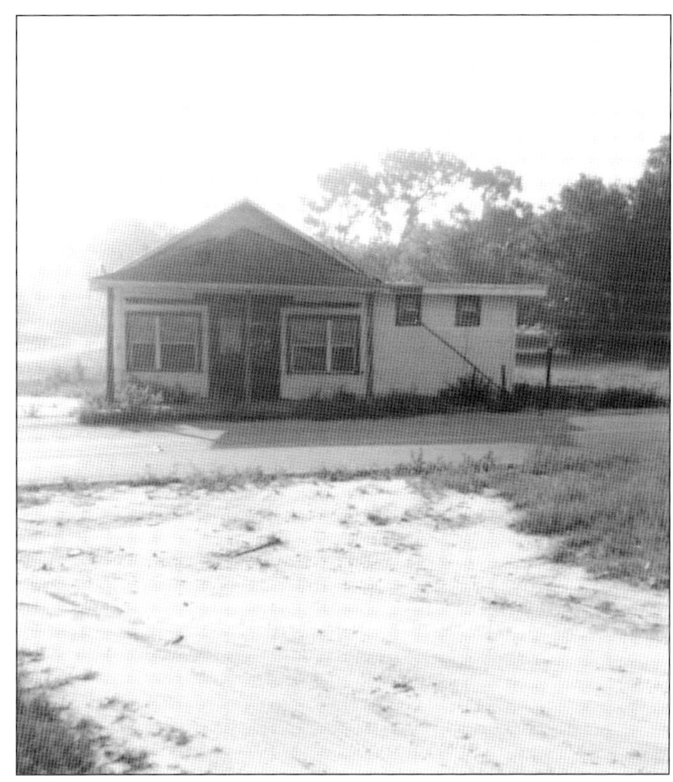

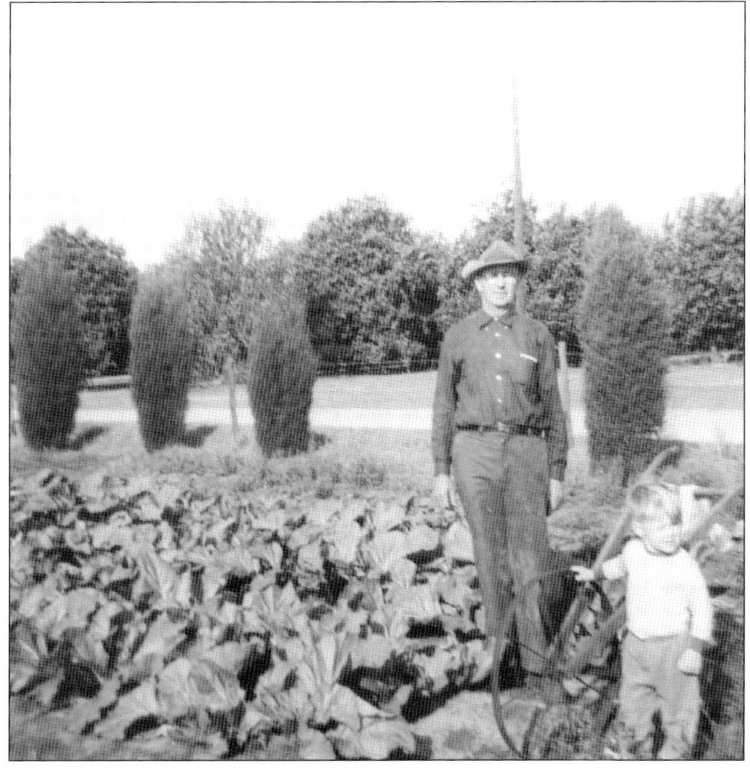

Will Padgett and his son Bill are pictured tending their collard greens, with a push tiller in their family garden, in this 1951 photograph. Padgett worked for W.G. Frankenburger as a grove caretaker and lived behind the Goff's Grocery Store (above), which was owned by Frankenburger. Later, Padgett became foreman of Stenger Grove Service and moved his family to a home on Stenger Road in Lake Garfield. (Courtesy of Shirley Padgett Johnson.)

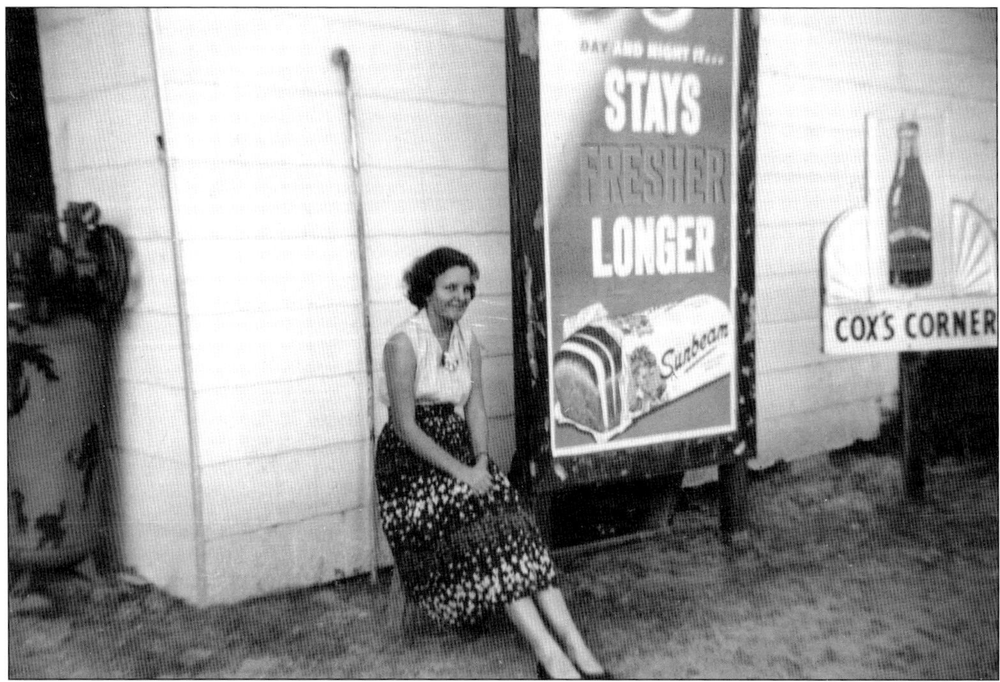

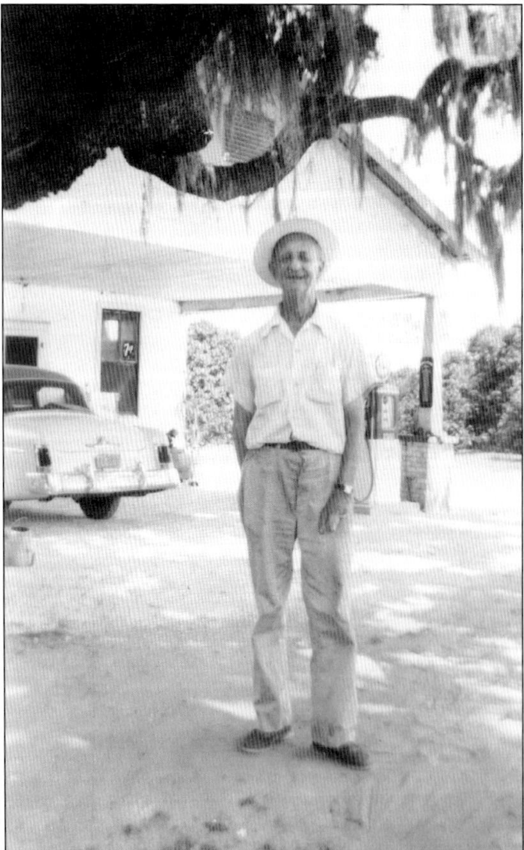

Cox's Corner Store was located at the corner of Cox Road and the 80 Foot Road in Lake Garfield. Mariline Tiebeau is taking a breather at the store—the "getting place" for a cold drink and a snack—in the 1950s picture. Tiebeau was visiting her cousin Shirley Padgett, who, as a young person, worked many years as a cashier at the store. (Courtesy of Shirley Padgett Johnson.)

Prior to the 1940s, Cox's Corner Store's original proprietor was Dirven Vickers. The original store name at that time is unknown. Leila Ione Cox and her husband purchased the general store from the Vickers and named it Cox's Corner Store. The Cox family recreated it into a family-friendly environment that sold gas and groceries. Leila's daughter and son-in-law, Murray and Catherine Harrison, took ownership in the 1950s. Pictured here in 1954 is Murray's father, who was lovingly called Grandpa Harrison by the community. Later, the Hegler family bought the store. Jerry and Glenda Porter were the last known proprietors before the doors closed in the 1970s. (Courtesy of Shirley Padgett Johnson.)

Four

The Churches

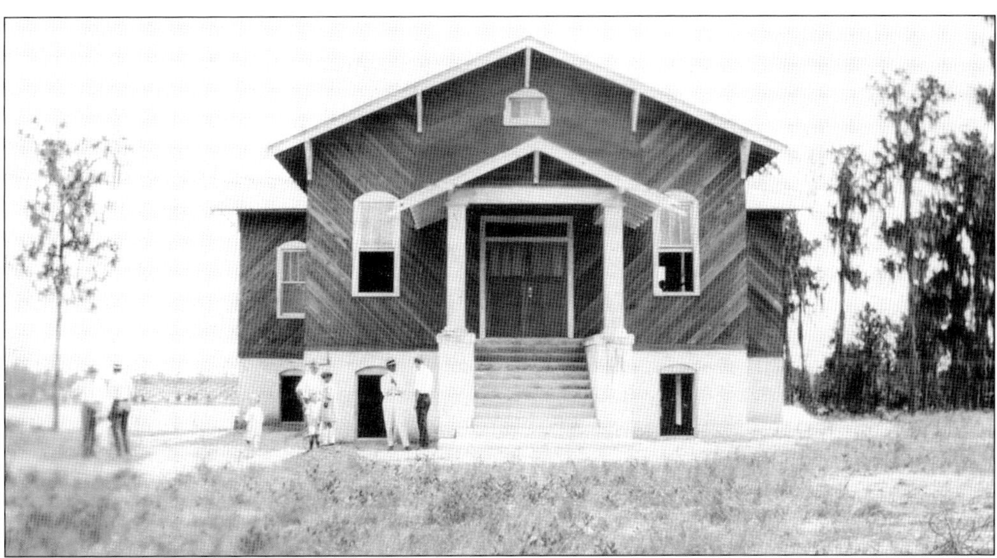

From the beginning of the area's history, life in Alturas and Lake Garfield revolved around the faith of their people. Over time, organized churches came to life and created a solid faith foundation for the building of the two small communities. The Alturas Methodist Church congregation began their services in the upstairs room of the recently constructed Seiler Hotel in 1915. This was the first photograph taken that shows completion of their new church building in 1924. Victor E. Voigt oversaw construction with F.J. Rosenburg as his assistant. In 1968, this church became affiliated with the United Methodist Church. (Courtesy of Linda King.)

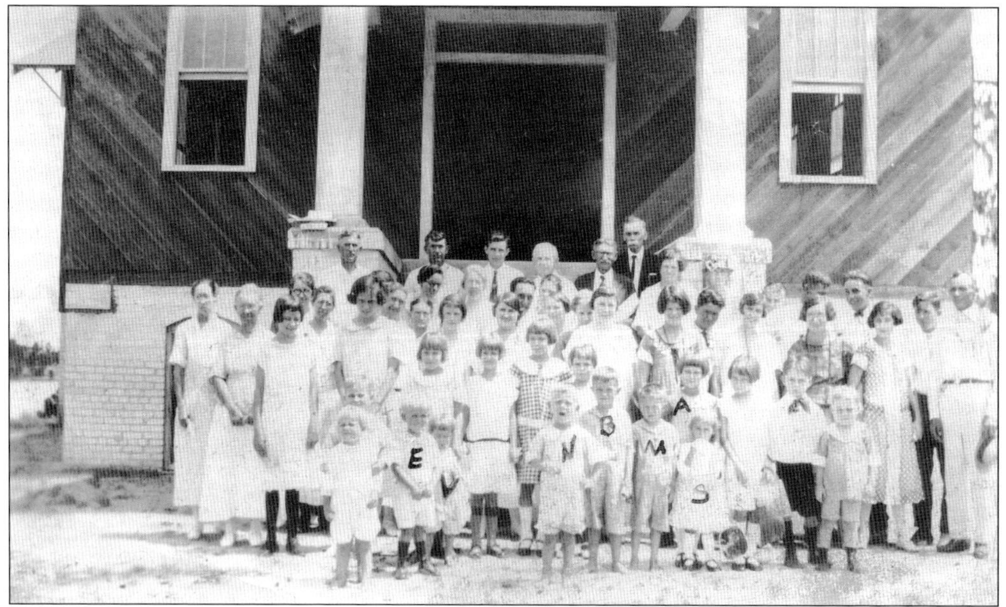

The Alturas Methodist Church members gathered in front of their church in 1924. It is interesting to note that the church exterior of rough pine is still present at this time. These big timbers were locally cut, milled, and donated by Benjamin Brookes Register Sr., affectionatey known as "Pappi." The high-water level of Star Lake is clearly visible on the west side of the church building. The cornerstone of the church was laid with the following names: Rev. W.H. Herndon, V.E. Voigt, Noah Swartsel, Sadie F. Connell Swartsel, R.G. Newcome, F.J. Rosenburg, and W.A. Barr. (Courtesy of Karen Kelly.)

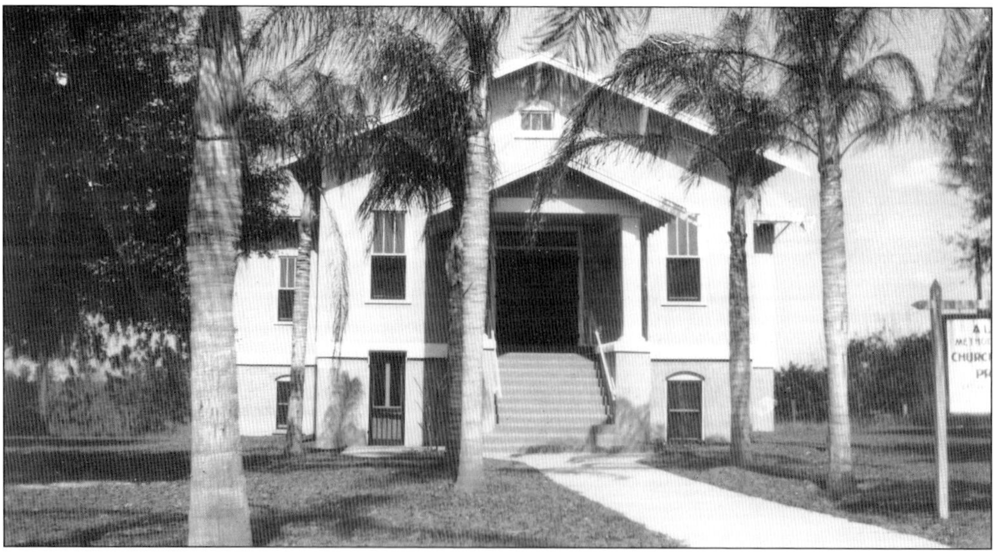

A stucco finish was added to Alturas Methodist Church, which covered the rough pine exterior. It is pictured here in the 1940s. The beautiful, locally grown palm trees in the landscape were donated by Victor Voigt. Some noteworthy history is that the Pittsburgh Development Company owned the Alturas town site in the 1910s and 1920s. The church traded its original site, which was gifted to them by the company, for this lakefront lot to build a church. The church paid an additional $500 for the trade. (Courtesy of Karen Kelly.)

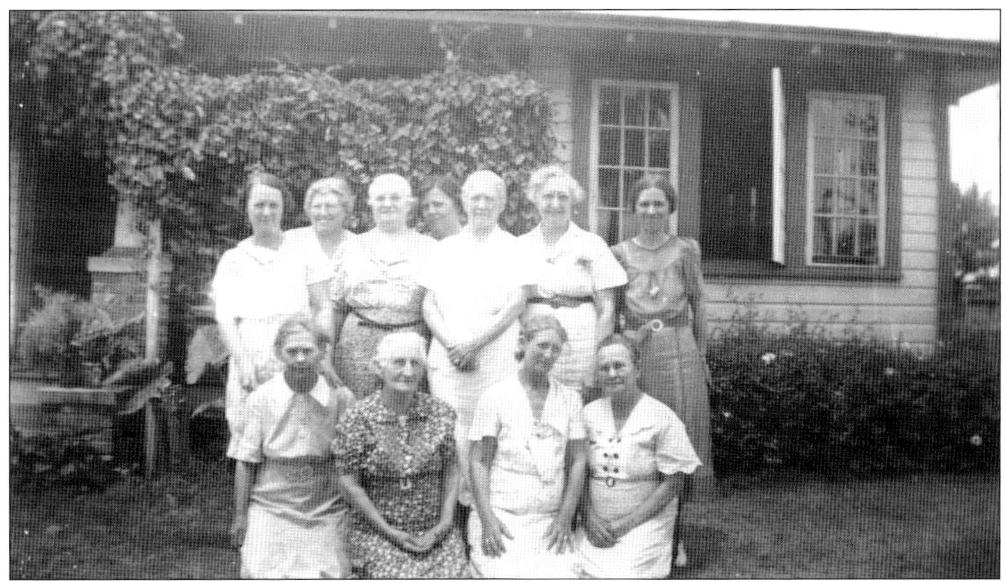

The newly formed Ladies Aid Society of the Alturas Methodist Church met at the home of John and Maude Patton in 1938. Those pictured, from left to right, are (first row) Nellie Swartz, Annie Leytham, Maude Patton, and Isabel Chitty; (second row) Ethel Gadau, Myrtle Hains, Winnie Knauff, Dorothy Godwin, Georgia Sheldon, Anna Newcome, and Mrs. M.E. Myers (pastor's wife). Later in its history, the group's name changed to the Woman's Missionary Society. (Courtesy of Linda King.)

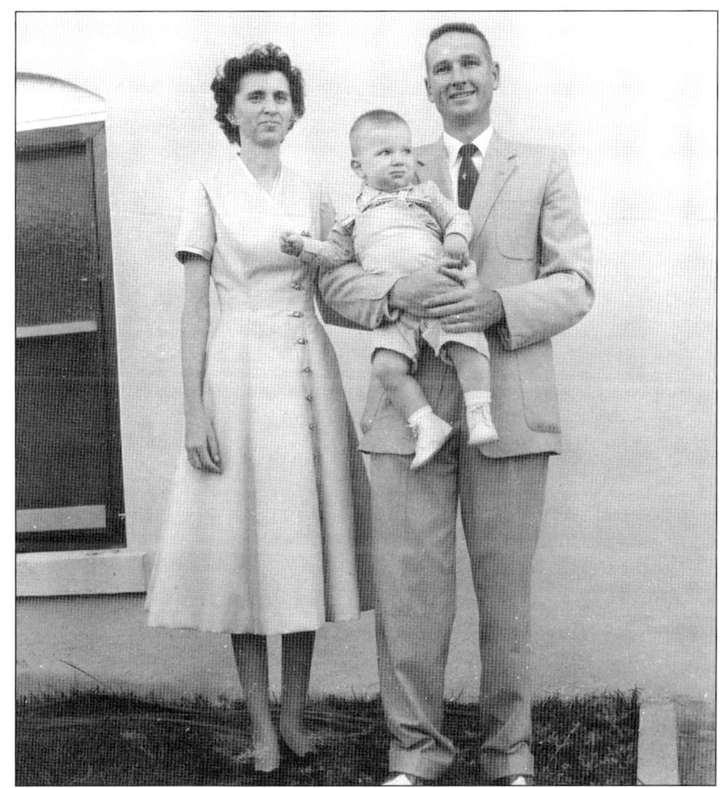

In June 1953, Rev. William P. Trobough became the first full-time pastor of the Alturas Methodist Church. In 1956, he also served a second appointment at this church as the fourth full-time pastor after he received additional ministerial education. This photograph was taken on January 13, 1957, and shows Trobough with his wife, Alma, and their son, Little John. This day of celebration was for the ground breaking of the new Sunday school room building. (Courtesy of Linda King.)

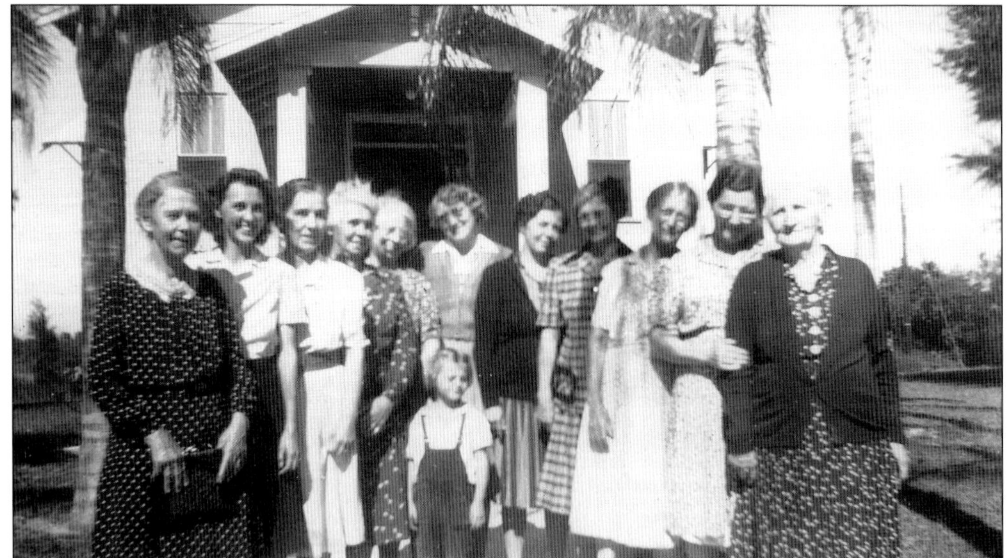

The Alturas Methodist Church's Ladies Aid Society played an integral role in the church's development and growth. The society sponsored community suppers to raise funds to pay off the $500 mortgage for the lakefront property. Pictured above from left to right are Nellie Swartz, Sylva Swartz, Mrs. V.O. White, Ester Wilson, Zula Voigt, Della Voigt, Dorothy Godwin, Hazel Lander, Maude Patton, Mrs. Woodward (pastor's wife), Annie Elizabeth Leytham, and an unidentified child. (Courtesy of Linda King.)

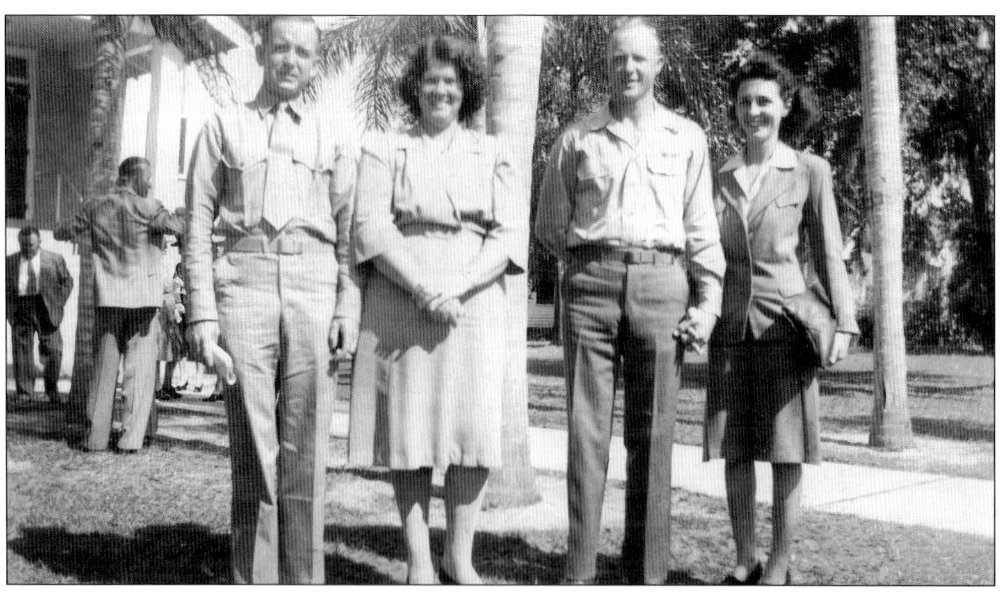

Alturas servicemen Fred Smith (left) and Jessie Kelly (right) are on leave from World War II in 1945. They are pictured here with their future wives, Marguerite Voigt and Sylva Swartz, on the Sunday that Marguerite joined the membership of the Alturas Methodist Church. In the background are father and son, Victor and John Voigt. (Courtesy of Karen Kelly.)

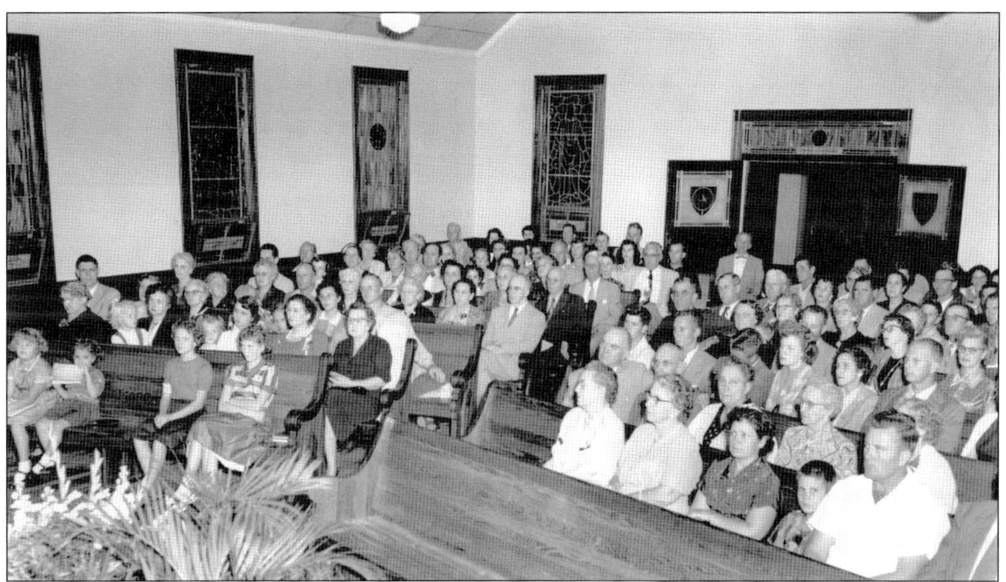

In April 1955, Alturas Methodist Church members celebrated the dedication of the beautiful stained-glass windows that graced their sanctuary. Each window was donated by a church family, often in memory of a loved one who had passed away. The windows were artistically created by a stained-glass company from St. Petersburg, Florida. Over the years, additional windows were added to complete the collection in the sanctuary. (Photograph by Robertson Studio; courtesy of Linda King.)

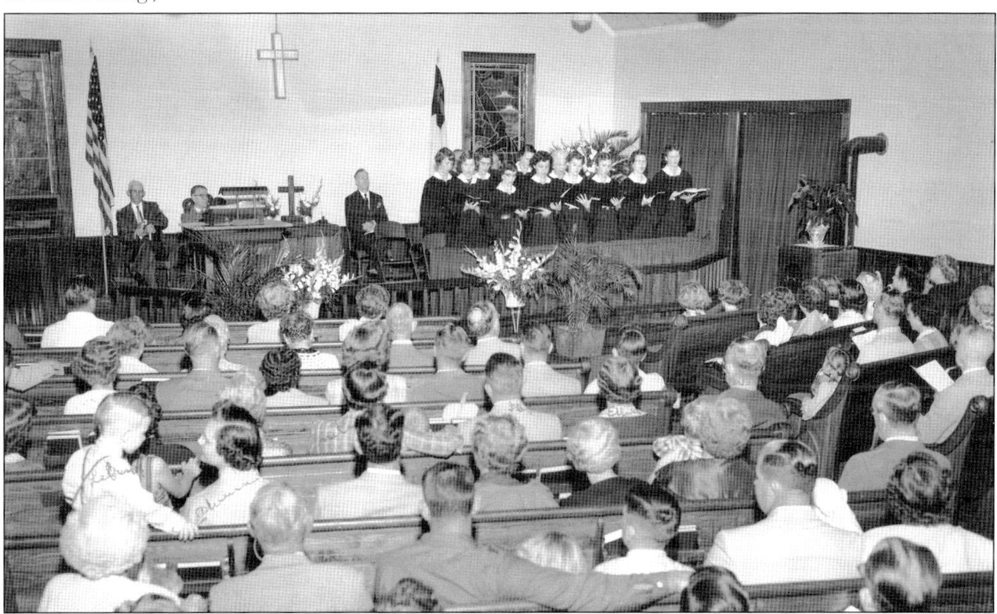

In April 1955, during the stained-glass dedication service in the Alturas Methodist Church sanctuary, the beautiful lighted cross is visible as well as one of the ornate stained-glass windows. Choir members, pictured from left to right, are Christine Underwood, Sue Murphy, Ruth Stevens, Doris Odell, Mrs. George Wiseman (pastor's wife), Gloria Estes, Zula Voigt, Gail Stevens, Leila Allen, an unidentified woman, and Bessie Voigt. (Photograph by Robertson Studio; courtesy of Linda King.)

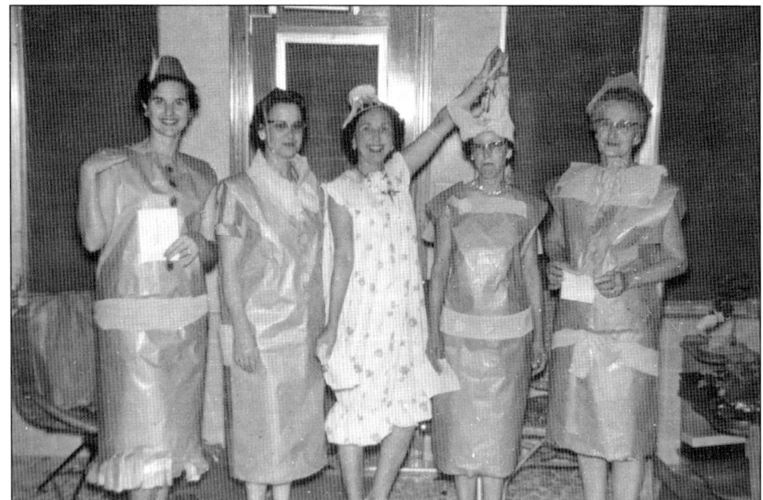

Fun was always to be found at gatherings of the Alturas Methodist Church ladies. Those featured in this photograph, from left to right, are Wanda Young, Ruth Odowski, Sylva Kelly, Alta Mae Jenkins, and Vera Howard. (Courtesy of Karen Kelly.)

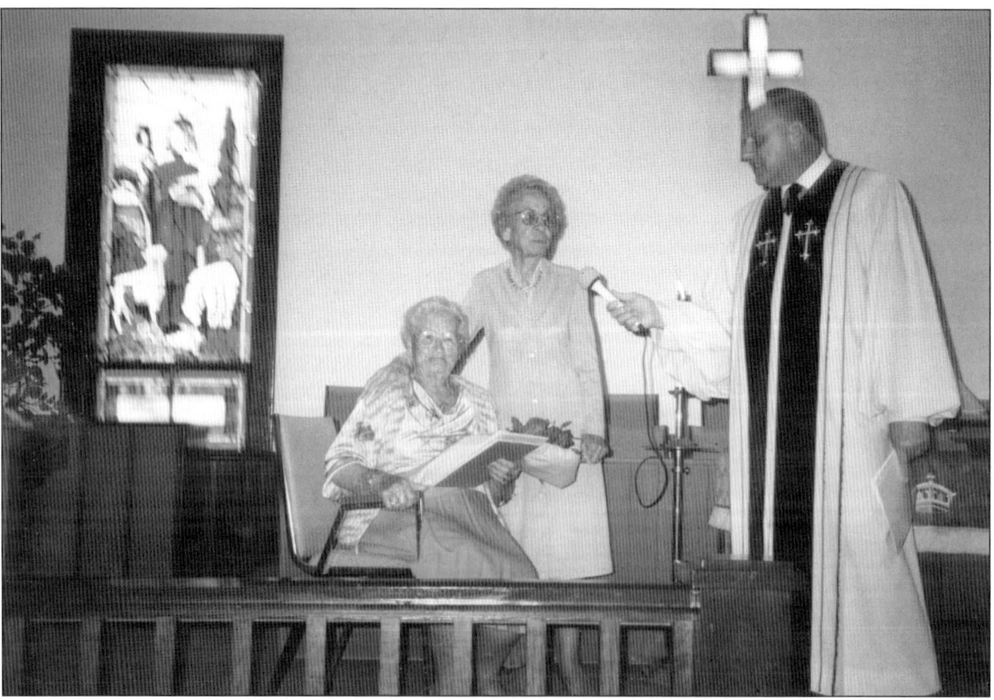

Charter members Irene Richey and Ruth Perdue (seated) are pictured here with pastor Bob Grant of the Alturas United Methodist Church in 1993. Other pastors were Robert White, a Mr. Lufsey, W.H. Herndon, A.M. McFarland, H.H. McAfee, C.W. McConnell, J.W. Austin, E.J. Gates, J.T. Mitchell, O. Sewell Palmer, M.E. Meyer, E.O. McMullen, Joseph E. Woodard, John B. Gill, H.L. Wiggins, William P. Trobough, George W. Wiseman, William H. Cadwell, L.E. Denslow, L. John Larson, Jesse L. Baker, Paul O'Brien, Dean W. Witten, David A. Day, W.E. Rowell, Joe B. Hughes, John W. Finkell Jr., Otis Melvin Andrews, Oscar C. Poole, Horace G. Murry, Robert E. Grant, Robert Harding, Craig Paul, Armando Rodriguez, Dennis Lewis, Barbara Herr, Carroll Phillips, David C. Groves, Curtis Cain, Douglas Hallman, Mathew Kern, and Kathleen Durbin. (Courtesy of Linda Smith.)

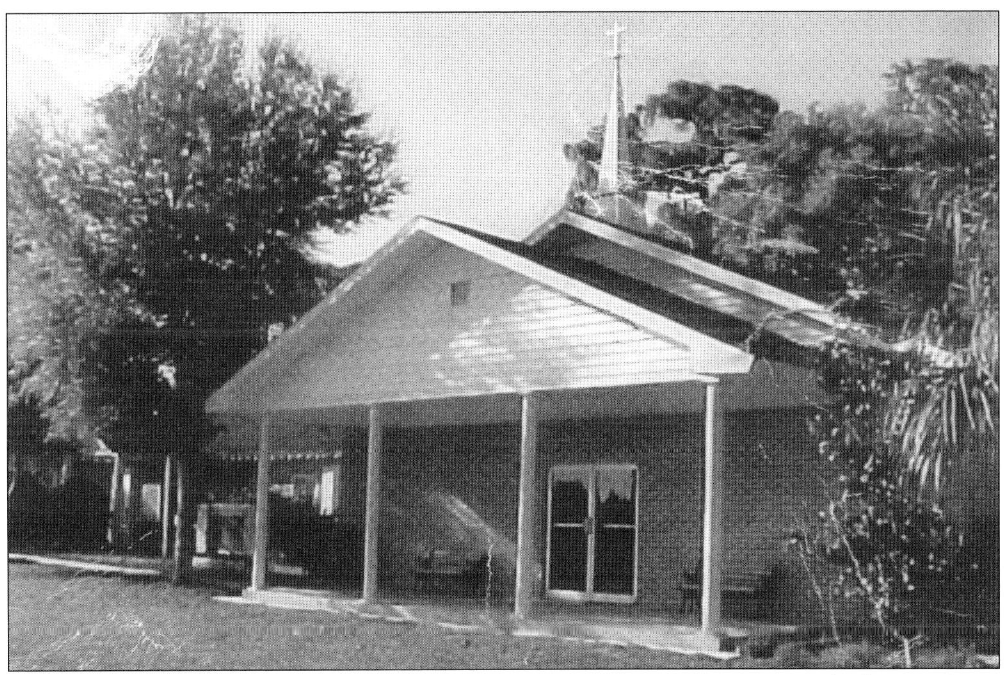

The First Baptist Church of Alturas began as a fellowship in August 1949 in the home of D.L. Mercer. As the group grew, they met in the old Alturas Elementary schoolhouse. The fellowship was adopted as a mission by the First Baptist Church of Bartow and Rev. Zelon Page was called as the first pastor. The mission purchased land in 1950 to build a church, and construction started on August 19, 1951. The First Baptist Church was established on December 9, 1954, with Rev. H.T. Ward as pastor. (Courtesy of Alturas Baptist Church.)

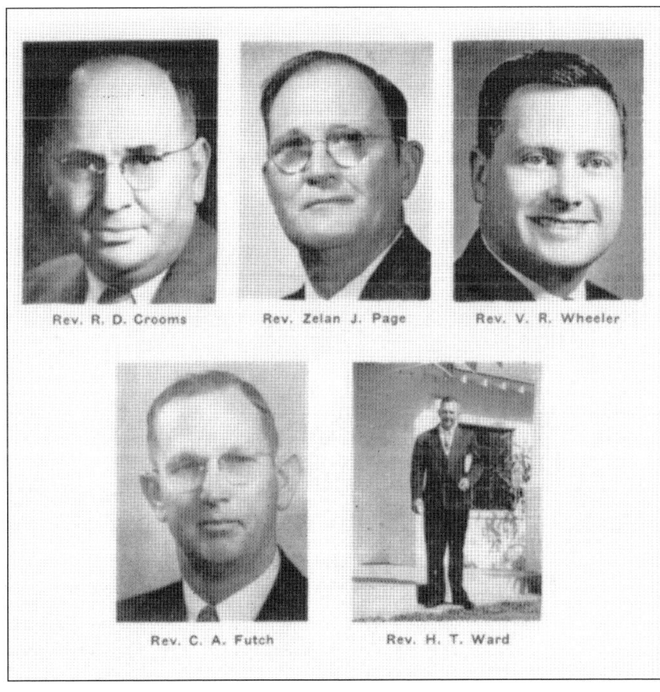

Five of the earliest pastors of the First Baptist Church of Alturas are pictured here. Other pastors were Paul Cartledge, Joe Speight, R.T. Barrett, Aaron Singletary, Harrison Crews, Russell Barefoot, Alvin Parker*, Cecil Brock, Otto Hansen, Bill Bledsoe, Paul Dixon, Raymond Carroll*, Larry Gandy, Kenneth Allaby*, J. Burton Nightingale, Ed Bryant, Michael Vosbrink, Gene Hitchcock*, Wayne Maberry*, Mark Koruschak, Randy Seiver, Walter Strohmaier, Bill Anderson*, and Richard Counts. (The star* by a name indicates interim pastors.) (Courtesy of Alturas Baptist Church.)

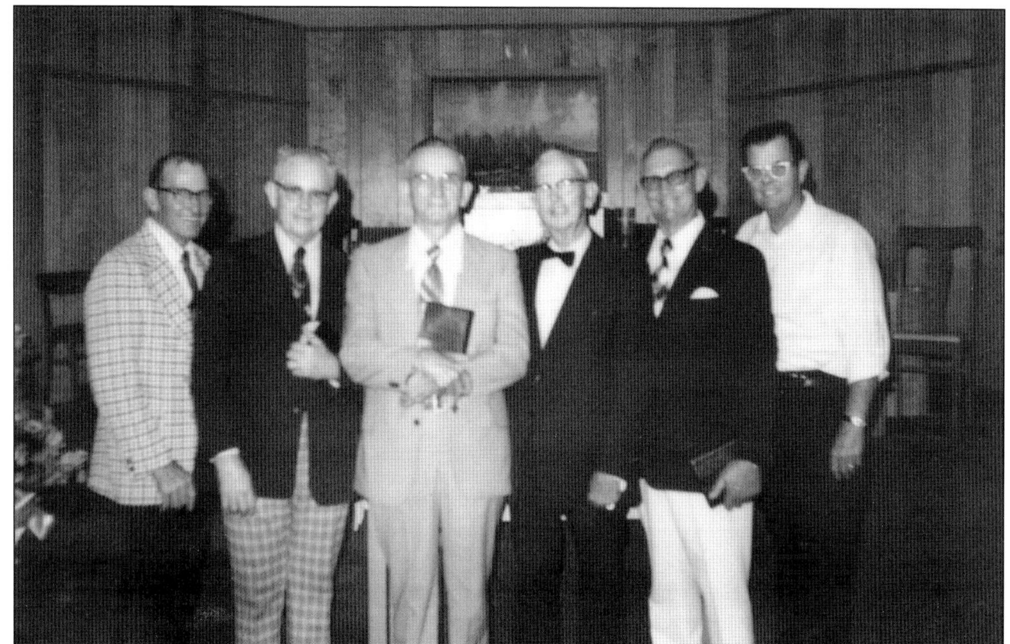

On March 14, 1976, at the 22nd Homecoming of First Baptist Church of Alturas, this photograph was made of several former pastors and minister friends of the church. Pictured from left to right are Carol Rhoden, Lester Burke, Russell Barefoot, Clyde Futch, Otto Hansen, and Robert T. Barrett. (Courtesy of Alturas Baptist Church.)

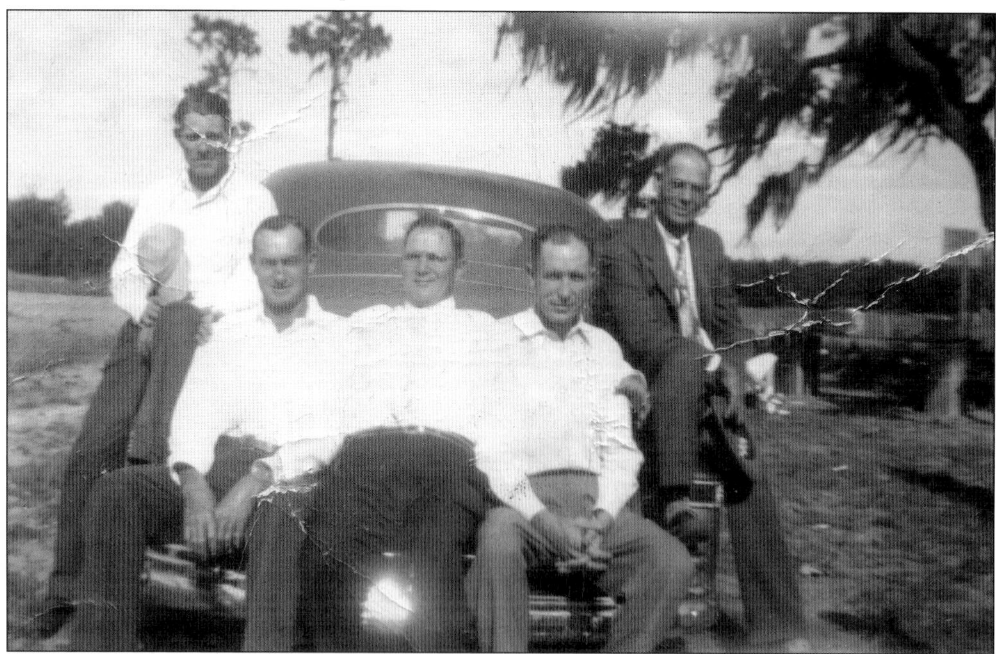

This c. 1949 photograph shows mission leaders of the soon-to-be-established 1954 First Baptist Church of Alturas. The photograph was taken in front of the old Alturas Elementary schoolhouse, where the fellowship met before its church was built. From left to right are Gilbert Register, Henry Young, Rev. Zelon Page, Mr. Barfield, and John Wynn. (Courtesy of Sherry Maberry.)

On May 21, 1972, from left to right, Deacons Riley Young, Harold Graddy, Quince Radford, Carl Hielscher, and Dan Young of the Alturas Baptist Church are "breaking the ground" to build their new sanctuary. They used a "Golden Shovel" as a symbol of a new era. The sanctuary was started under the pastorate of Bill Bledoe and completed under the guidance of carpenter and pastor Otto Hansen. The older church building was named Hanson Hall in honor of Reverend Hanson, who was instrumental in the completion of the structure in 1976. (Courtesy of Alturas Baptist Church.)

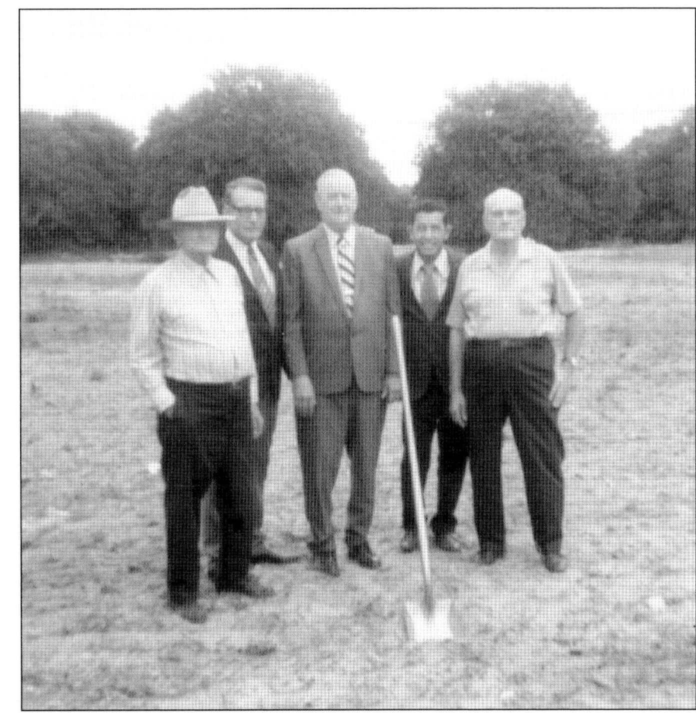

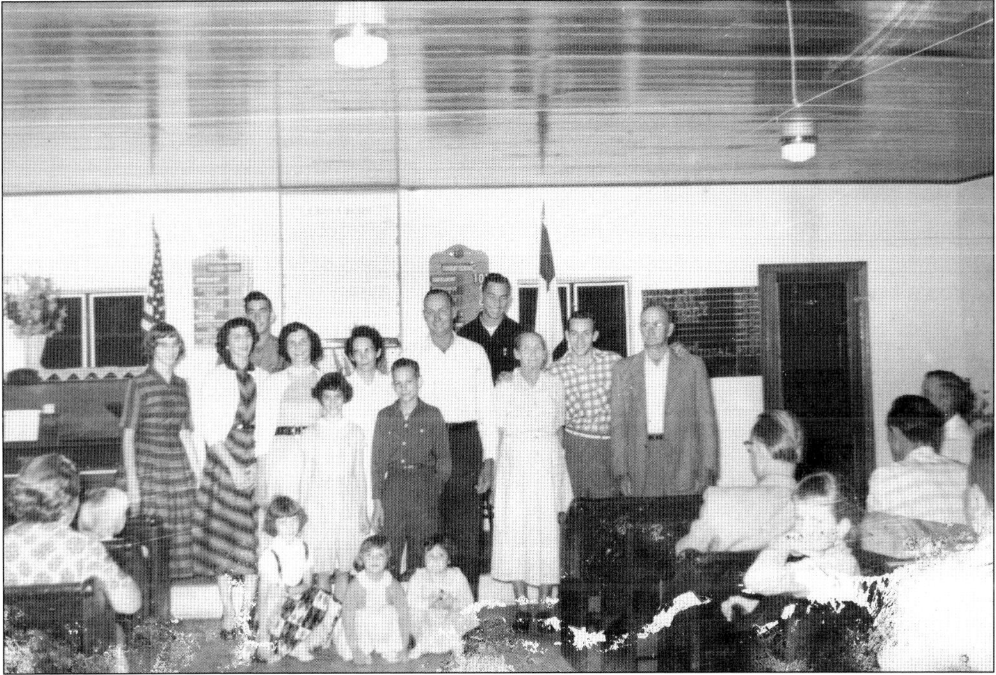

The Riley Young family, the Henry Young family, the Merlin Hielscher family, and the Carl Hielscher family are spotlighted in this 1959 photograph taken in the infancy of the established First Baptist Church of Alturas. Note the enrollment on the attendance board of 100 active members. Church functions were at the heart of events for most families in this rural community, and many held a strong Christian faith. (Courtesy of Sherry Maberry.)

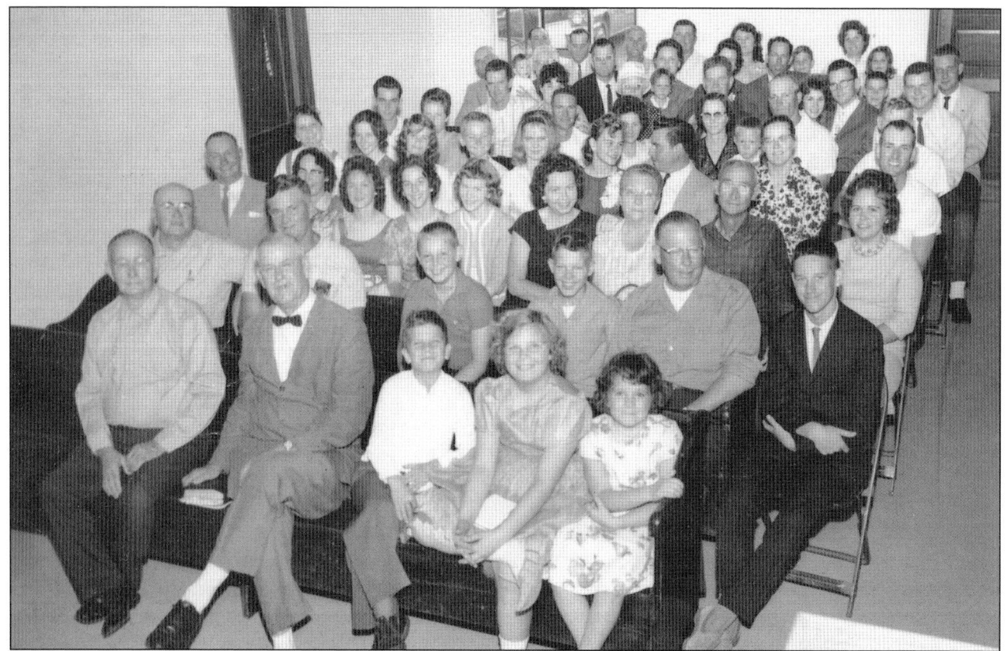

The 10th Homecoming celebration of Alturas Baptist Church was held on March 15, 1964. Pictured here in the first couple of rows are, from left to right, (first row) Riley Young, Quince Radford, Billy Green, Ginger Langford, and Janell Peacock; (second row) Dan Young, Roy Smith, Randy Hogan, Richard Daughtry, T.J. Langford, and Johnny Radford. (Courtesy of Alturas Baptist.)

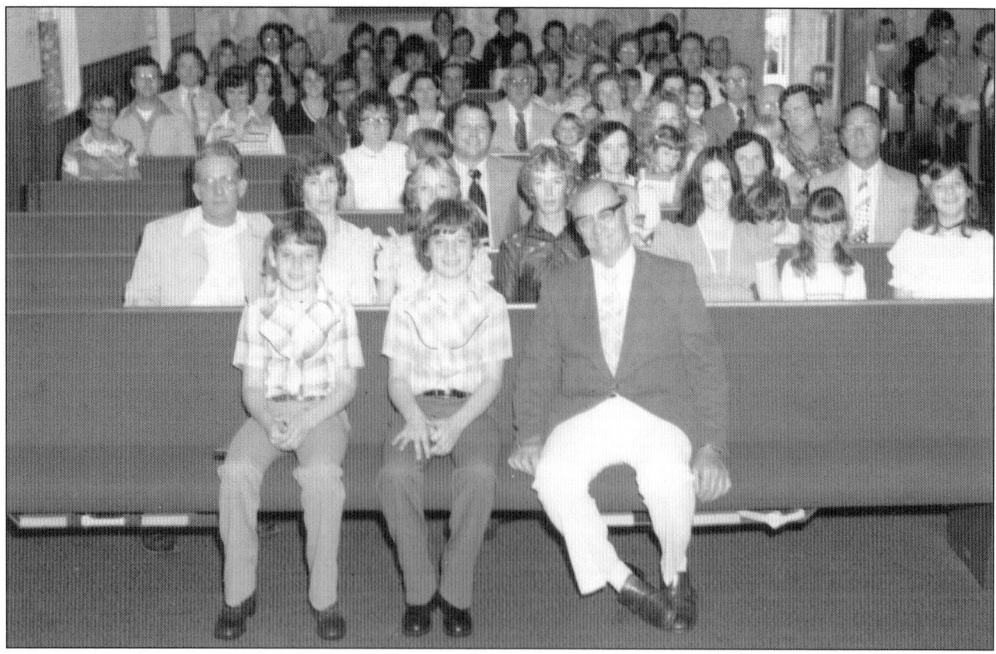

The 24th Homecoming celebration of Alturas Baptist Church was held in March 1978. Pictured here in the first couple of rows are, from left to right, (first row) Wayne Graddy, his twin brother Dayne Graddy, and Rev. Otto Hansen; (second row) Harold Graddy, Flora Graddy, Janan Graddy, Graeme Sellers, Doniece Bennett, Karyn Bennett, and Lorianne Bennett. (Courtesy of Flora Conley.)

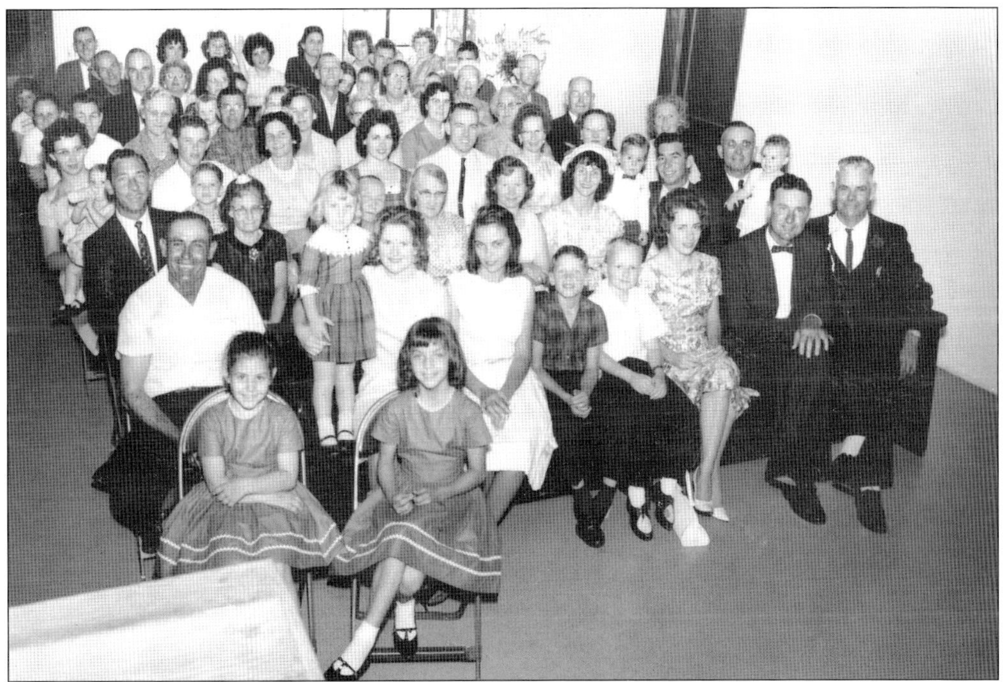

The 10th Homecoming celebration of Alturas Baptist Church was held on March 15, 1964. Pictured in the first several of rows are, from left to right, (first row) Vicki Hielscher and Sherry Hielscher; (second row) Grady Lane, Leanne Hielscher, Nancy Radford, Dorothy Carr, four unidentified, and Luke Radford; (third row) Merlin Hielscher, Annie Lee Smith Peacock, Molly Palmer Young, Cora Young, Louise Rhoden Radford, Raymurl Young Hielscher, Kevin Hielscher, Carl Hielscher, Rev. Russell Barfoot, and Elizabeth Barfoot. (Courtesy of Alturas Baptist.)

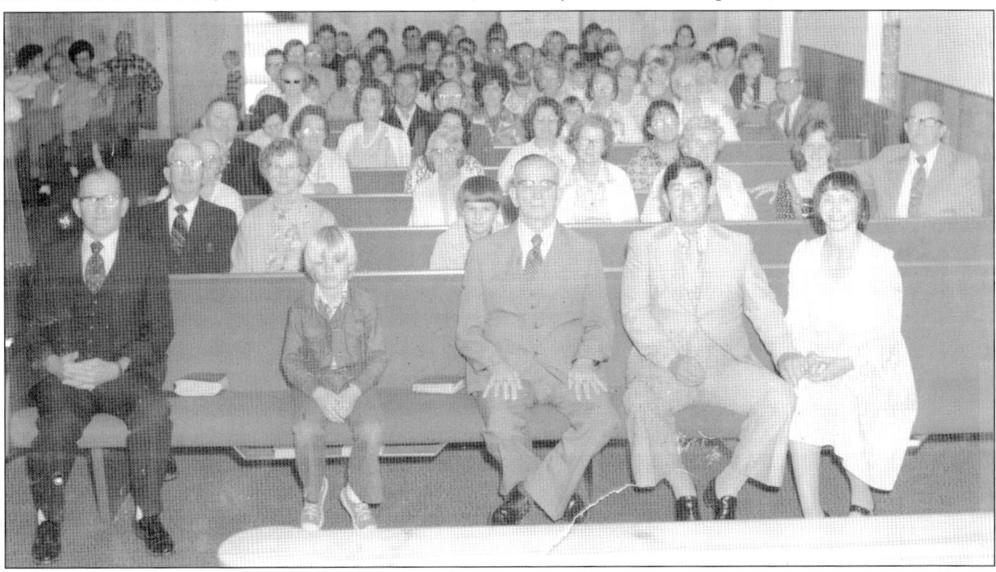

The 24th Homecoming celebration of Alturas Baptist Church was in March 1978. Those pictured in the first two rows are, from left to right, (first row) Rev. Carol Rhoden, two unidentified, Carl Hielscher, and Raymurl Young Hielscher; (second row) Rev. Clyde Futch, his wife (name unknown), and unidentified. (Courtesy of Flora Conley.)

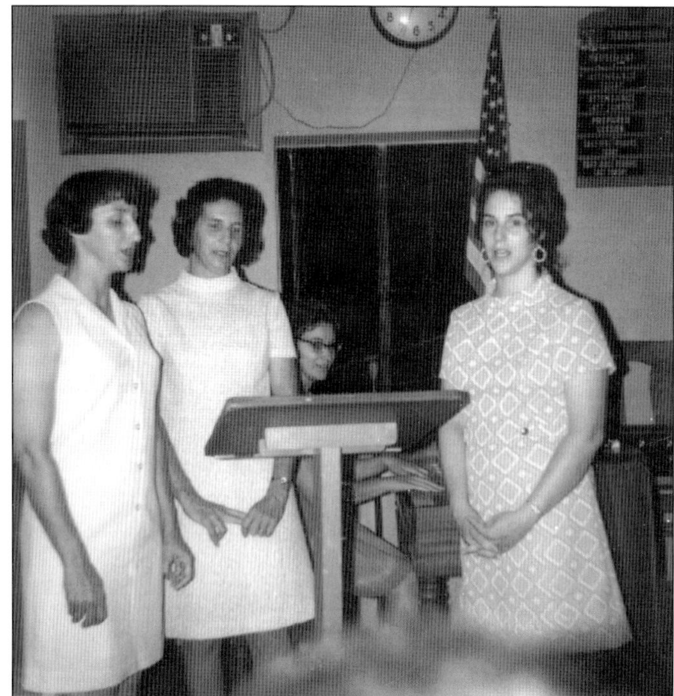

Pictured in this late-1960s photograph are, from left to right, sisters Raymurl Young Hielscher, Evelyn Young Hielscher, Flora Young Graddy (piano), and Doniece Young Bennett, four of the original 69 charter members of Alturas Baptist Church. One of their favorite hymnals was the 1939 *Favorite Songs and Hymns*. Flora played the piano at most every church service from age 14 until long after she was married to Harold Graddy and had three children, Janan and Wayne and Dayne (twins). (Courtesy of Sherry Maberry.)

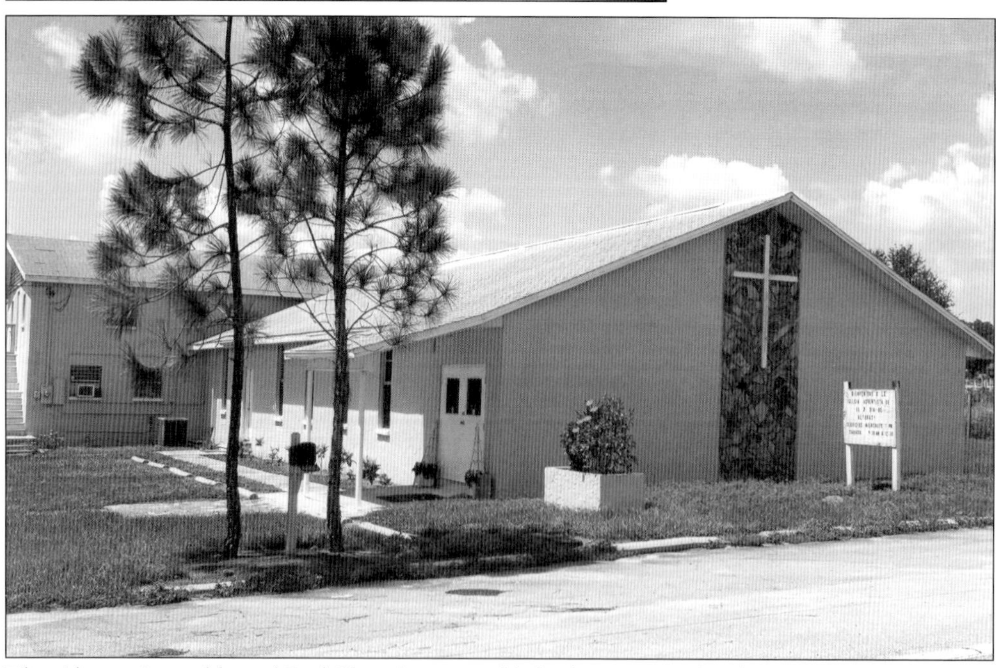

The Alturas Assemblies of God Church was established in 1934 and its building was constructed around 1942. Rev. John King was the first pastor. A Pentecostal church, it was the second denomination started in the Alturas community. The church building was located on the south side of the township. Sadly, the once vibrant congregation closed its doors in the mid-1990s. Today, the building has an active Hispanic Seventh-day Adventist membership. (Courtesy of Sherry Maberry.)

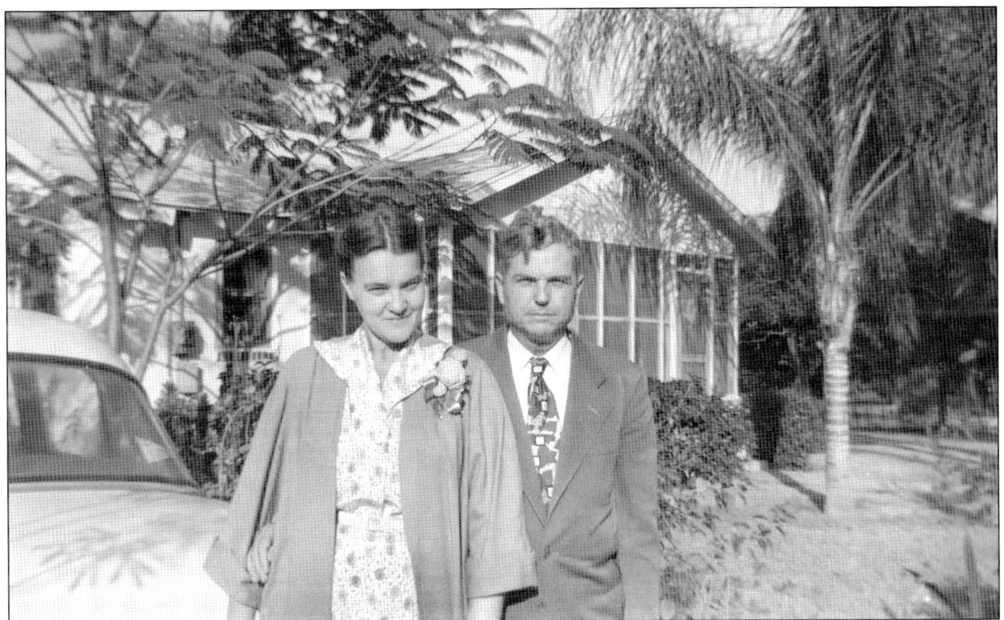

Rev. J.H. Powell, pictured here with his wife, was the pastor of the Alturas Assemblies of God Church in 1955. Other pastors were John King, J.W. Hause, Ernest Williams (he made $5 per week), Florence DeLancy, E.M. Ready, G.W. Cook, W.H. Day, John Mooneyham, D.L. Kelly, A.A. Rowan, W.A. Hill, James Powell, Donald Holton, Alva Wyatt, Rocky Scott, David Crout, James Hendershot, and Wayne Pitts. (Courtesy of Shirley Skipper.)

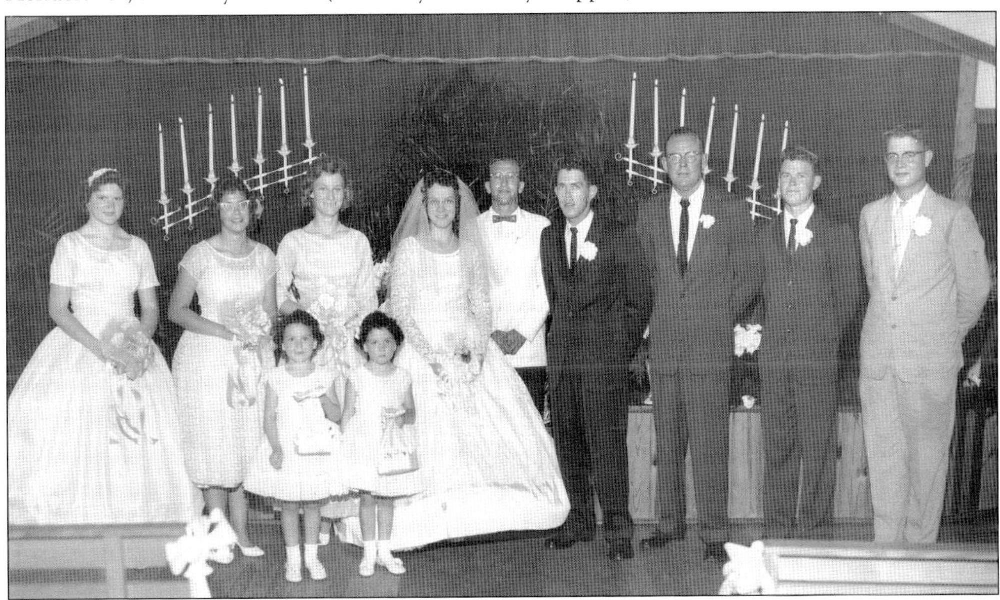

On June 5, 1960, Shirley Radford, daughter of Willie Mae Bennett and George Radford Sr., married LeRoy Skipper, son of Rufus and Vera Mercer Skipper, at the Alturas Assemblies of God Church. Rev. John Mooneyham performed the ceremony. Attendants were, from left to right, Nancy Radford, Nina Skipper, Lenore Radford Smothers, Bill King, Ray King, and George Radford Jr. The flower girls were Kay and Fay Mooneyham (twins). Willie Mae made her daughter's dress, and Juanita Voigt made the veil. (Courtesy of Shirley Skipper.)

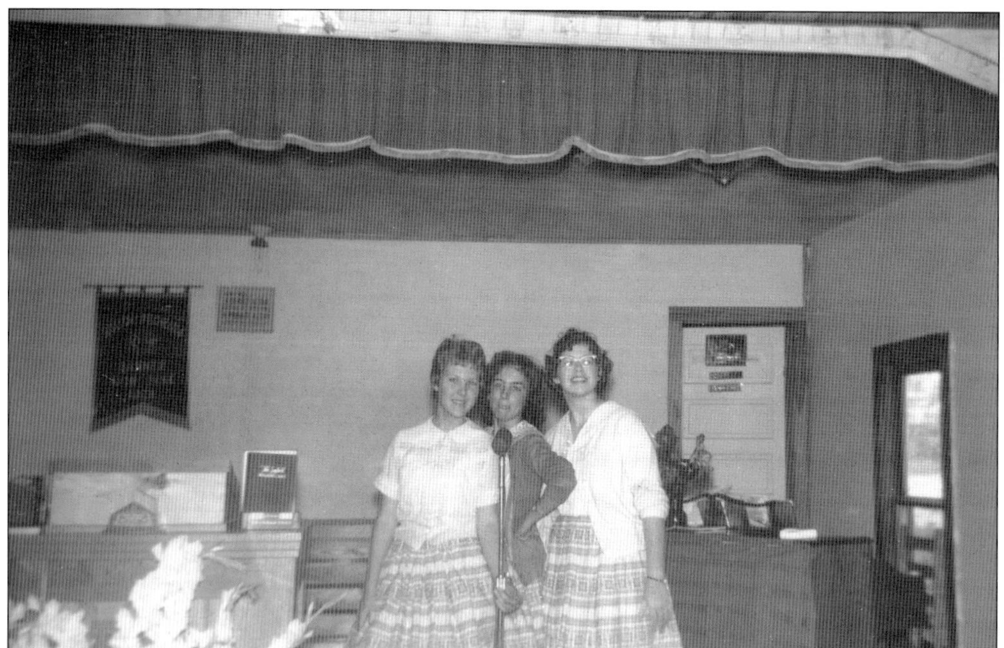

Pictured from left to right in 1959, the Radford sisters, Lenore, Peggy, and Shirley, are standing in the sanctuary of the Alturas Assemblies of God Church. Their parents were Willie Mae and George Radford Sr. The family was charter members of the Alturas Assemblies of God Church. The sisters formed a trio and sang with angelic voices. Peggy was the pianist. Their husbands were Carrey Smothers and John Mooneyham (Lenore); Tommy Smothers and George Trapp (Peggy); and LeRoy Skipper (Shirley). (Courtesy of Shirley Skipper.)

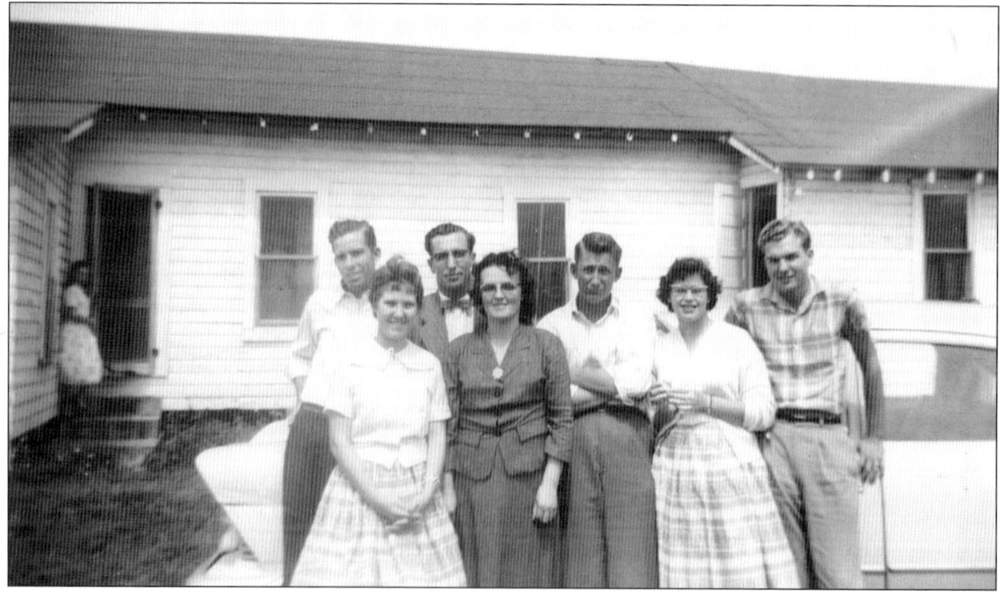

This was the Alturas Assemblies of God Church youth group in 1959. Those pictured, from left to right, are Jack Benton, Sandra King, John Mooneyham (pastor), Grace Mooneyham, Carry Smothers, Nina Skipper, and Marvin Powell. The church building is seen in the background from the south side. (Courtesy of Shirley Skipper.)

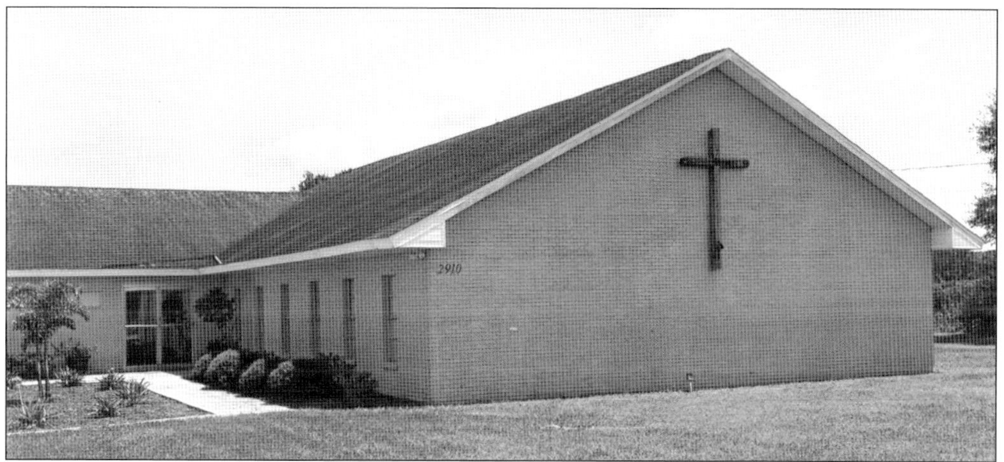

The Harvest Time Fellowship, established on February 4, 1973, as an Independent Full Gospel Church, was in the Reynoldsville area of Alturas. The first pastor was Rev. R.E. Cooper, a pilot. Other pastors were Gary Ebby, Bill Lamb, David Wine, Mike Aycock, Jim Jones, Jim Minor, and Justine Keyt. Early church members were Janie Wallace; Weita and Floyd Wiggins; and Johnny, Diane, and Mike Aycock. All Things New Church is the new name of the church. (Courtesy of Sherry Maberry.)

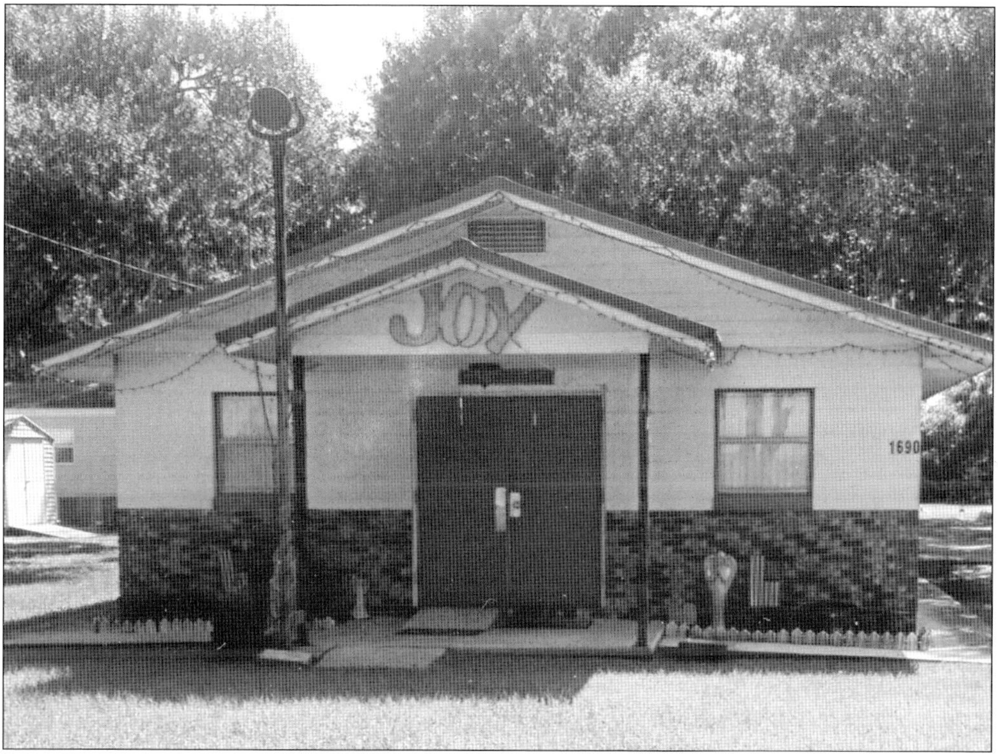

The Alturas Primitive Baptist Church was built in the late 1960s. Services were held once a month. Sadly, the building sat unused for many years until October 22, 2000, when the congregation became a nondenominational, charismatic congregation under the leadership of Rev. James Waycaster and his wife, Connie. The name was changed to The Church. James was an accomplish guitarist and singer. He formed a Southern gospel group called The Vessels. (Courtesy of Sherry Maberry.)

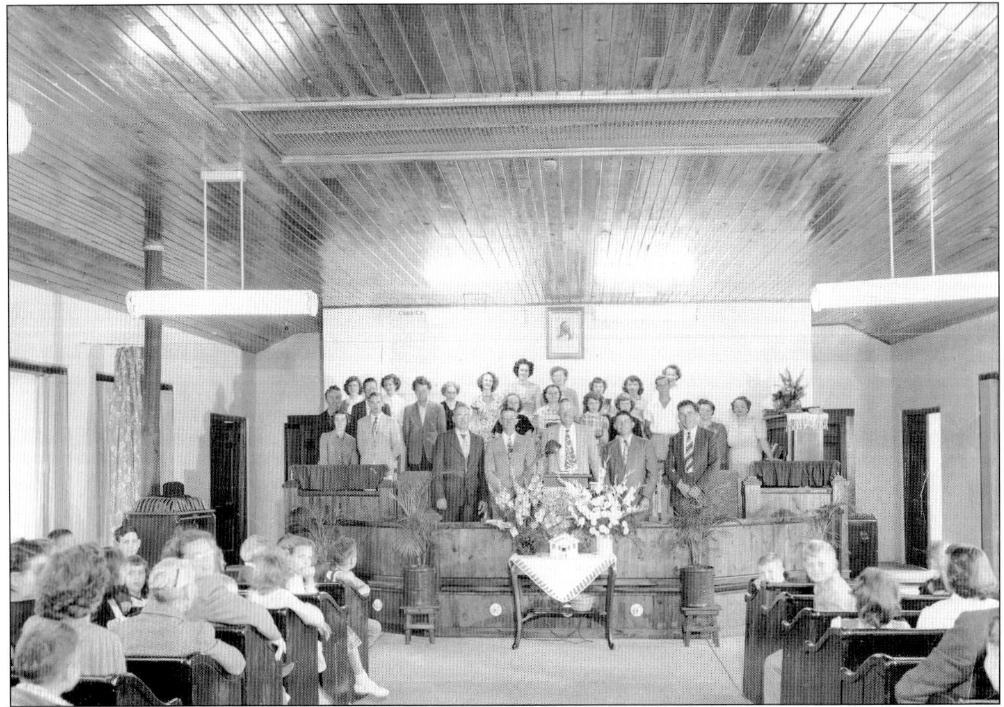

The Lake Garfield Baptist Church was established in 1946 when it split from the Peace Creek Baptist Church. The fellowship began as a mission of the First Baptist Church of Bartow and met for months at Lake Ann School. This is a 1946 Sunday morning service in the new building with pastor L.W. Mills. The deacons and the adult choir are pictured in the front. (Courtesy of Lake Garfield Baptist Church.)

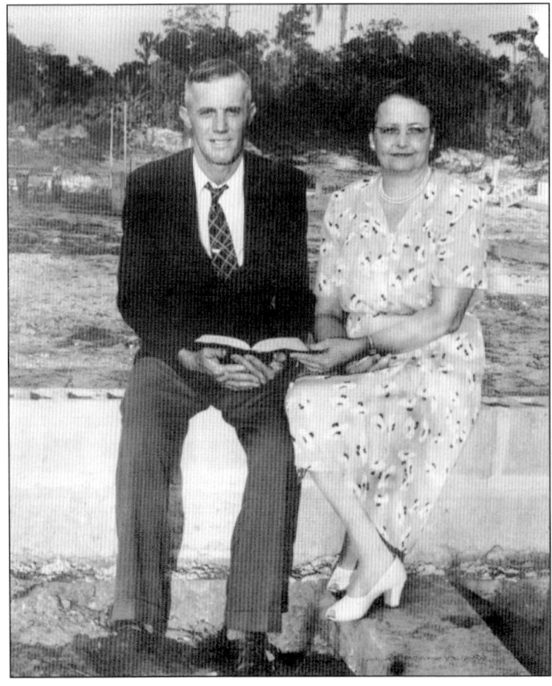

The Lake Garfield Baptist Church pastor, L.W. Mills, and his wife, Ruby, are pictured in this 1946 photograph. Ruby was the pianist for the church. (Courtesy of Lake Garfield Baptist Church.)

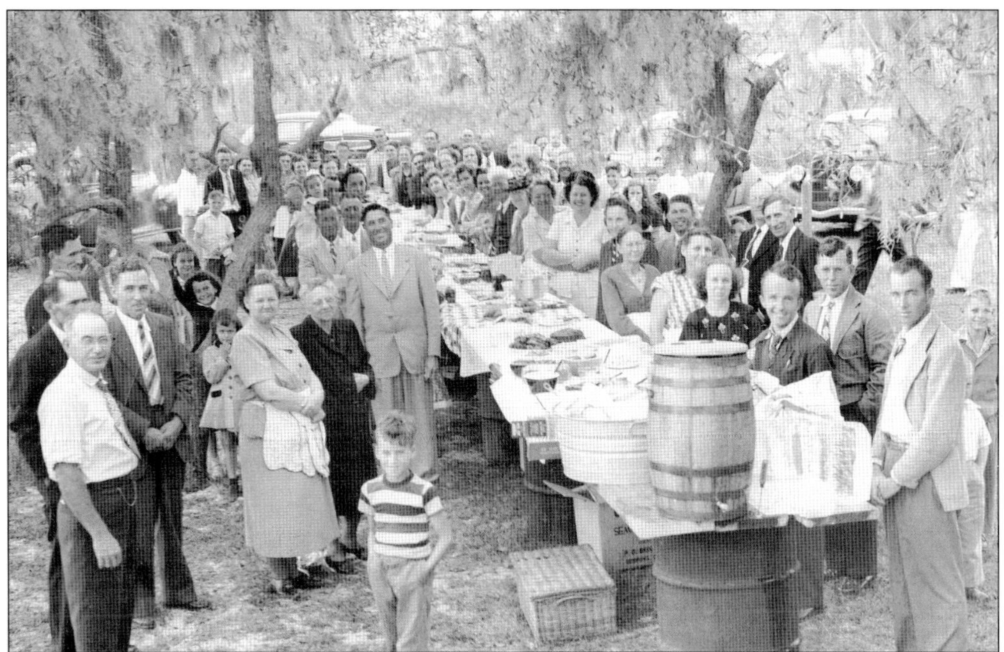

At Lake Garfield Baptist Church, "dinner on the grounds" was a time for food and fellowship. The dinner featured chicken and dumplings with sweet tea. In this c. 1946 photograph, the man in the white shirt is Charlie Brown, next to him is Lloyd Auton, the lady in the apron is Myris Porter, and the woman behind the barrel is Shorty Waters. (Courtesy of Lake Garfield Baptist Church.)

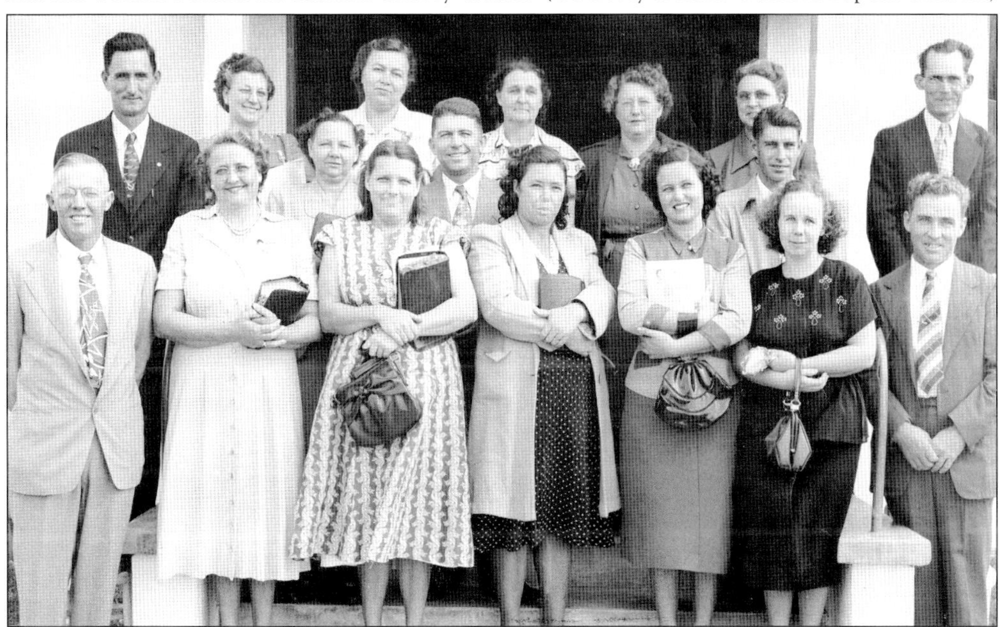

The Sunday school teachers of Lake Garfield Baptist Church are seen here around 1946. They are, from left to right, (first row) Pastor L.W. Mills, Ruby Mills, Bernice Geiger, Mrs. Parker, Louise West, Shorty Waters, and Lloyd Auton; (second row) Mr. Scott, Myris Porter, Jim Porter, Mr. Cain, and Ernest Geiger; (third row) Gussie Westbrook, Geneva Scott, Lillian Gandy, Minnie Lou Thompson, and Ethel Brown. (Courtesy of Lake Garfield Baptist Church.)

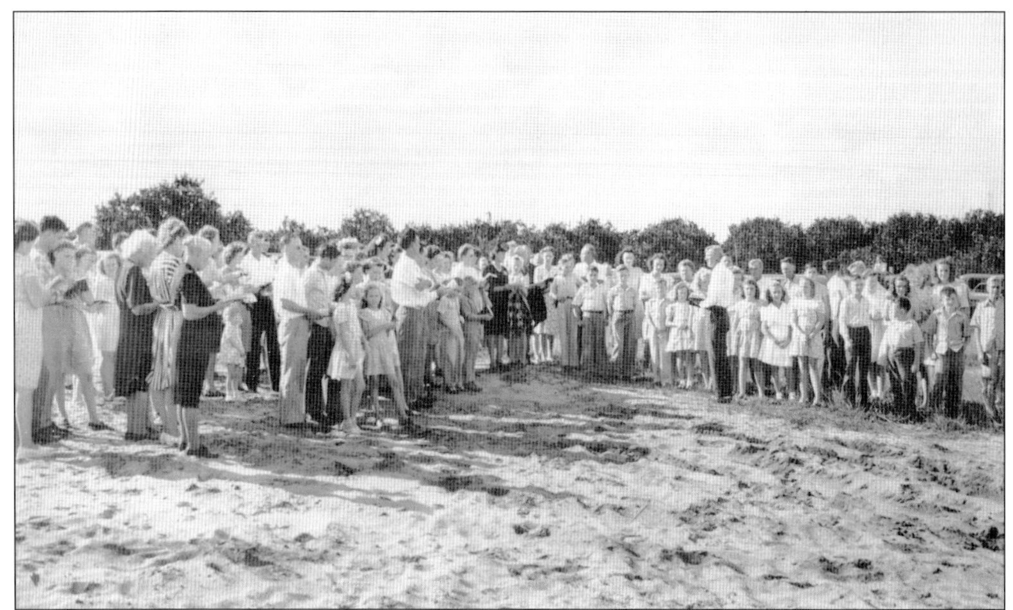

In 1946, Lake Garfield Baptist Church gathered for baptisms at Flora Lake, located between Alturas and the Lake Garfield Community. Pastor L.W. Mills is on the far left, and Deacon Jim Porter is on the far right. Deacon Porter helped with the baptism that day since there were so many. The 20th person from the left is Jessie Brown. (Courtesy of Lake Garfield Baptist Church.)

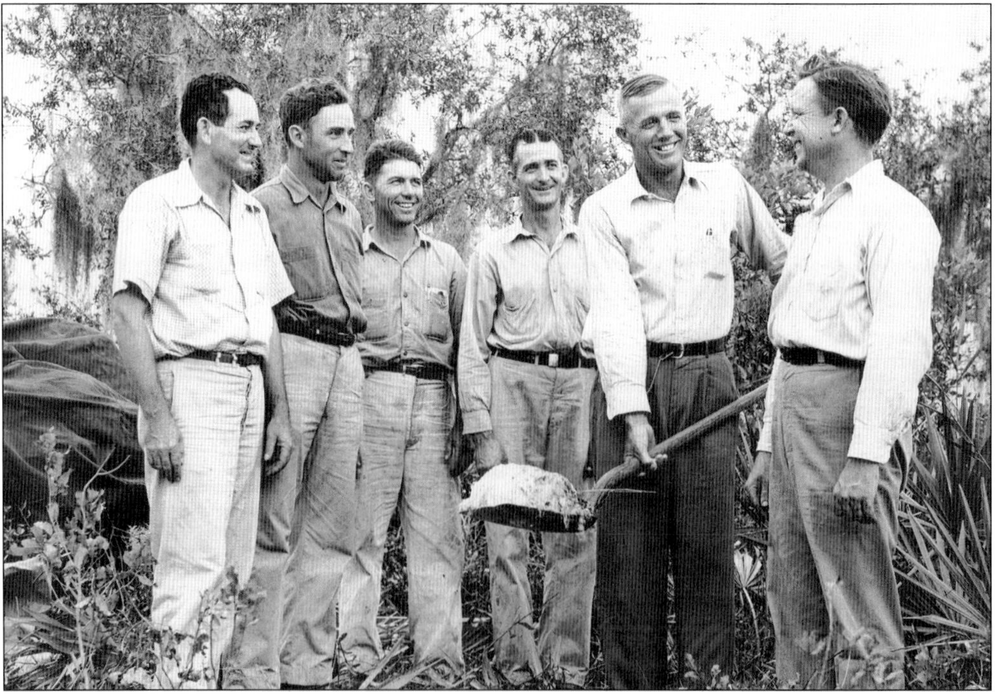

Deacons of the Lake Garfield Baptist Church and its pastor, Rev. L.W. Mills, are breaking ground for the construction of new building in 1946. From left to right are Joe Blocker, Lloyd Auton, Jim Porter, Benny Thompson, pastor L.W. Mills, and Joe Gandy. (Courtesy of Lake Garfield Baptist Church.)

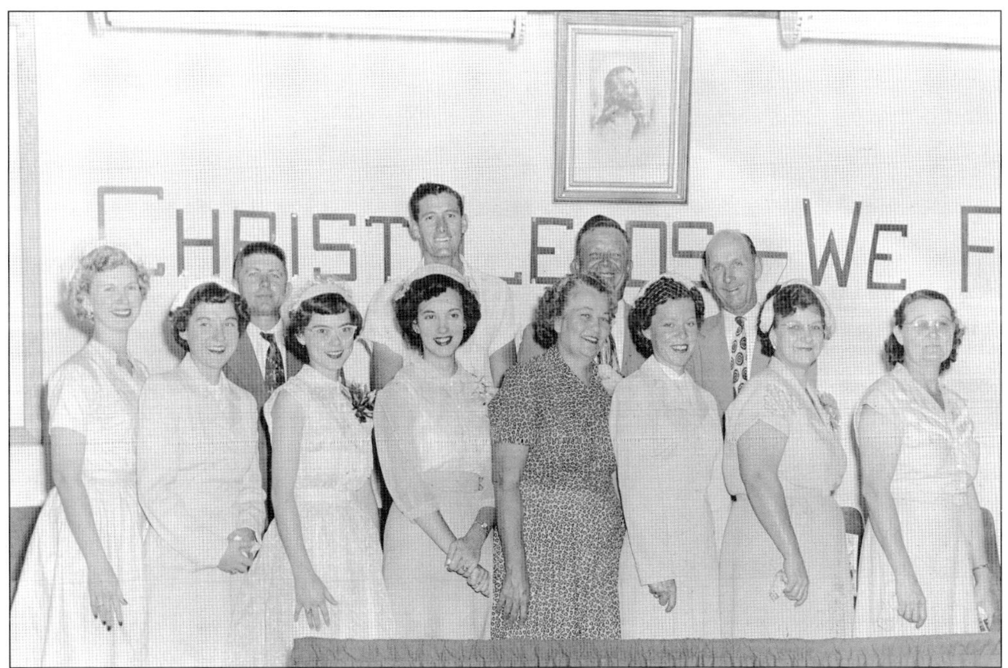

The adult choir at Lake Garfield Baptist Church is featured in this 1953 photograph. Their pastor was Rev. Kenneth Hawkins (not pictured). From left to right are (first row) Odell Broadrick, Eileen Auton, Imogene Gandy, Clarice Henson, Flossie Reynolds, Francis Gandy, Mrs. Westbrook, and Lillian Gandy; (second row) Jim Porter, Arthur Smith, Joe Gandy, and unidentified. (Courtesy of Lake Garfield Baptist Church.)

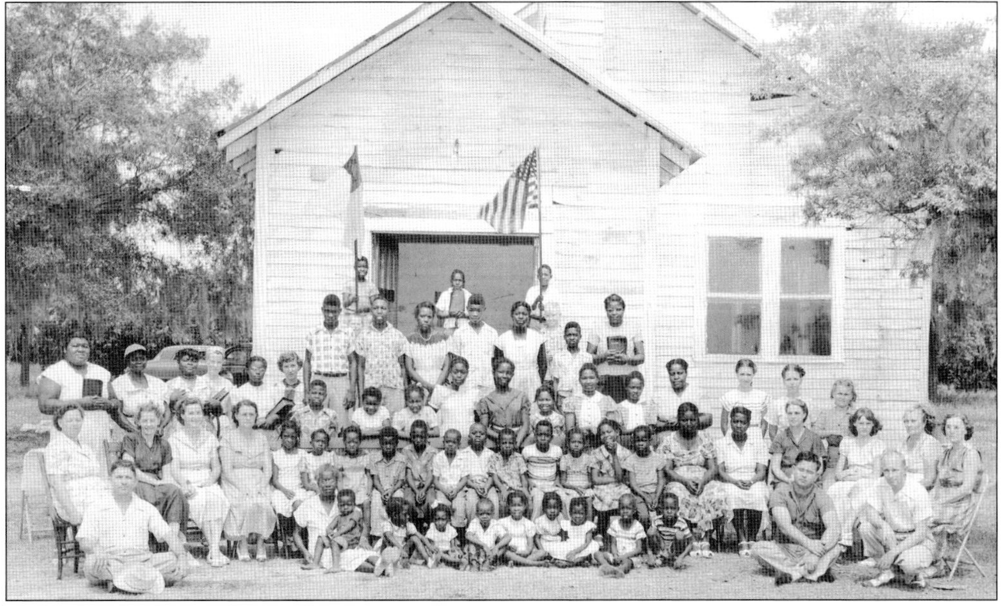

In 1953, the congregation at Lake Garfield Baptist Church, under the leadership of Rev. Kenneth Hawkins, led a Vacation Bible School program at their sister church, the Macedonia Baptist Church. This church was attended by the black residents in Lake Garfield. (Courtesy of Lake Garfield Baptist Church.)

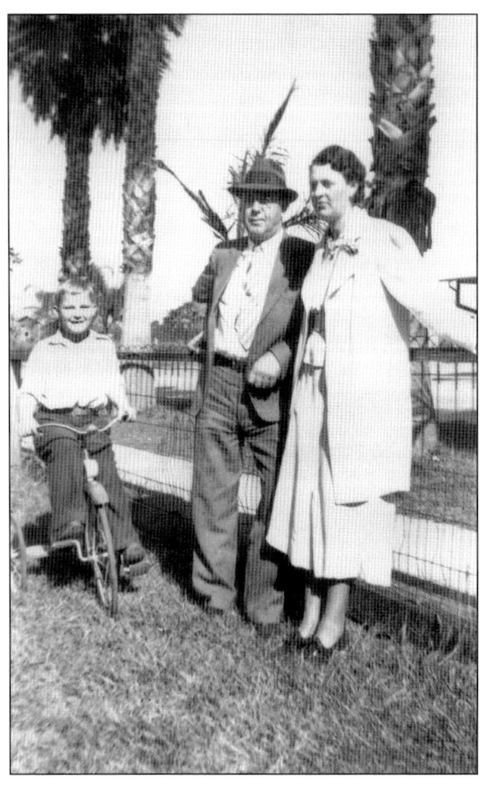

Junius Warren (J.W.) and Mae Bell Huff, with their son Warren Patrick, are pictured relaxing in their Lake Garfield front yard after a Sunday church service in 1937. Services were held in a small building used as an auditorium when the circuit pastors came through the community. Every year, a weeklong revival was attended by many of the local families there. The auditorium was located across the road from the Roux Crate and Lumber Company's Commissary. (Courtesy of W. Patrick Huff.)

Reverend Will Padgett, holding his Bible, is pictured here with his daughter Shirley. They are standing in front of their Lake Garfield home on Stenger Road in the early 1950s. Padgett was a Church of God supply pastor in Central Florida, where he filled pulpits and held revivals throughout the area. Padgett's parents were John Autry Padgett and Charlotte Martha Ramer Padgett, of the Florida Panhandle. Will moved to Lake Garfield, Florida, in the early 1920s, seeking work as a sawmill laborer. He and his widowed mother lived across the road from the Roux Crate and Lumber Sawmill. Padgett married Sara Elizabeth Fahrenback on December 15, 1928. Sara's parents were William Henry and Lillian Carrie Fahrenback, who moved from Georgia to Lake Garfield in the early 1920s. They lived across the road from the packing house. In the 1940s, Padgett became the foreman for Stenger Grove Service. His fellow workers often remembered him praying aloud while working in the groves. The Padgetts had four children: John William, Shirley Jo, Thomas Dalan, and William "Bill" Samford Jr. (Courtesy of Shirley Padgett Johnson.)

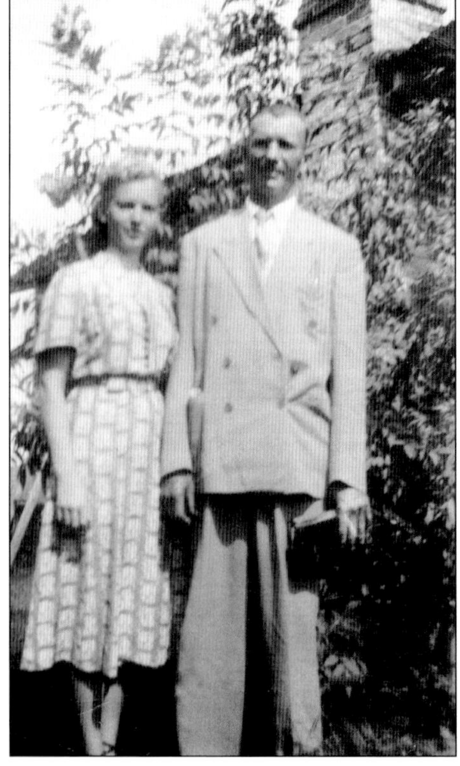

Five

The Alturas Woman's Club

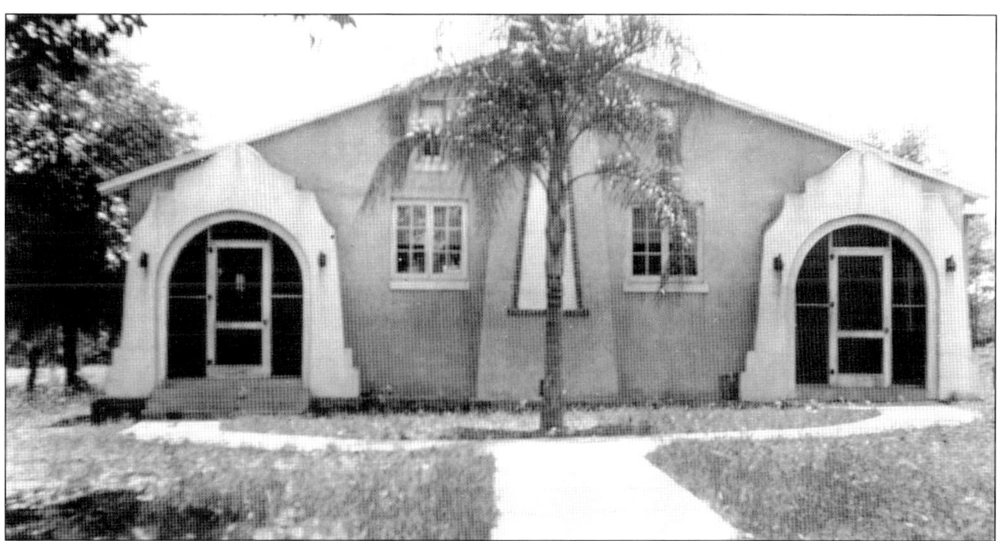

In 1922, the Alturas Woman's Club was given land on Crystal Lake by the Pittsburg Development Company to build a community house. The Alturas Fruit and Land Company donated much of the funds. The building burned in 1923. Again, the Pittsburg Development Company gave land to the club to build, but this time near Star Lake. The new building was completed in 1927. This is a 1935 photograph of the beautiful clubhouse. (Courtesy of Linda Smith.)

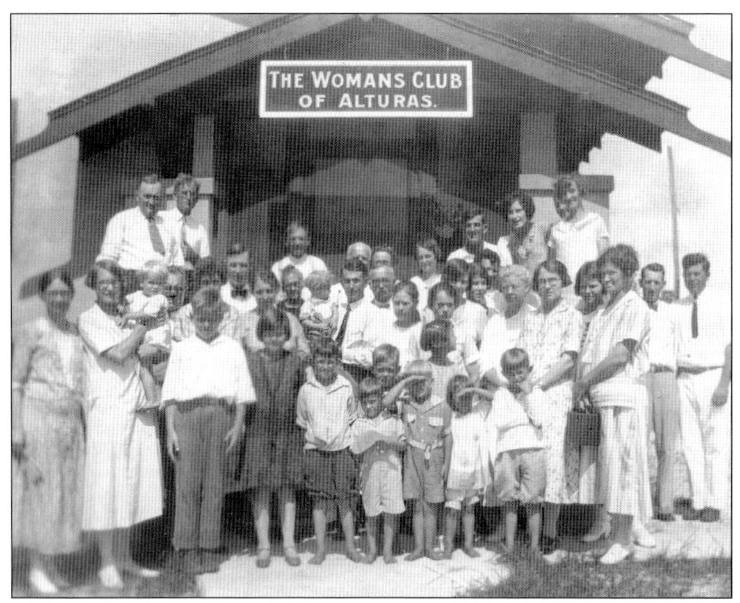

The West Salem Club, who were former residents of West Salem, Illinois, organized in June 1926. Many members came to Florida after Alturas resident Harry Rothrock gave a favorable report to them about the benefits of living in Florida. This 1927 photograph shows the newly built Alturas Woman's Club, which the West Salem Club used for its monthly meetings. (Courtesy of Linda King.)

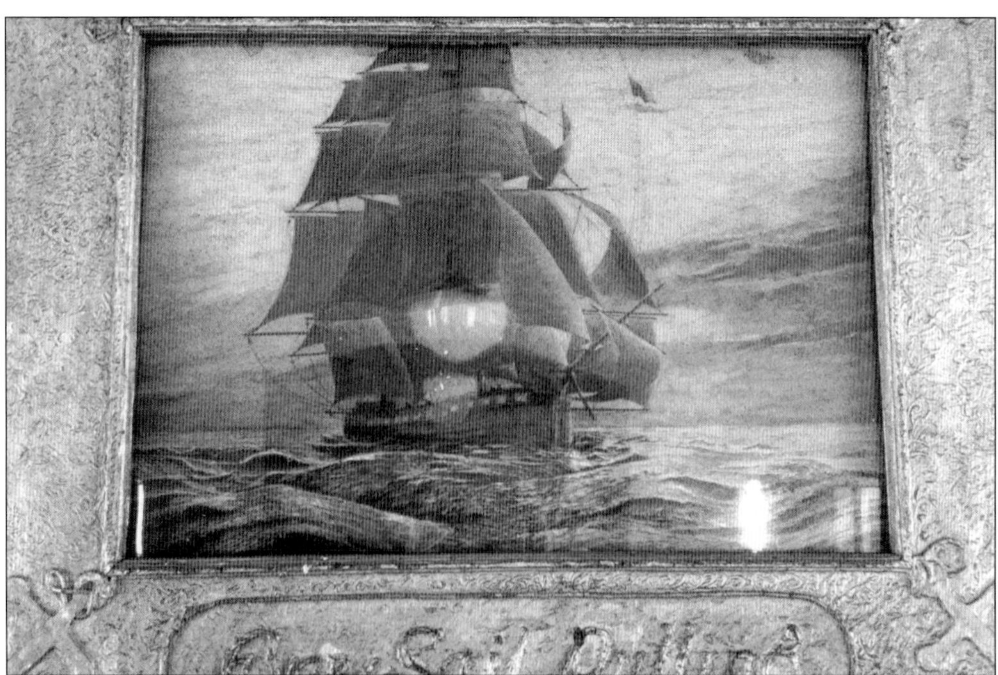

In April 1928, artist U.S. Huggins presented to the Alturas Woman's Club one of his famous paintings, which to his mind expressed the club's purpose of forever moving forward. It is a beautiful oil painting of a ship in full sail entitled *Every Sail Pulling*. The painting found its permanent home over the mantel of the fireplace in the clubhouse. U.S. Huggins also painted the beautiful mural on the club's stage curtain. (Courtesy of Sherry Maberry.)

In 1923, the Pittsburg Development Company owned much of the township of Alturas and gave property to the Alturas Woman's Club for a second building, since the first one was destroyed by fire earlier that year. D.W. Wallace, pictured here with his wife, Mary, was caretaker for the company. "Ma" and "Pa" Wallace lived near the clubhouse on Peanut Alley and took an active part in the Alturas community. In 1928, the Wallaces donated a large hand-painted stage curtain, painted by renowned artist U.S. Huggins, to the club. The mural on the curtain illustrates a beautiful tropical scene of palms trees swaying on a breezy ocean front with ships sailing on the open sea. The inscription of the curtain states, "Presented to the Alturas Woman's Club by Mr. and Mrs. D.W. Wallace and dedicated to Mrs. G.M. Cranston and her building committee." Nan Cranston was the club president at that time. Additional inscription reads, "Painted by U.S. Huggins in loving remembrance of his wonderful friends, 'Pa' and 'Ma' Wallace." Remarkably, the curtain is still used today. (Both, courtesy of Linda King.)

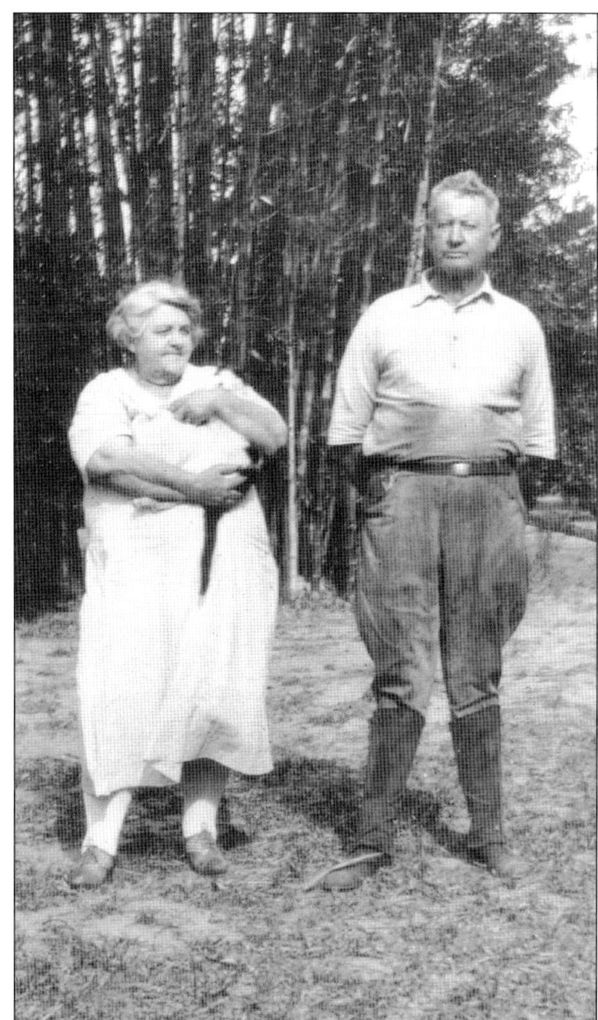

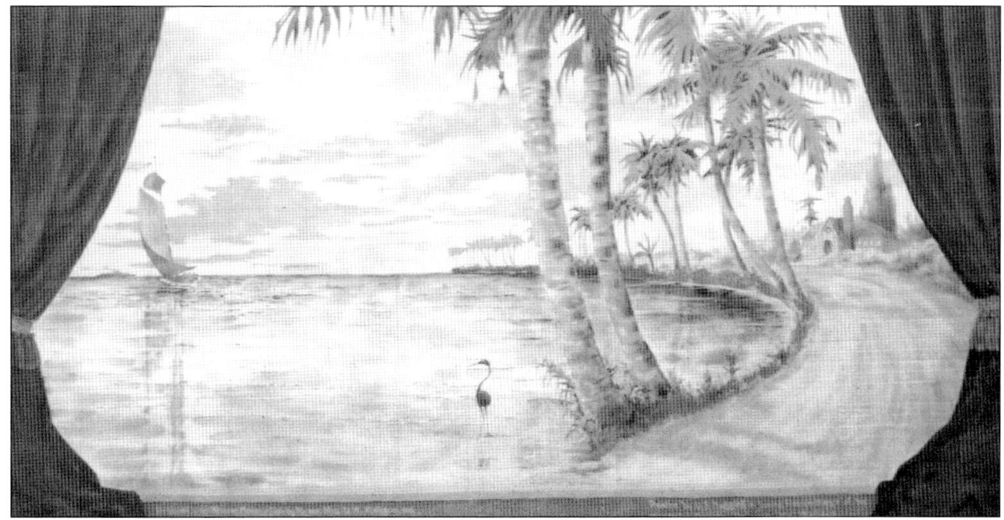

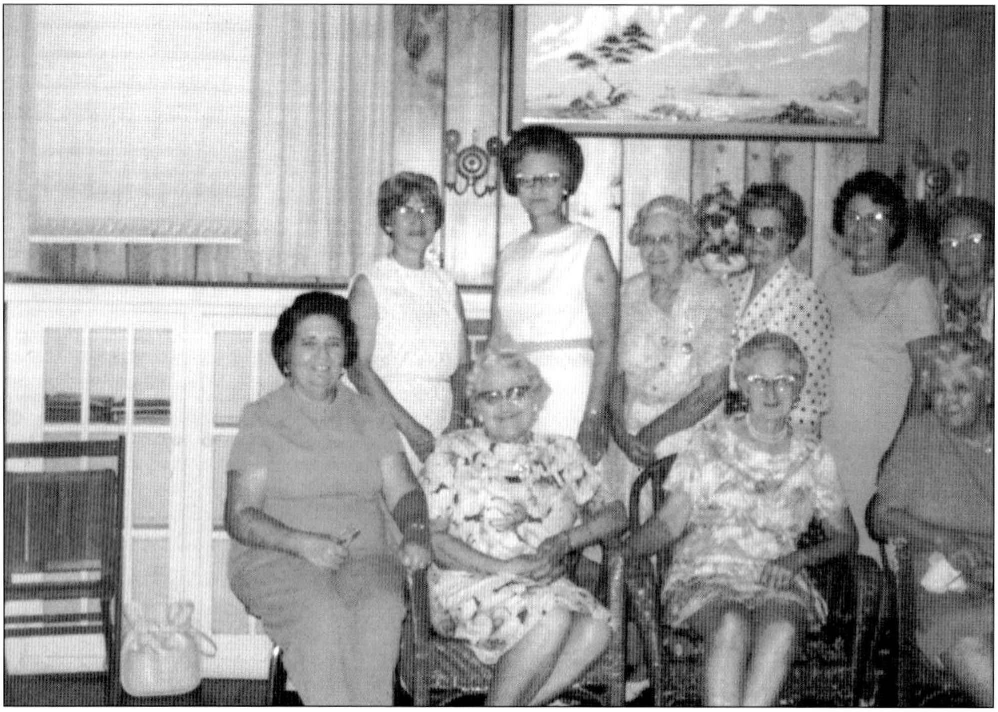

The ladies in this 1960s picture were some of the active members of the Alturas Woman's Club. They are, from left to right, (first row) Lena West, Della Voigt, Vera Howard, and Blanche Cronquist; (second row) Mary Warner, Alvena Smith, Nell Voigt, Ruth Stevens, and Ethel Wojteczko. (Courtesy of Cathy Curtis.)

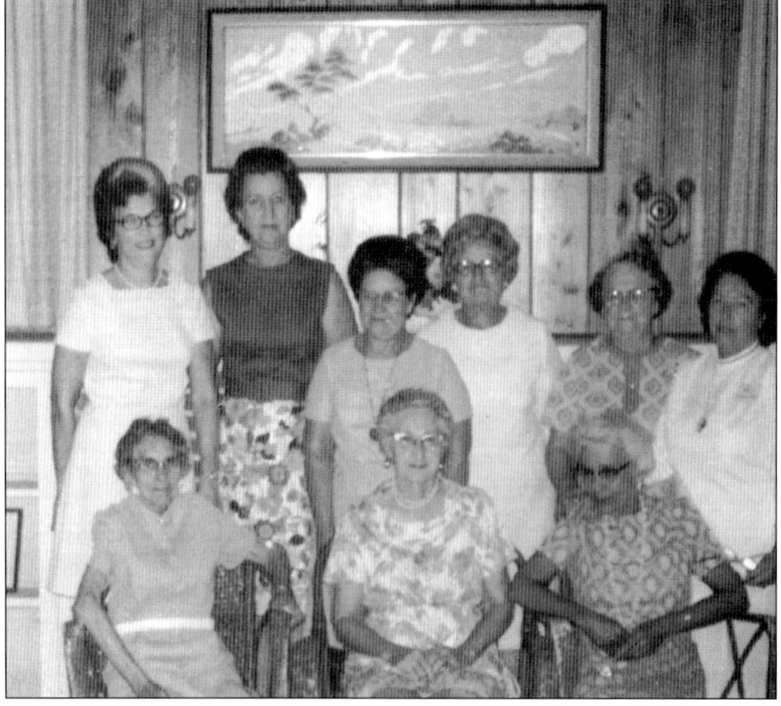

Pictured here in the 1960s are some of the active members of the Alturas Woman's Club. From left to right are (first row) Lyda Frankenburger, Vera Howard Leytham, and Hazel Landers; (second row) Eileen Varner, Ruth Odoswski, Martha Underwood, Ruth Perdue, Ethel Gadau, and unidentified. (Courtesy of Cathy Curtis.)

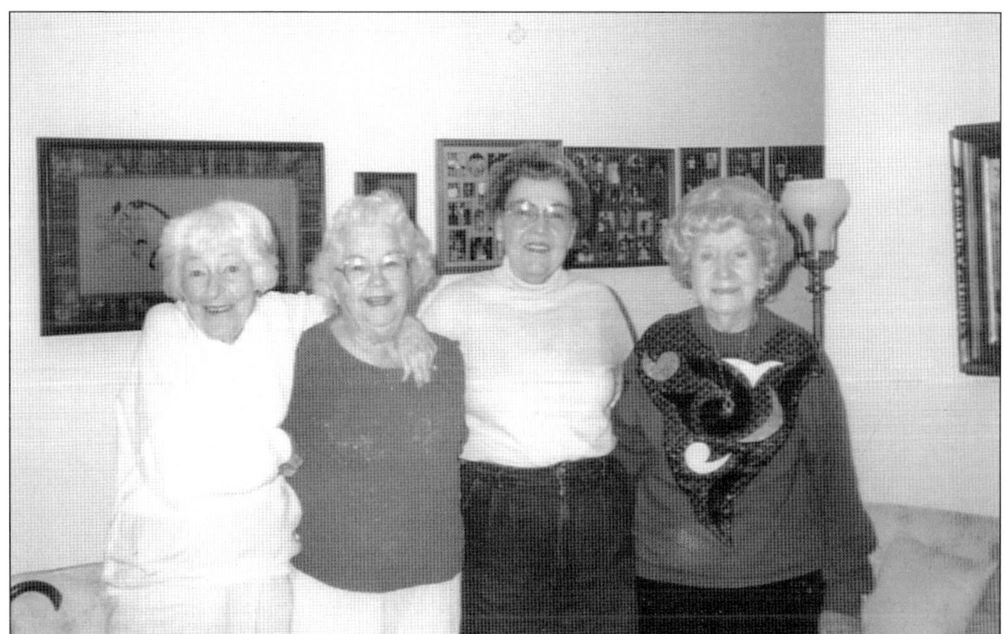

These ladies from the 1960s bridge club in the Lake Garfield/Alturas community, pictured from left to right, are Bertha Kitchens, Zara Huff Frankenburger, Inez Estes, and Ruby Register. (Courtesy of Cathy Curtis.)

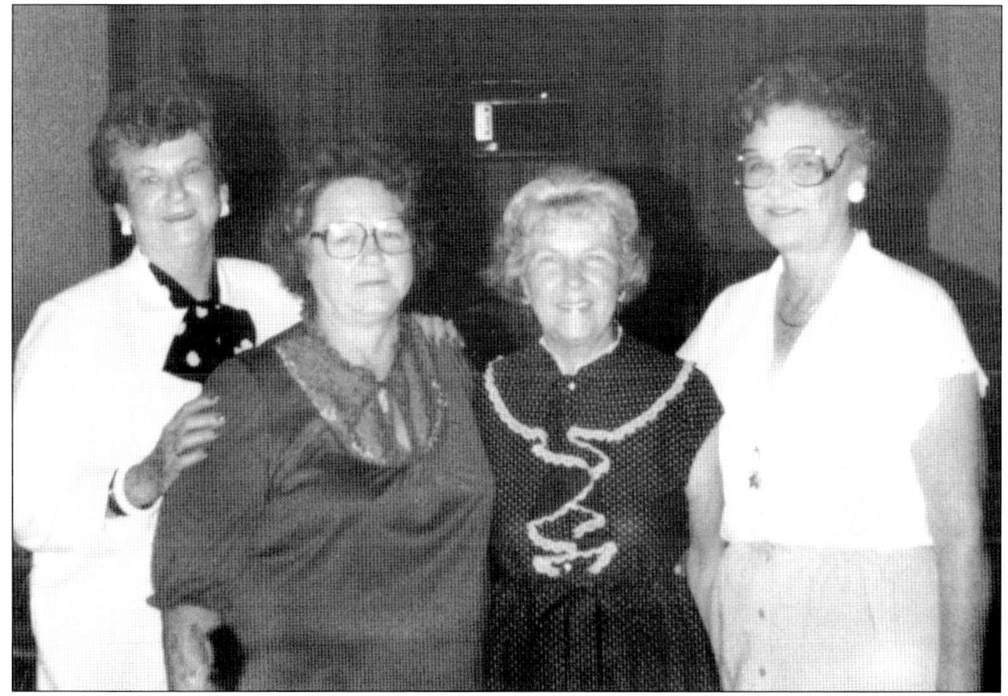

The ladies in this 1970s picture were some of the active members of the Alturas Woman's Club. They are, from left to right, Nita Albritton, Juanita Voigt, Mary Werner, and Alvena Smith. (Courtesy of Karen Kelly.)

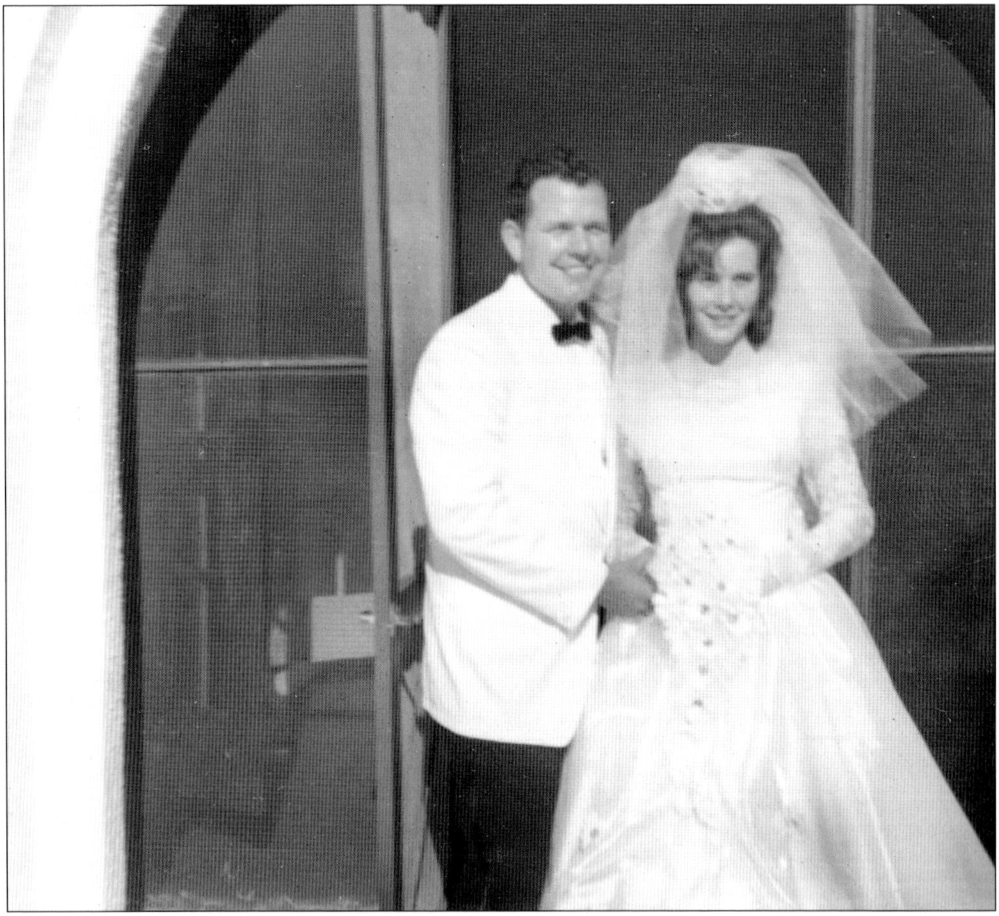

Elon Sowell and Dee Hielscher were married at Alturas Baptist Church on March 30, 1969. Their wedding reception followed at the Alturas Woman's Club. As the newly wedded couple left for their honeymoon, rice was tossed into the air to wish them happiness and riches. (Courtesy of Sherry Maberry.)

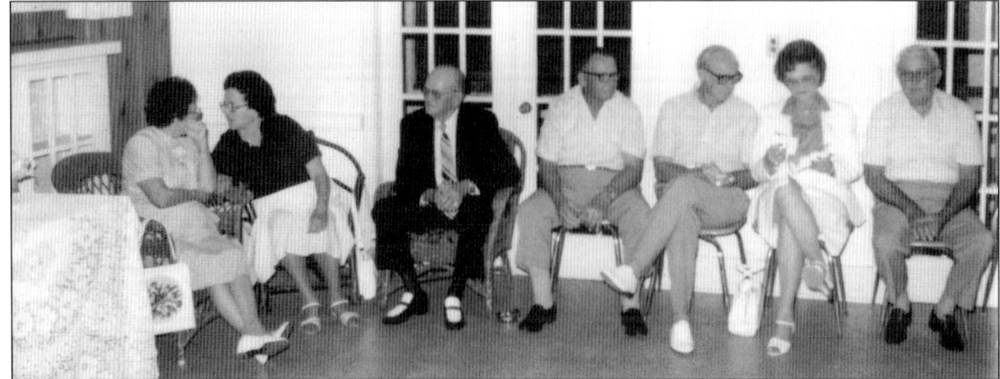

The Alturas Woman's Club was a popular venue for wedding receptions, birthday parties, and community events. This 1980s photograph is a typical scene of Alturas community members attending a local event. Pictured are, from left to right, Flora Lee Young, Margaret Perdue, Joe Perdue, Isaac Albritton, Doug Smith, Alvena Smith, and Joe Underwood. (Courtesy of Scott Young.)

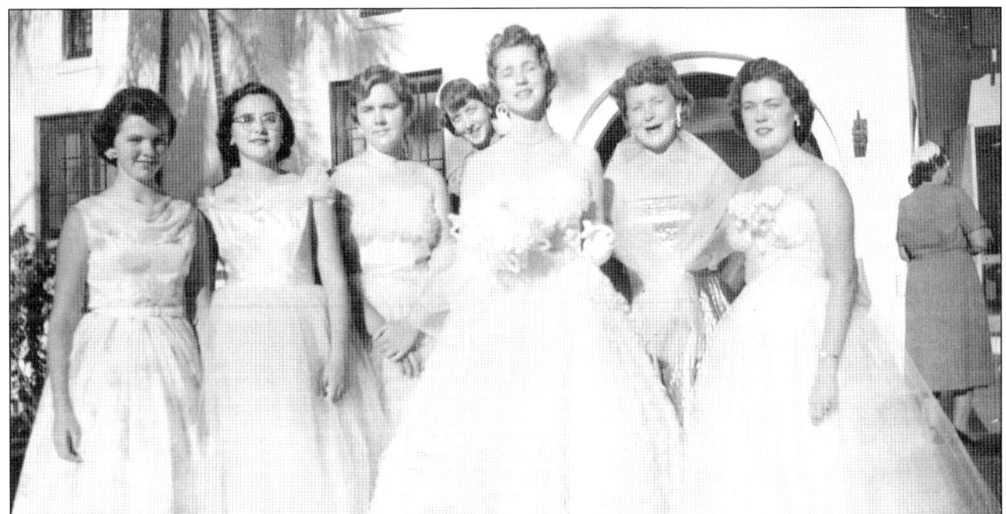

Betty Ann West married Larry Clark at the Alturas Methodist Church in the late 1950s. Their reception was held at the Alturas Woman's Club, the most popular venue in the little community of Alturas. Pictured here at the reception, from left to right, are Allene Voigt, Phyllis Voigt, Jeannette Voigt, Lucille Frost Clements, Betty Ann West, Juanita Voigt, Anadelle Fullington, and Guynnell Voigt. (Courtesy of Teresa Skeen.)

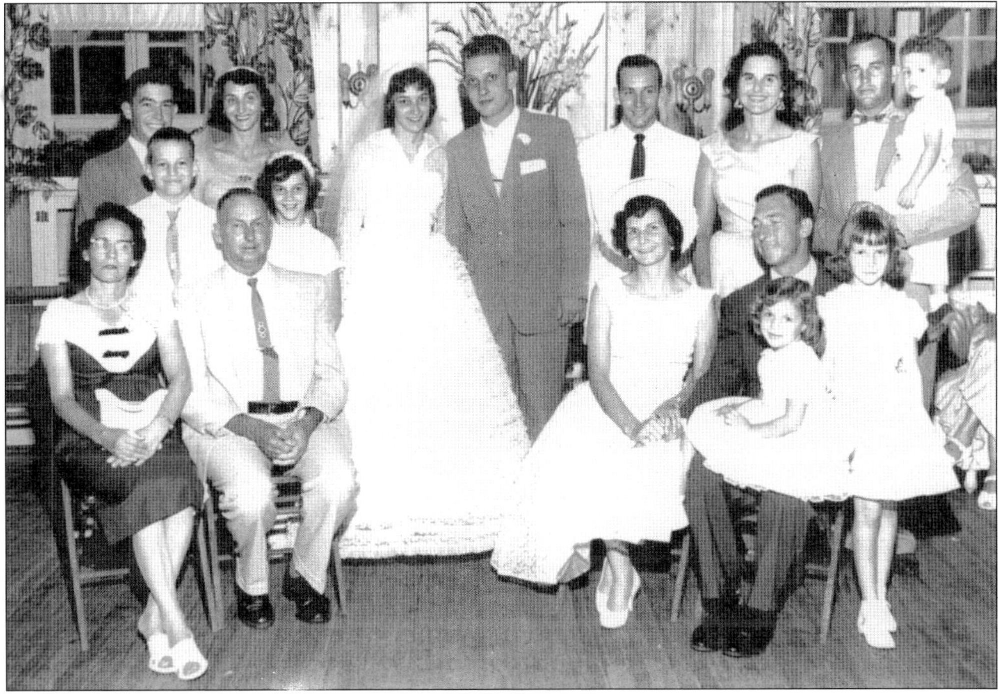

Flora I. Young and Harold Graddy married at Alturas Baptist Church on July 17, 1959. Their reception was held at the Alturas Woman's Club. Pictured are, from left to right, (first row) Flora Lee and Henry Young, Evelyn and Merlin Hielscher, Dee Adams (later Hielscher), and Sherry Hielscher; (second row) Allen and Donnie Young; (third row) Carl and Raymurl Hielscher, Flora and Harold Graddy, James Young, Wanda and Leland Young, and Scott Young. (Courtesy of Flora Conley.)

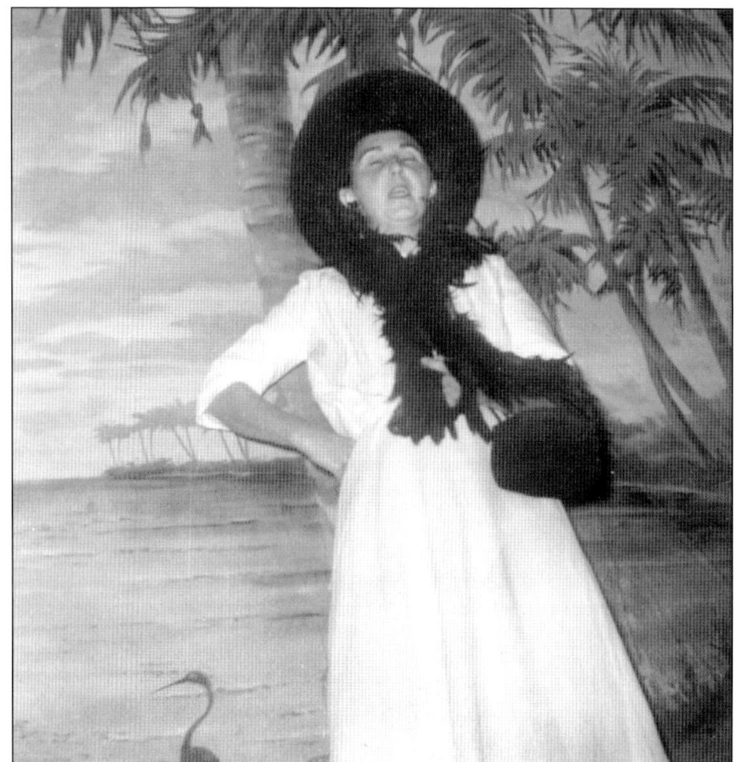

The Alturas Woman's Club held many community variety shows to raise money to support the upkeep of the club. Sylva "Skylenski" (also known as Sylva Kelly) was a crowd favorite when she performed her famous comedic operatic routine. (Courtesy of Karen Kelly.)

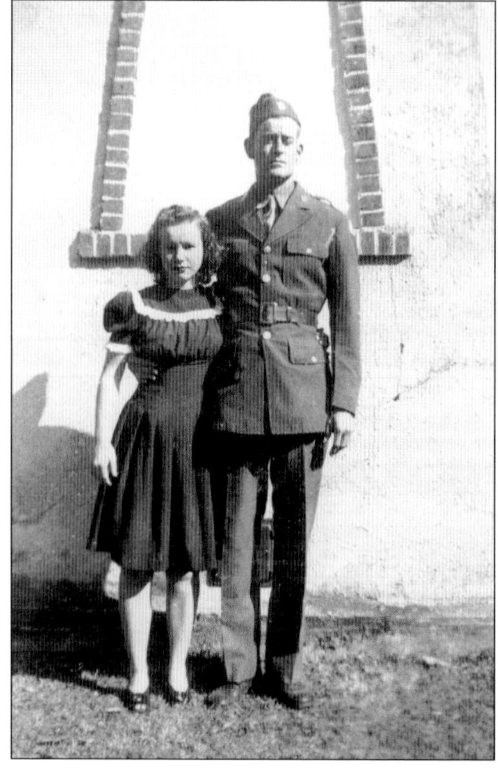

Irene Rhoden and Quince Radford were married on November 10, 1943. They had two daughters, Nancy and Cathy. Quince was drafted into the 31st Infantry in the Pacific soon after his marriage. As a civilian, he worked at the Armour Fertilizer Plant. Irene was a school crossing guard and a homemaker. The couple are standing in front of the Alturas Woman's Club in this 1940s photograph. (Courtesy of Cathy Radford Grace.)

Six

The Lakes

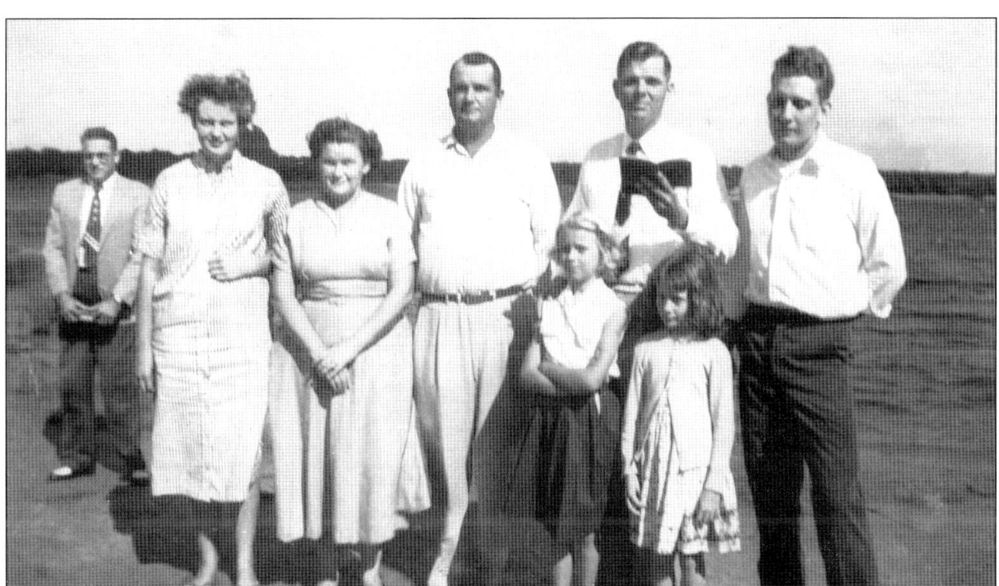

Flora Lake was located between the two communities of Alturas and Lake Garfield on Cox Road. The Baptist churches used this lake for their baptisms. In 1958, the First Baptist Church of Alturas's pastor, Rev. Robert T. Barrett (second from right), is reading scripture before a baptism. Song leader Howard Peacock is standing at left. Those being baptized were Jimmie Sue Grubbs, am unidentified couple, Harold Graddy and children, Janice Woods, and Dee Adams Hielscher. (Courtesy of Sherry Maberry.)

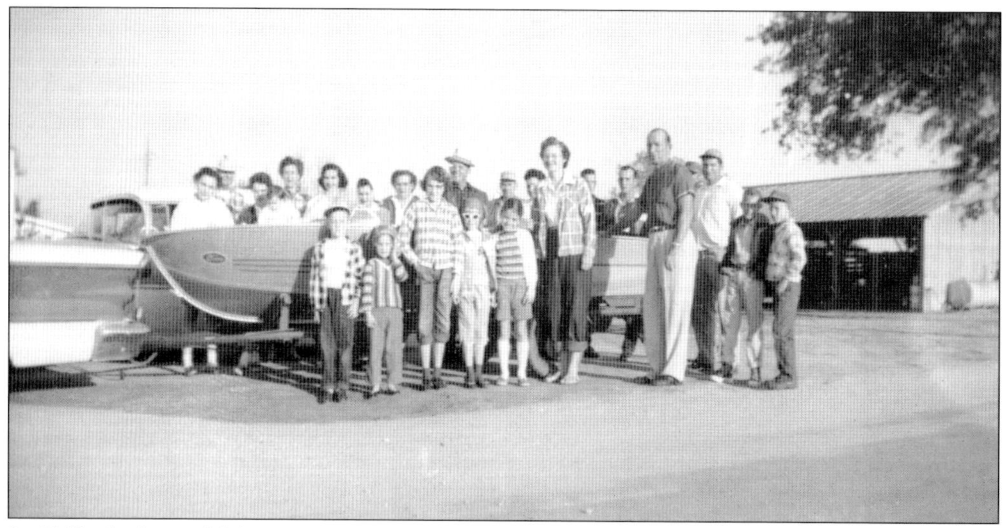

In 1958, the love of fishing among several Alturas residents led to the formation of the Alturas Boat Club. Monthly outings were planned with lots of fun enjoyed. In no particular order are Louis Voigt, Ronnie Voigt, Verdon Voigt, Alvena Smith, Inez Estes, Doug Smith, Rosemary Estes, Elenor Odowski, Dixie Serdynski, John Serdynski, Leland Young, and Wanda Young. (Courtesy of Scott Young.)

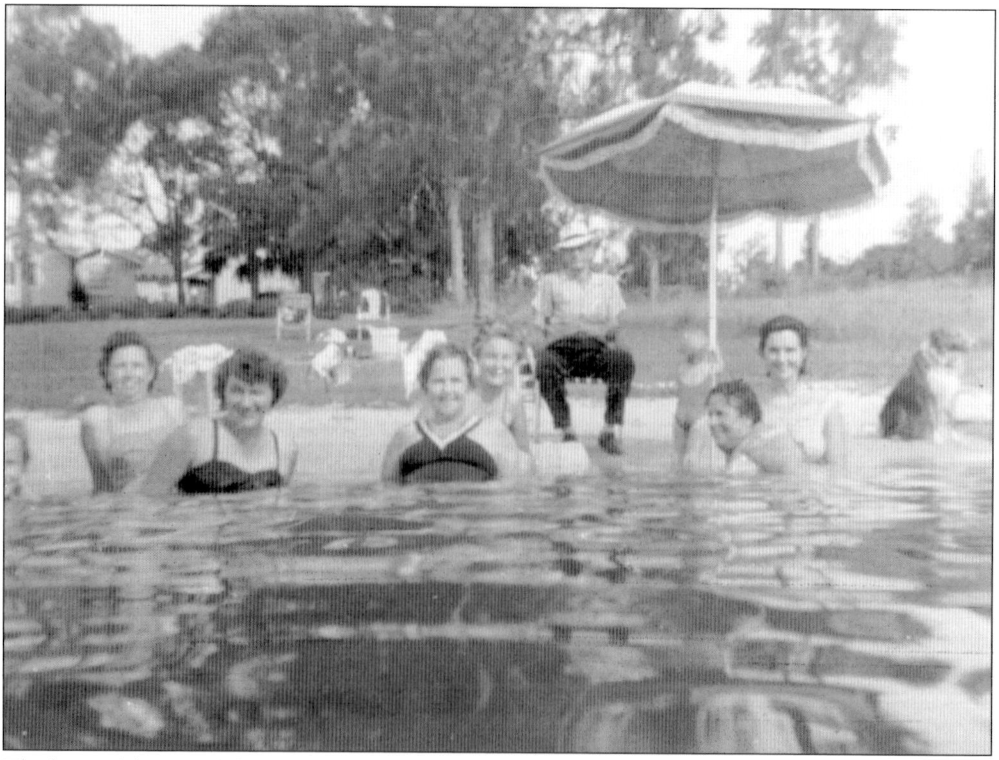

The beautiful spring-fed Star Lake was a favorite swimming hole for most everyone around Alturas. It was very deep; many said it was "bottomless." This 1961 photograph shows, from left to right, Lena West, Ethel Wojteczko, Clara Perdue, Alvena Smith, Joe Perdue (sitting), Dixie Serdynski, and Wanda Perdue Young. (Courtesy of Scott Young.)

Fishing was a popular pastime with so many lakes located around Alturas. W.N. Gadau caught this 12.5-pound fish in the lake near his home. Most people referred to it as Gadau Lake, but it had previously been known as Booth Lake, named after local businessman Strother Booth. The bamboo pole was cut from a stand of bamboo nearby. Little Alvena Gadau was admiring her Daddy's catch in this 1921 photograph. (Courtesy of Linda King.)

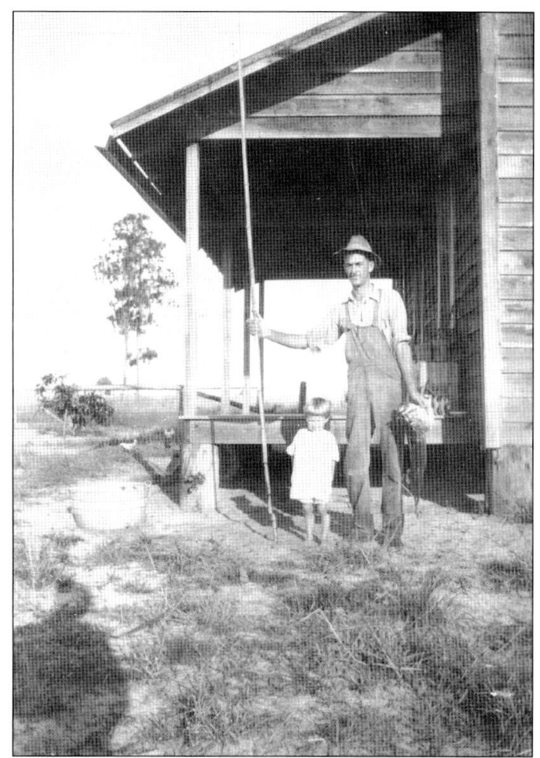

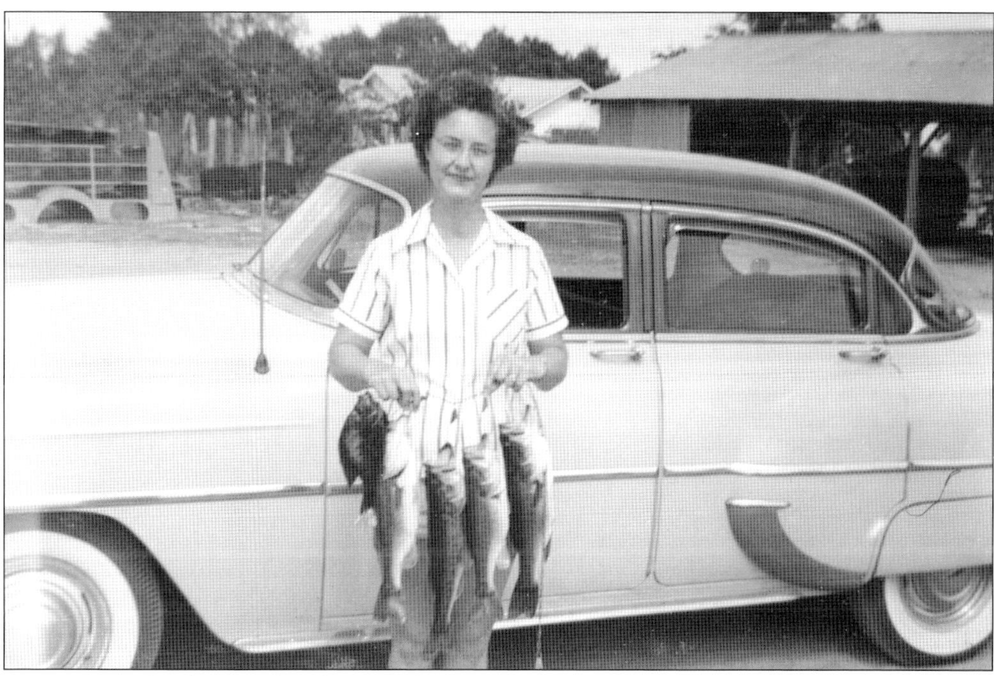

Juanita Voigt (and her husband, Bunk) loved to fish. This photograph shows "Nita" in the 1960s with a mess of fish caught from Lake Garfield, which was located behind their home in Alturas. Nita was well known in the community and was an active member of the Alturas Methodist Church and the Alturas Elementary School PTA. (Courtesy of Teresa Voigt Skeen.)

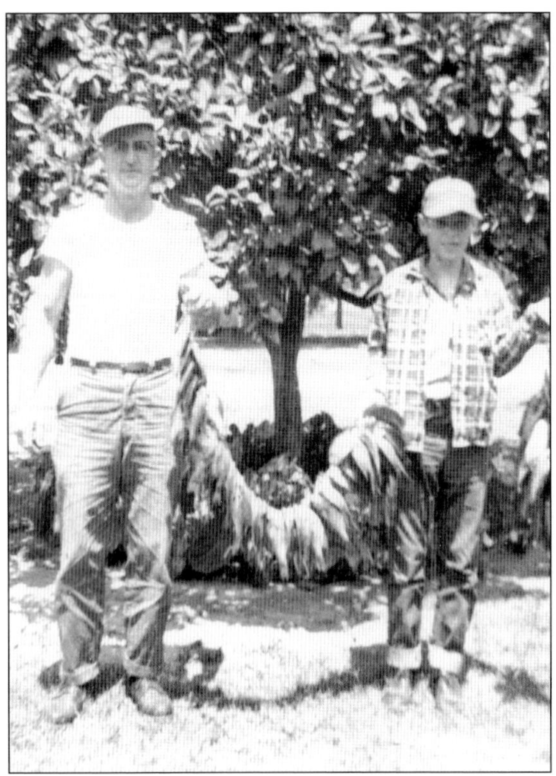

On May 14, 1960, Jesse Kelly and his son Wayne caught this large mess of fish in Lake Garfield. This lake was well-known to the fishing community because it had an easy access road and a boat ramp. Few dared to swim in this alligator-invested lake. (Courtesy of Karen Kelly.)

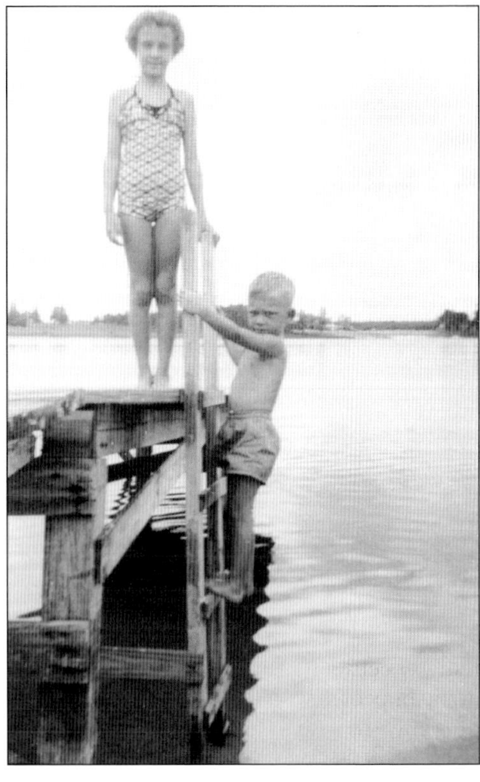

Growing up in Alturas usually involved swimming in Star Lake. As more and more families homesteaded on lakefronts, docks were built to enjoy getting closer to the water. Here, Linda and Leland Smith are enjoying their dock in 1955. Note that orange trees are visible in this photograph on the far right. (Courtesy of Linda Smith King.)

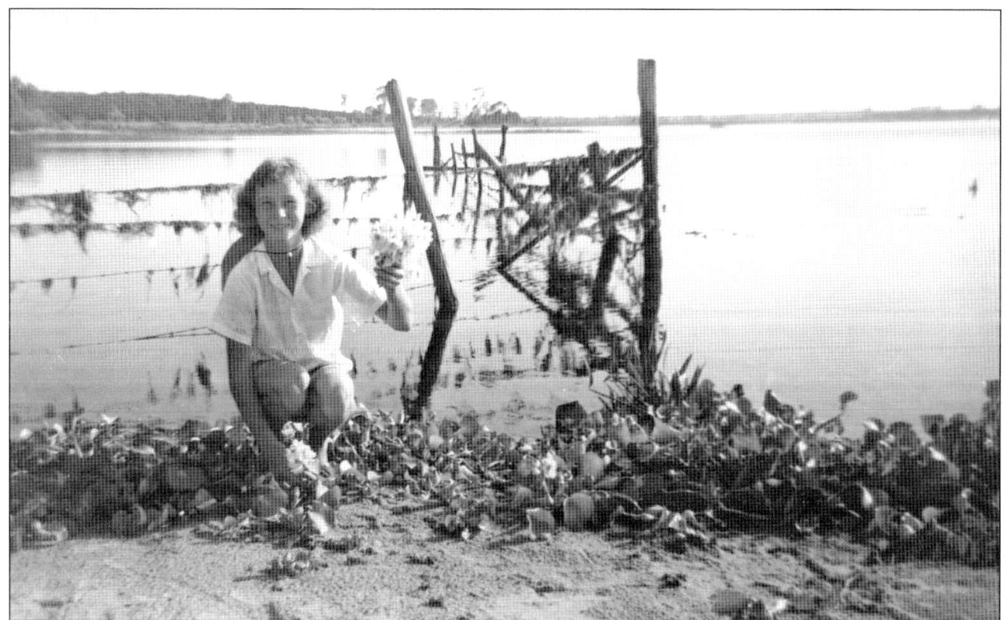

In 1960, Karen Kelly is sitting at the boat ramp of the picturesque Lake Garfield. Note the lovely hyacinths and cattails near the bank. Lake Garfield, the lake, was located east of the Lake Garfield tract and in closer proximity to Alturas than it was to the community for which it was named. The lake was a busy place for fishermen but was never a place for swimming due to the abundance of alligators. (Courtesy of Karen Kelly.)

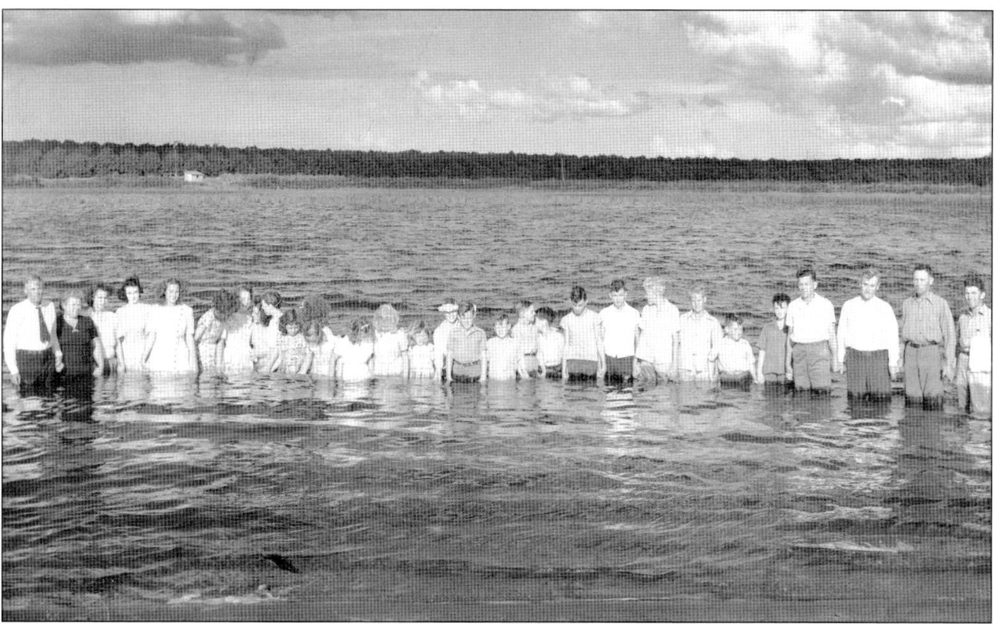

The Lake Garfield Baptist Church held baptisms at Flora Lake, which was located on Cox Road halfway between Alturas and the Lake Garfield community. In this 1946 picture, there is a large group of people waiting to be baptized. Rev. W.L. Mills is at far left, and Deacon Jim Porter is at far right, there to assist the pastor. The 20th person from the left is Jessie Brown. (Courtesy of the First Baptist Church of Lake Garfield.)

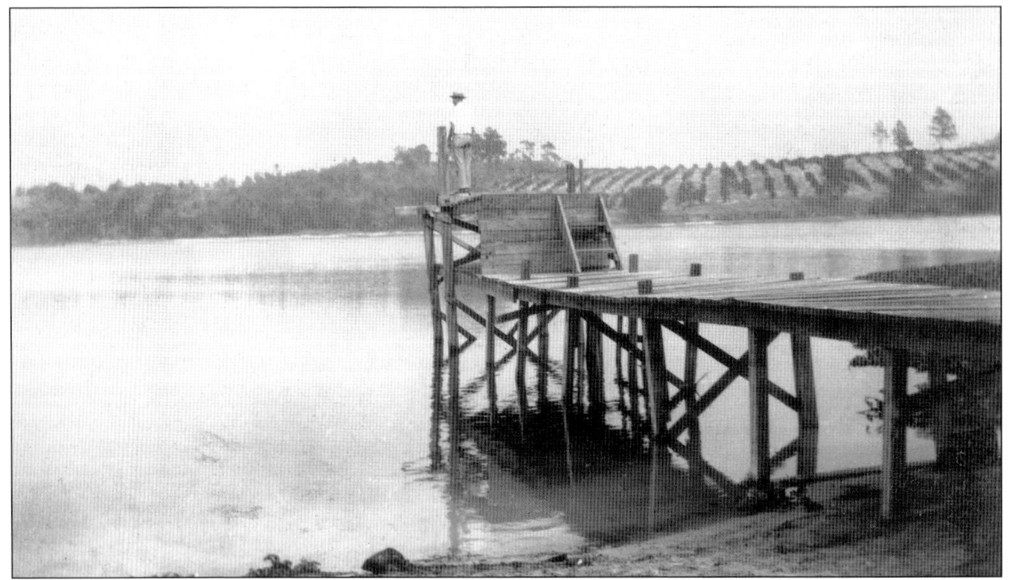

Early settler Louis Stenger is standing on the dock of Beulah Lake, which was located remarkably close to his home in Lake Garfield. The lake, like many others in that area, was destroyed by mining by the IMC phosphate company and no longer exists. Stenger was a prominent resident and owned Stenger Grove Service. His younger brother, John, later bought the company, and it remains in the family, owned and operated by John's son Michael Stenger. (Courtesy of Jackie Stenger Stoltz.)

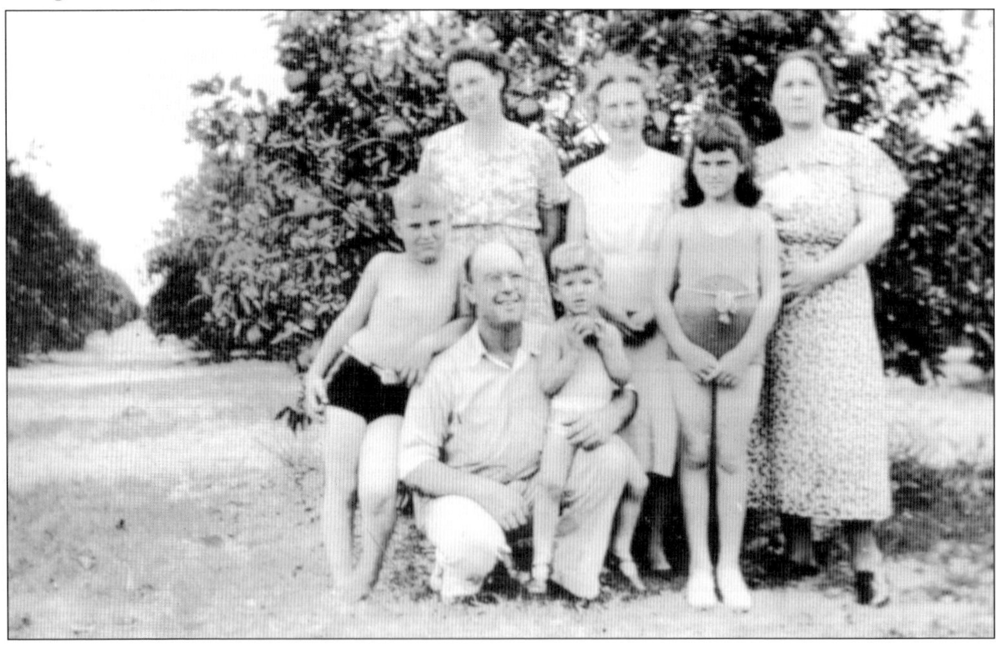

Junius W. and Mae Belle Huff with their son Patrick are entertaining out-of-state relatives from Texas and Mississippi in 1938. They took the group to Star Lake for a swim, and a picture was made in an orange grove to show the folks back home. Star Lake in Alturas was a favorite swimming spot for residents of Lake Garfield. Pictured are W. Patrick Huff (first row, left); his father, J.W. Huff (first row, second from left); and Mae Belle Huff (second row, left). (Courtesy of W. Patrick Huff.)

Seven

The Schools

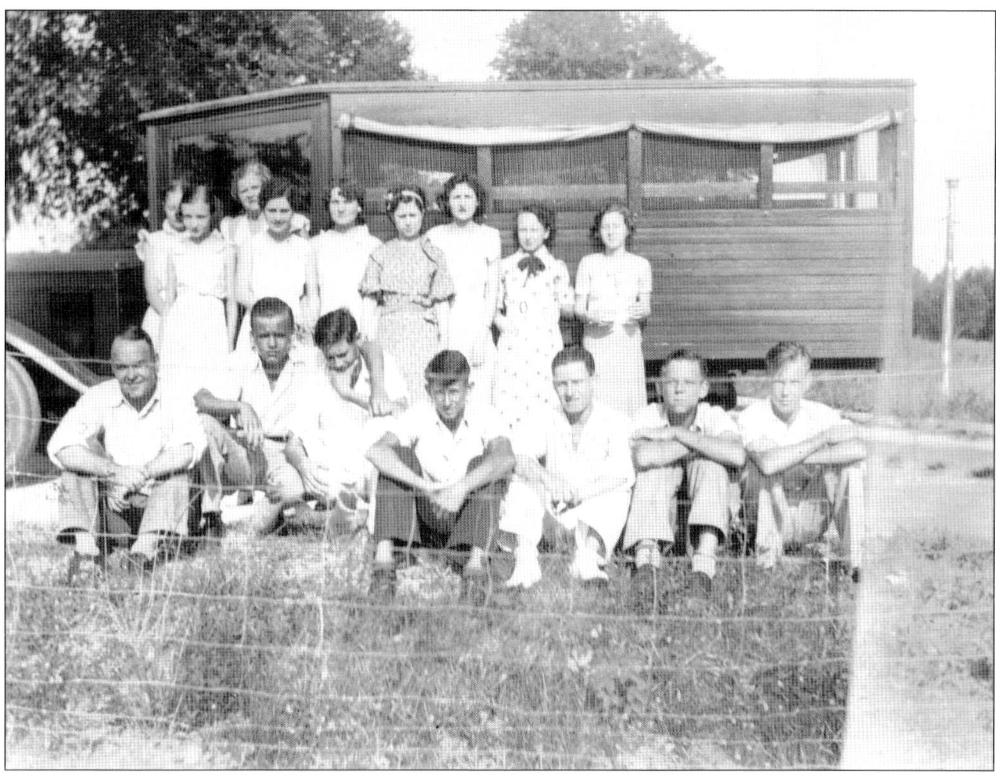

Alturas students affectionately named their school bus "Tin Can Willie," which is pictured here in 1934. Grammar-school children rode the bus to Alturas Elementary. Older students rode the bus from Alturas to Summerlin Institute in Bartow, Florida, a 12-mile ride one way. The two students identified are Edward Voigt (first row, second from left) and Noble Gadau (first row, second from right). Bus driver Harry Shepard, a Scottish immigrant (first row, first person on the left), met and married Marie Voigt in West Salem, Illinois. They moved to Texas, where Marie passed away around 1930. After her death, Shepard moved to Alturas and married Alturas resident Ella Mae Harris. (Courtesy of Linda Smith King.)

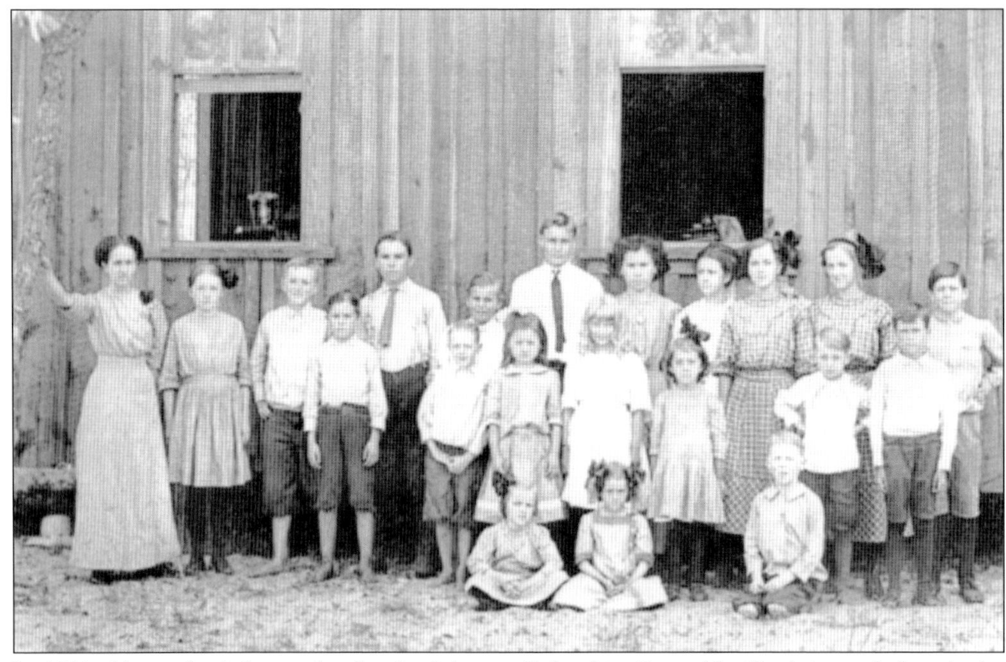

In 1911, Alturas had three schools: the Johnson School in Reynoldsville (pictured above), the Surveyor's Lake School at Murphyville, and Alturas Elementary School. In this Johnson School photograph are, from left to right, (first row) Clemmie Colton, Hilda Starling, and Paul Colton; (second row) Troy Tyson, Albert Colton, Viola Tyson, Florida Feddern, Melba Bryan, Cecil Johnson, and Cleo Starling; (third row) teacher Mayme Langford, Pearle Colton, George Colton, Tezzie Tyson, Gussie Feddern, Walter Feddern, Lillie Tyson, Nolie Bryan, Kate Colton, Ruth Colton, and Olen Bryan. (Courtesy of the *Lakeland Ledger*, 1984.)

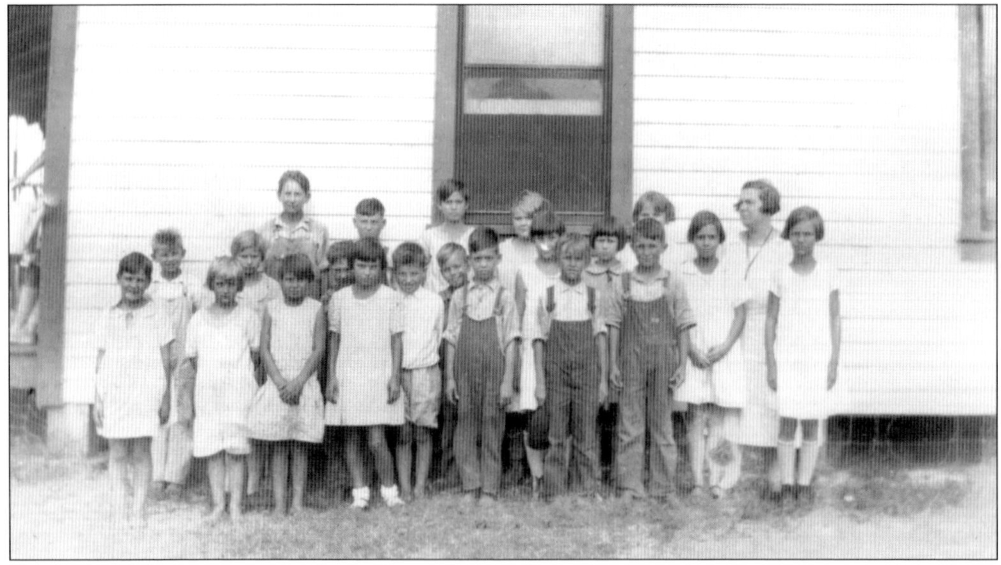

The original 1920s Alturas Elementary School was located behind the homes on Peanut Alley and directly south of the Alturas Woman's Club. The schoolhouse had two classrooms and two outhouses. In the 1930s, a classroom was added, and bathrooms were built on the back porch. Ms. Gilbert was the teacher. (Courtesy of Linda Smith.)

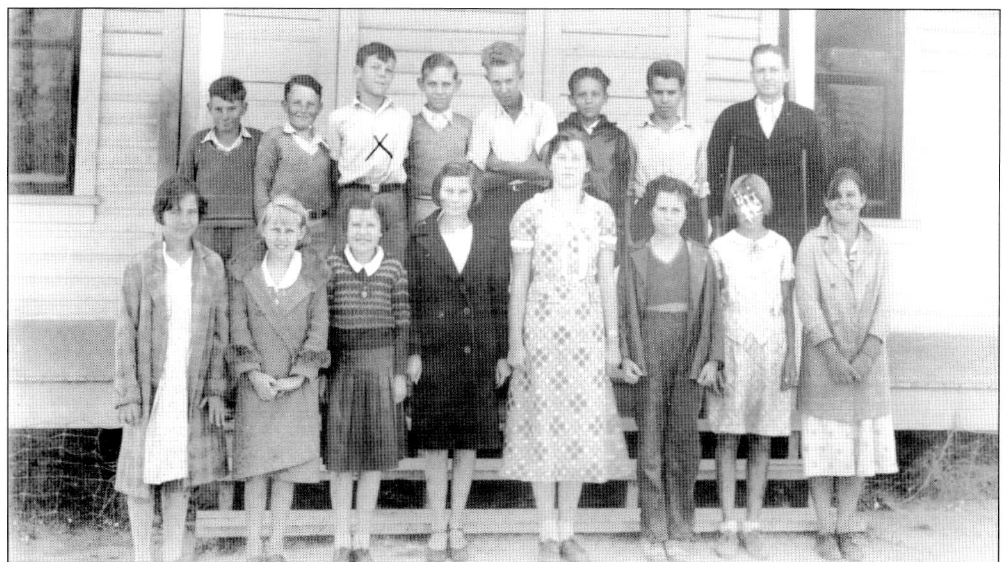

The sixth-, seventh-, and eighth-grade classes at Alturas Elementary School are pictured in 1934. From left to right are (first row) Dorothy Shepherd, Betty Jean Harris, Jean McCourt, Elsie Parker, Ruth McCourt, Virginia Godwin, Alice Wojteczko, and Dorothea Mimms; (second row) Verdon Voigt, Alfred Simpson, Nobel Gadau, Roy Kirkland, Narcys Odowski, William Serdynski, Floyd Reynolds, and teacher Carlos P. Mullins. (Courtesy of Linda King Smith.)

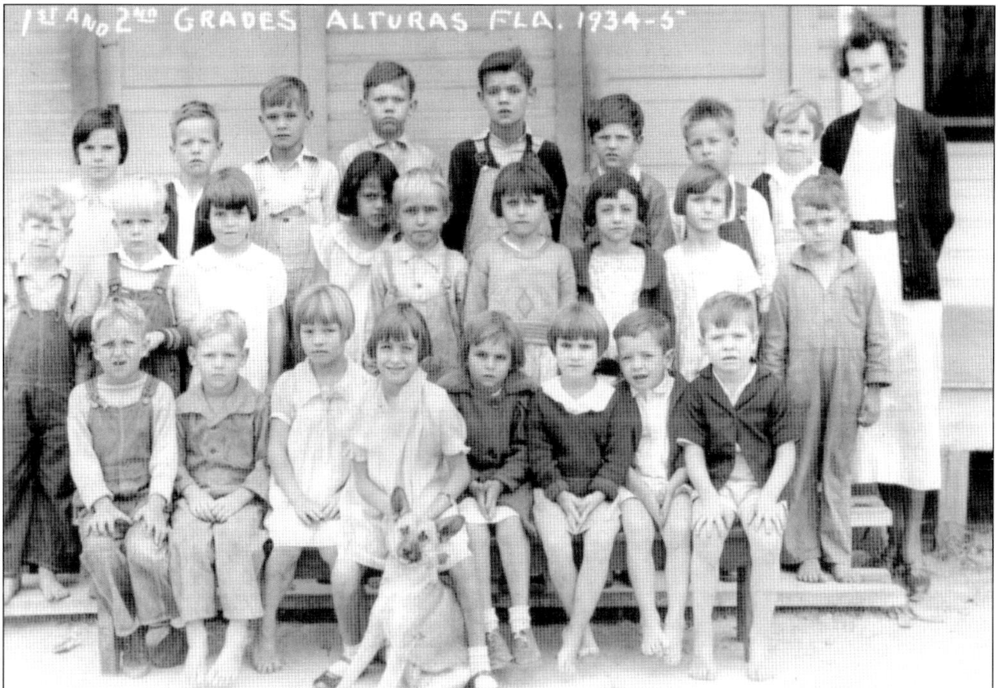

The first- and second-grade classes at Alturas Elementary School are pictured in 1934. Those identified are (in no particular order) Kelly ?, Rachel Cochran, Colon Tyson, Clyde Tyson, John Voigt, Joe Wojteczko, Richard Greene, Bobby Strickland, Howard Frost, and Elaine Harkey. (Courtesy of John A. Voigt.)

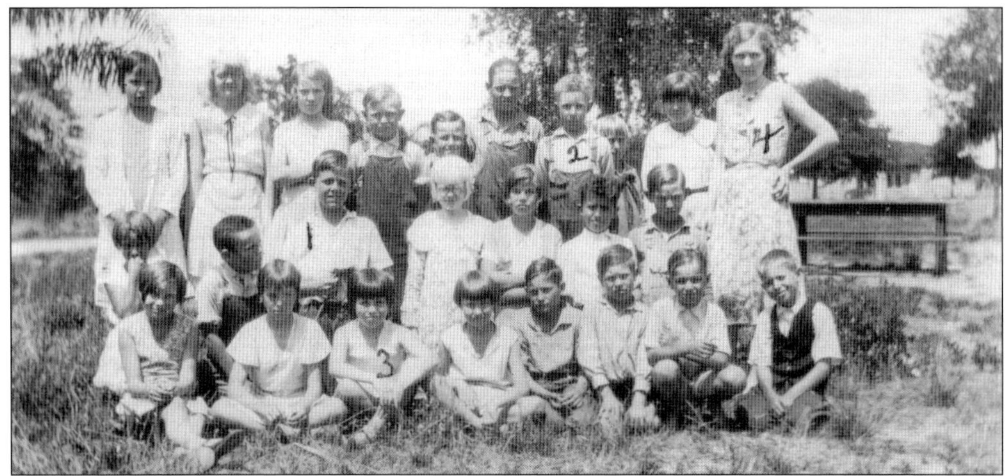

In the late 1920s, Alturas Elementary School teacher Blanche McKrey was standing outside with her students. She taught several grades and many different ages at one time, which was very common at that time in history. Students and teacher numbered in the photograph are (1) Noble Gadau, (2) Narcis Odowski, (3) Virginia Voigt, and (4) teacher Blanche McKrey. Perhaps this was the end of the school year, since the teacher has on a sleeveless dress and the weather would have been warm. (Courtesy of Linda Smith.)

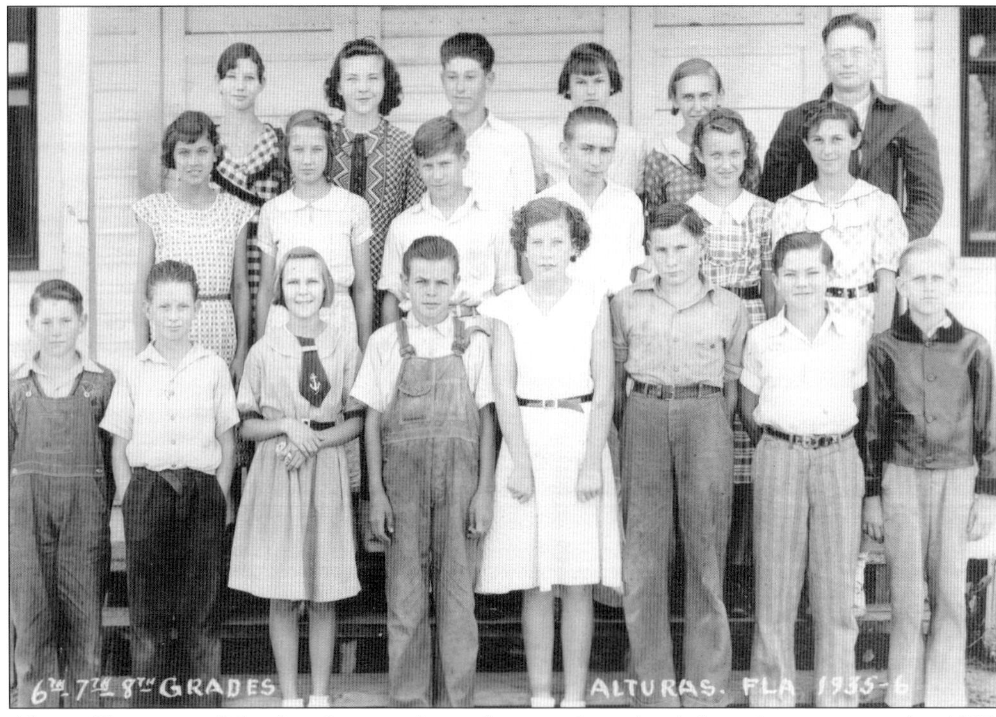

Alturas Elementary School students in the sixth, seventh, and eighth grades are pictured in 1935. From left to right are (first row) La Vern Voigt, Ralph Dees, Mary Wojteczko, Clayton Hill, Jean McCourt, Verdon Voigt, Archibald Bruce, and Richard Voigt; (second row) Juanita Greene, Doris Weatherington, J.B. Parker, Earle Tyson, Eunice Brown, and Sylva Swartz; (third row) Annie Durrance, Dorothy Ellis, Gordon Fortner, Flora Mae Stephens, Alice Wojteczko, and teacher Carlos P. Mullin. (Courtesy of Teresa Skeen.)

The first-grade class at Alturas Elementary School is pictured in 1938. The only child identified in this picture is Wanda Jean Perdue, who is seated in the third row, far right. (Courtesy of Scott Young.)

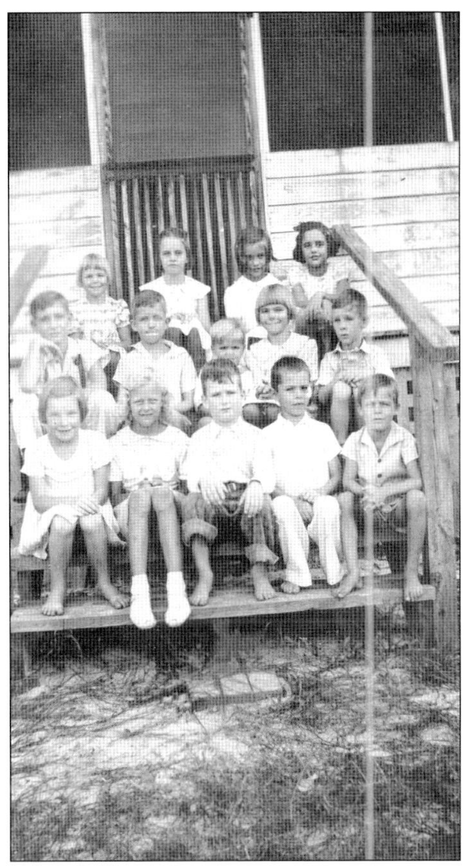

The Alturas Elementary School lunchroom ladies were often the children's favorite school personnel. The ladies cooked from scratch and gave each child generous amounts of food and big helpings of love. Those in this 1970s photograph are, from left to right, Barbara Griffin, Peggy Staton, and Elizabeth Watkins. Other cafeteria workers during the 1950s, 1960s, and 1970s were Dollie Rothrock, Doris Register, Rita Bomar, Lena West, Lou Stevens, Ruth Stevens, Iverdee Watkins, Mattie Lee Dixon, and Gloria Richardson Jones. (Courtesy of Alturas Elementary School.)

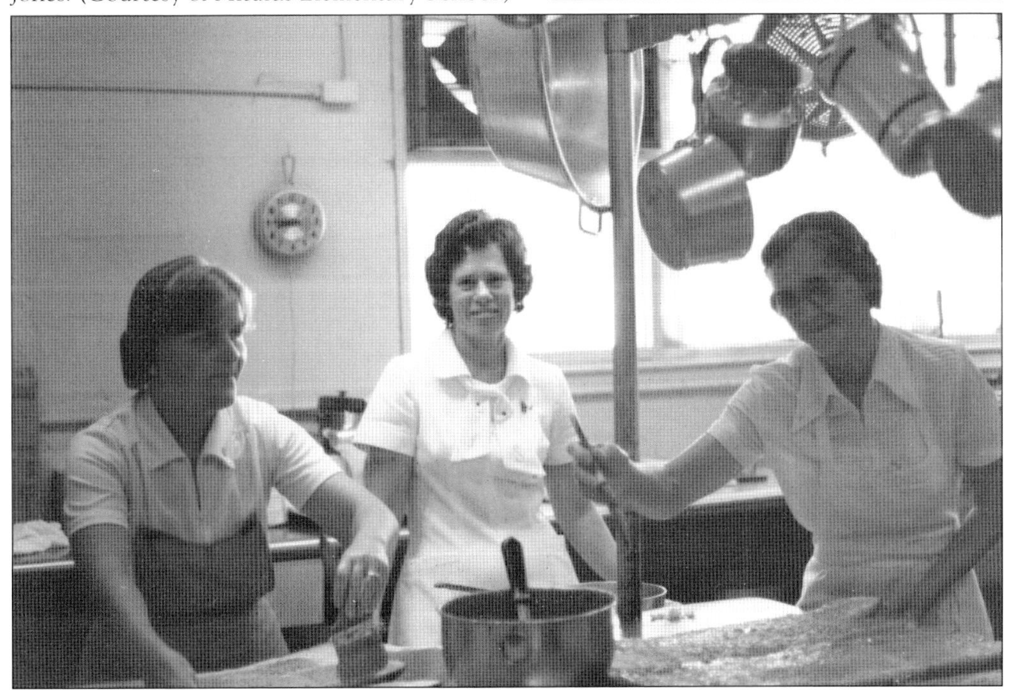

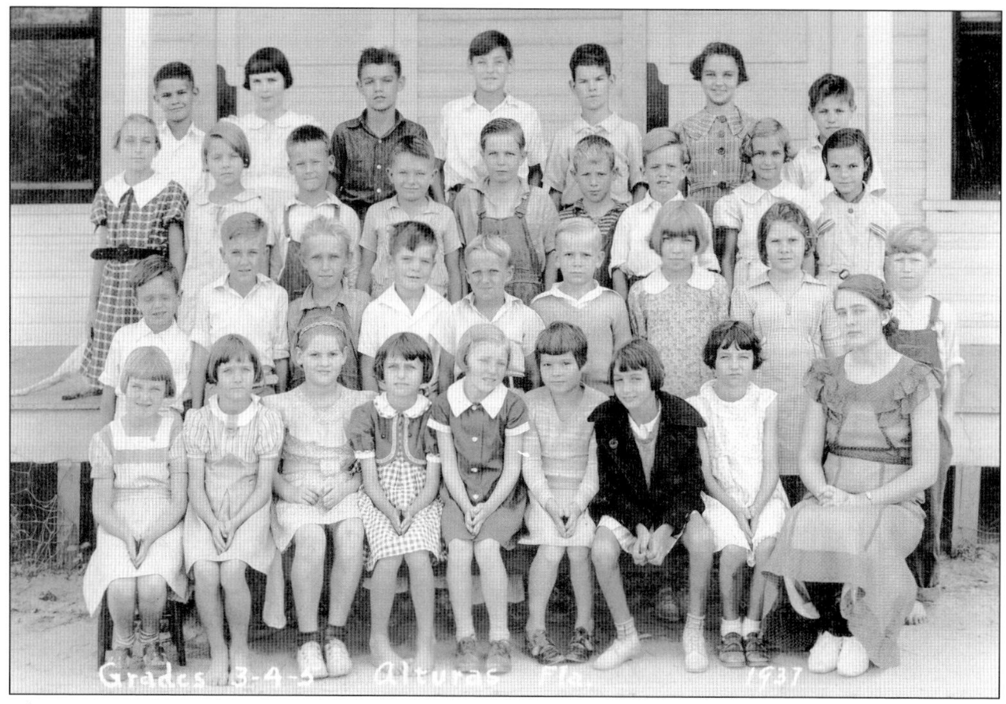

This is a 1936–1937 photograph of the third, fourth, and fifth grades at Alturas Elementary. This was the first year that teacher Annie Louise McLeroy taught at the school. She later married Robert H. Voigt. Pictured from left to right are (first row) Elaine Harkey, LaDonna Starling, Iris Minshall, Margaret Starling, Betty Hurst, Maxine Parker, Annie Belle Stephens, Agnes Black and teacher Miss McLeroy; (second row) Colon Tyson, Billie Hurst, Joe Wojteczko, Clyde Tyson, Junior Kelly, John Albert Voigt, Bonnie O'Neal, Barbara Minshall, and Junior Weatherington; (third row) Evelyn Kelly, Juanita Frost, Howard Frost, Oliver Tyson, Junior Hill, Vern Dees, Carlton Tyson, Jacqueline Kennedy, and Eloise Hill; (fourth row) J.B. Green, Sybil Harkey, Bobby Strickland, Jack Luna, Richard Cochran, Clara Schumacher, and Bill Luna. A noteworthy fact is that the Starling and Tyson children in this photograph were descendants of the original Alturas 1800s pioneers. (Courtesy of John A. Voigt.)

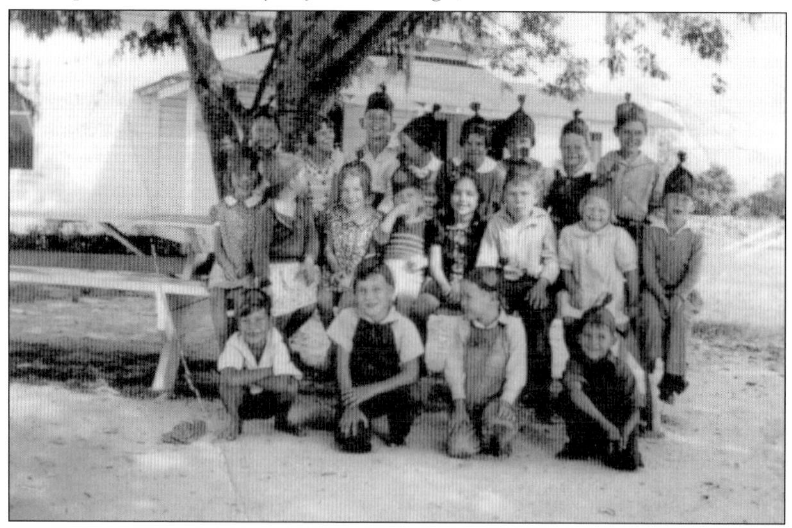

The first-grade class at Alturas Elementary School is pictured in 1937. The teacher was Lois Reynold. Leland Young is in the first row, far right. (Courtesy of Scott Young.)

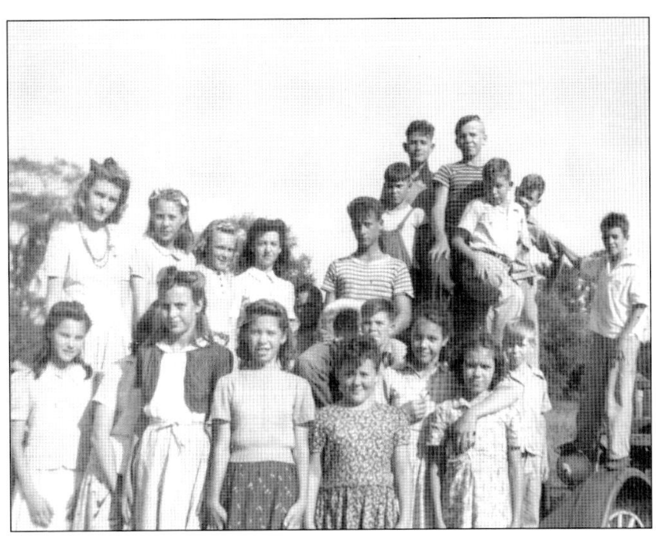

In 1943, Alturas Elementary School eighth-grade students were collecting scrap metal to help with the World War II effort. Students identified are Mary Joyce Luna (first row, first student from left) and Gladys Tyson (first row, third student from left), and on the second row are Elaine Harkey (second row, first student from left), Howard Frost (second row, fifth student from left), Colon Tyson (far right standing on wheel), and John Voigt (top right). (Courtesy of John A. Voigt.)

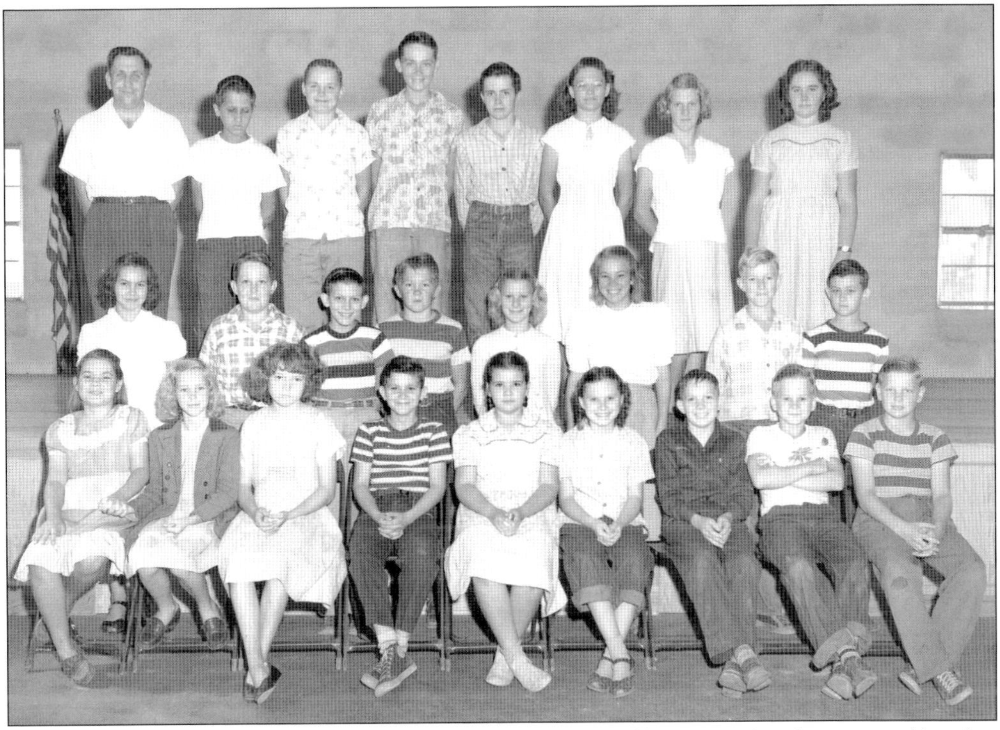

The sixth-grade class at Alturas Elementary School is pictured here in 1950. The principal/teacher was Mr. Teeter. From left to right are (first row) unidentified, Betty Ann West, Sybil Howell, unidentified, Bonnie Martin, Marcella Johnson, unidentified, David Garner, and Ralph Price; (second row) Clara Hill, Shelton Jones, David Ellis, Sherman Register, John Allen Smith, Lenora Radford, Betty Harrison, Shelton Jones, and George Rothrock; (third row) Nick Lazarko, Adrian Harkey, Robert Lolley, Hal Dixon, Inez Creech, Betty Bennett, and Jeanette Voigt. (Courtesy of Alturas Elementary School.)

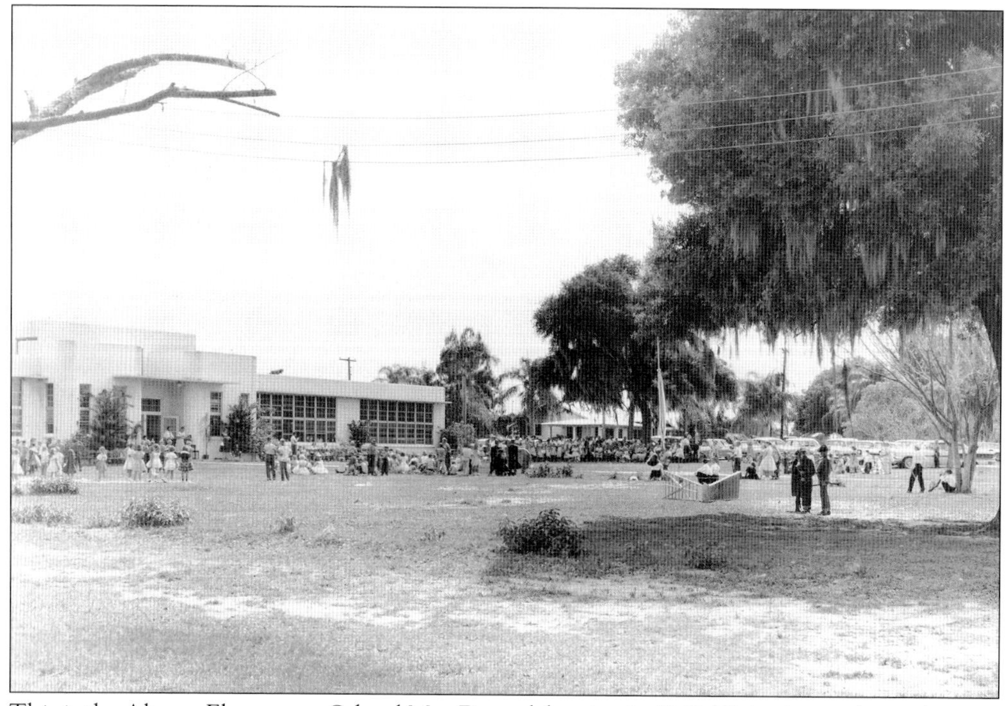

This is the Alturas Elementary School May Day celebration in 1960. This picture shows the west side of the main section of the school building. This larger building housed four classrooms. There was a smaller structure, located behind the main school building, which housed two classrooms. In 1969, the back two rooms began sinking due to a sinkhole. Those rooms were removed, and new structure was built back, in the very same place, but only after it had been fortified against sinkholes. (Courtesy of Alturas Elementary School.)

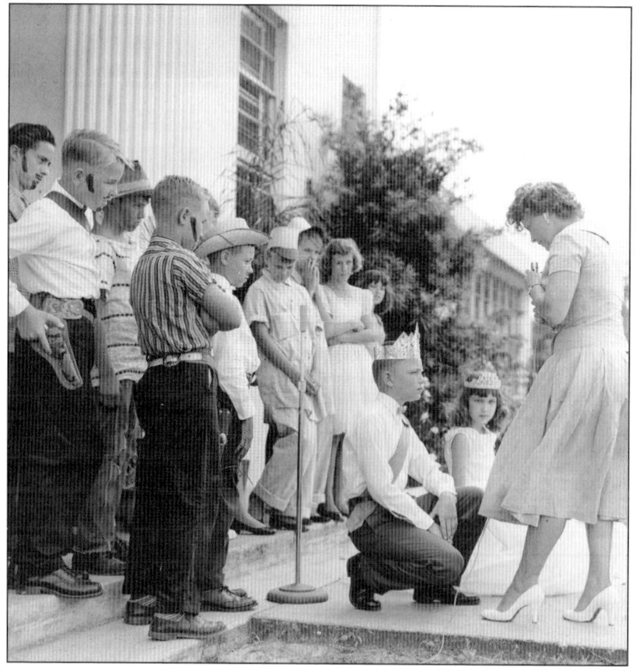

Juanita Voigt was a parent volunteer at Alturas Elementary School, and she is presiding over the May Day coronation of the newly crowned king, Mike Varner, and queen, Gwen Colvin, in 1958. The boy with the cowboy hat is Wayne Kelly, and the girl with her arms crossed is Sharon Jenkins. (Courtesy of Alturas Elementary School.)

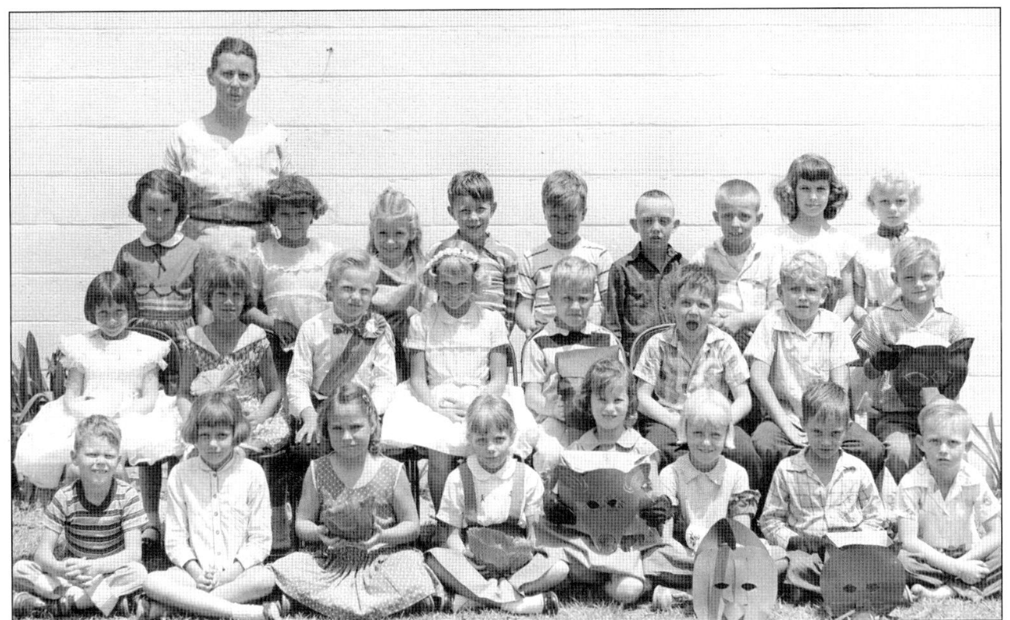

Ellen Campbell's second-grade class at Alturas Elementary School is shown at May Day in 1958. From left to right are (first row) Johnny Hadden, Sudie Moody, Bobbie Cannon, Charlotte Grace, Irma Jane Johnson, Sylvia Moody, Clark Houstin, and unidentified; (second row) Dee Adams Hielscher, Diane Green, Louis Earle Butts, Candy Voigt, Leon Seger, Floyd King, James ?, and Bert Bennett; (third row) Gloria Richardson, Charlotte Register, Barbara Scarborough, Emmett Kelly, Leon Seger, David King, Butch ?, Shirley Colvin, and Janis Woods. (Courtesy of Alturas Elementary School.)

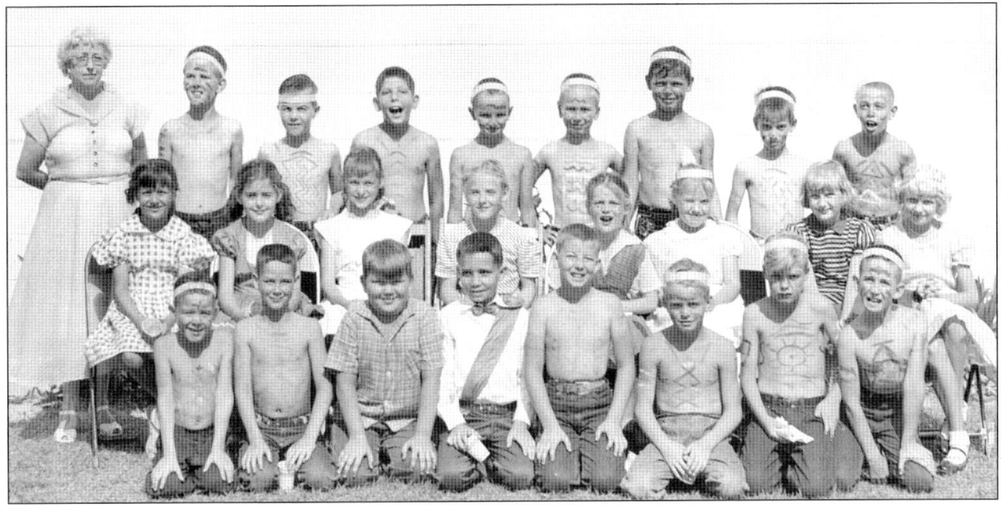

Mrs. Seville's third-grade class at Alturas Elementary School is shown in this picture on May Day in 1958. From left to right are (first row) Richard Daughtry, Johnny Radford, Jeffery Jacobs, Leon McDaniel, Perry Scott, Milford Richardson, Richard Moody, and Robert ?; (second row) Frances Palmer, Mary Waters, Karen Kelly, Carolyn Tyler, Margo King, Fay King, Mary Lou Werner, and Darlene Smith; (third row) Jimmy Young, Eddie Hadden, unidentified, Clove Tyler, Jimmy Lynn Young, Eddie Hadden, Johnny McKinney, Edward ?, Ricky Arter, unidentified, and Richard Green. (Courtesy of Alturas Elementary School.)

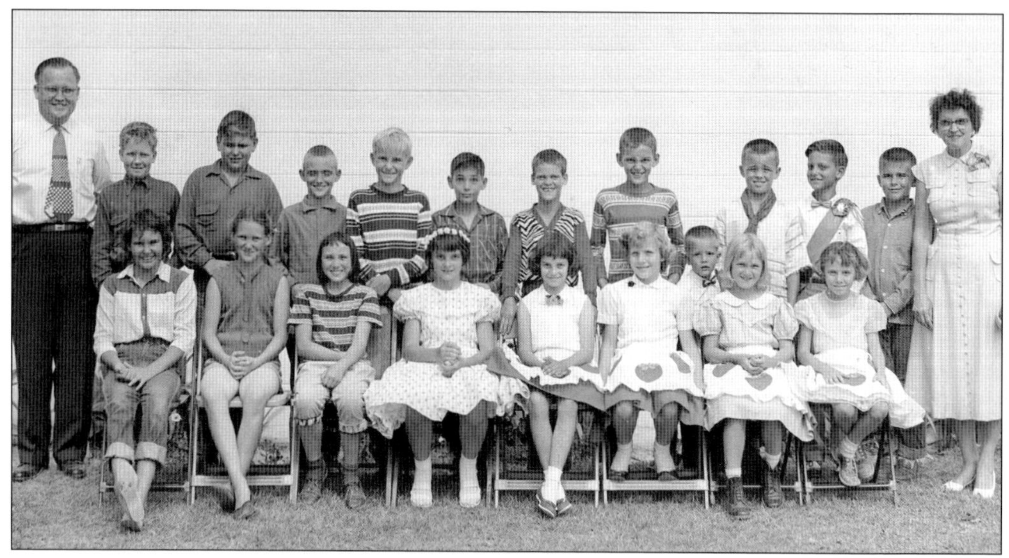

Mrs. Pealer's fourth-grade class at Alturas Elementary School is shown at May Day in 1958. From left to right are (first row) Johnnie Fay Hogan, Faye Durrance, Jackie Griner, Cheryl Duckworth, Doniece Bennett, Margaret Grace, and two unidentified; (second row) Principal Jack Keen, unidentified, Larry Braswell, Eddy Lee King, Butch Richardson, Steve Maddox, Roger Dale King, Eddy Bennett, Kevin Varner, Ronnie Voigt, Richard Waters, and ? Griner. (Courtesy of Alturas Elementary School.)

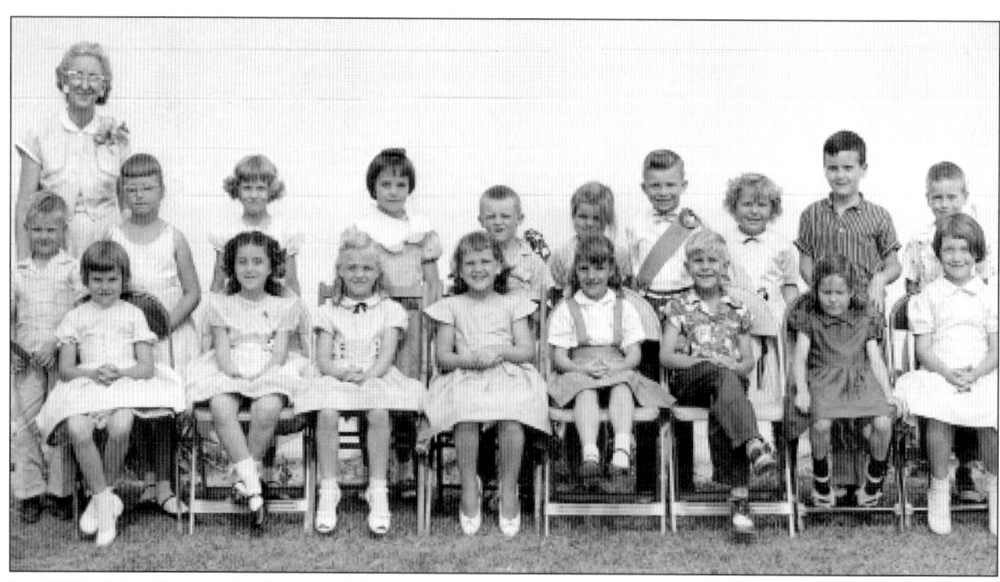

In 1958, May Day took place at Alturas Elementary School. Mrs. Chilton's first-grade class was part of the big celebration. Pictured are, from left to right, (first row) Teresa Voigt, Brenda Luna, Sheila King, Patsy Garner, Joyce Grace, Bobbie Green, Rachel Daughtry, and Linda Gail Parrish; (second row) Johnny Haddon, Cathy Voigt, Zena Jenkins, Bonnie Young, Harold Carnley, Karen King, Tommy Voigt, Pam Tyson, Randy Smith, and unidentified. Brenda Luna was the princess, and Tommy Voigt was the prince. (Courtesy of Alturas Elementary School.)

Alturas Elementary celebrated May Day each year with a special program and the crowning of a new king and queen from the outgoing sixth-grade class. In 1961, Karen Kelly was crowned queen, and Jimmy Young was crowned king. (Courtesy of Karen Kelly.)

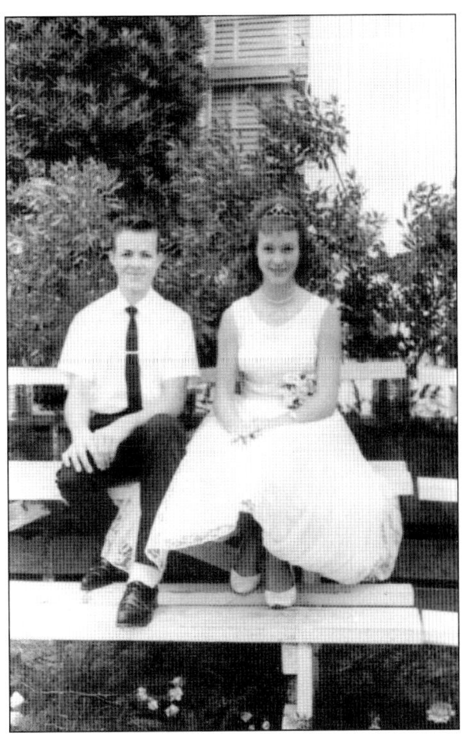

Pictured at the Alturas Elementary School May Day celebration in 1958 is the royal court. From left to right are (first row) Janice Colvin, Tommy Voigt, Brenda Luna, and Brian Varner; (second row) Louis Earl Butts, Candy Voigt, Leon McDaniel, and Rosemary Estes; (third row) Ronnie Voigt, Cheryl Duckworth, Elon Sowell, and Linda Smith; (fourth row) queen Gwen Colvin and king Mike Varner. (Courtesy of Alturas Elementary School.)

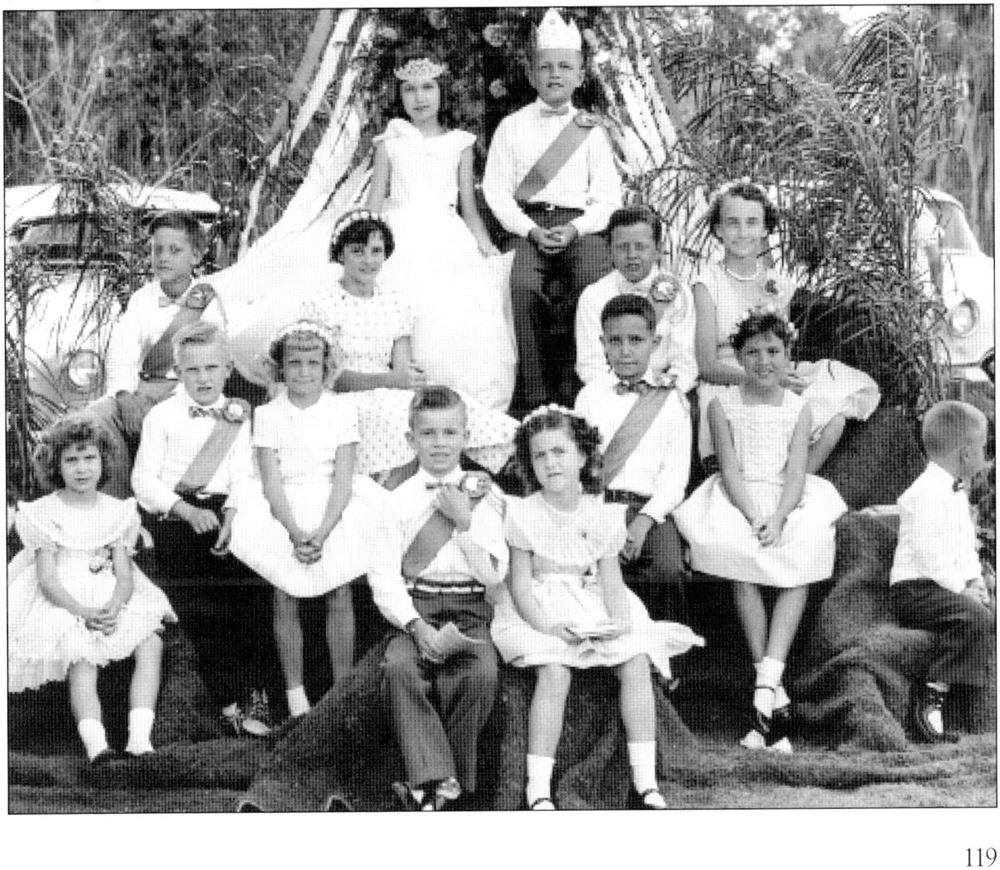

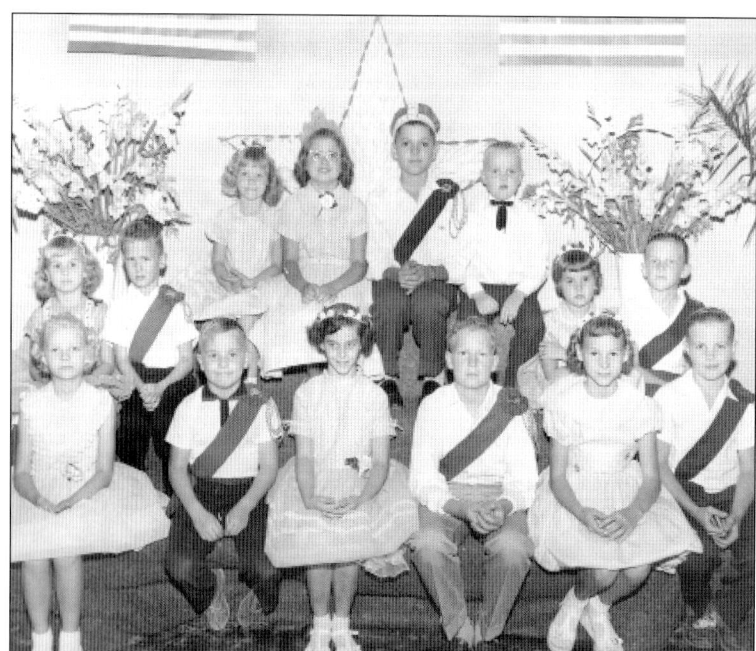

At the Alturas Elementary School May Day Celebration 1959, the royal court was, from left to right, (first row) Janice Woods, unidentified, Doniece Young, Nick Fuqua, Karen Kelly, and Jimmy Young; (second row) LaDonna Jones, ? Barrer, Teresa Voigt, and Leland Smith; (third row) Sherry Woods, Dinah Gabriel, Donnell Parrish, and Teddy Young. (Courtesy of Alturas Elementary School.)

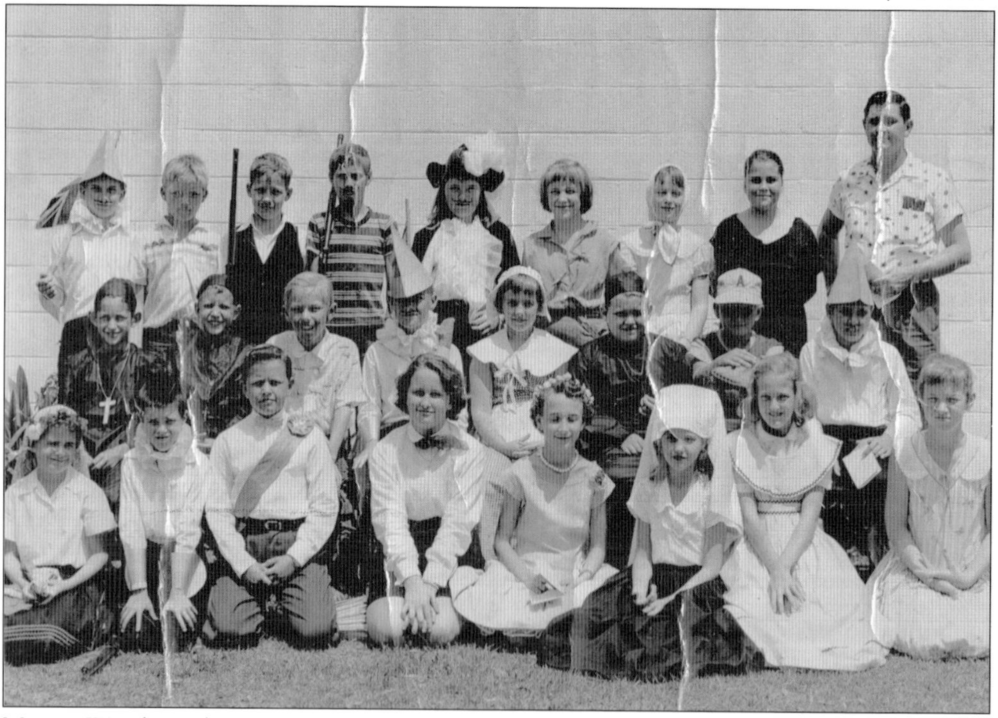

Marion Wood's sixth-grade class is featured at the 1959 May Day celebration. Pictured are, from left to right, (first row) Dinah Kay Gabriel, Donald Luna, Elon Sowell, Mary West, Linda Smith, Shirley Luna, Sara Barbara, and Mary Byrd; (second row) Louis Voigt, David Odowski, John Byrd, unidentified, Sybil Young, Charles Register, unidentified, and Donnell Parrish; (third row) two unidentified, Larry Grace, ? Skipper, Cheryl Voigt, Lanell Parrish, Kathy Radford, and Johnnie Mae Cannon. (Courtesy of Linda Smith King.)

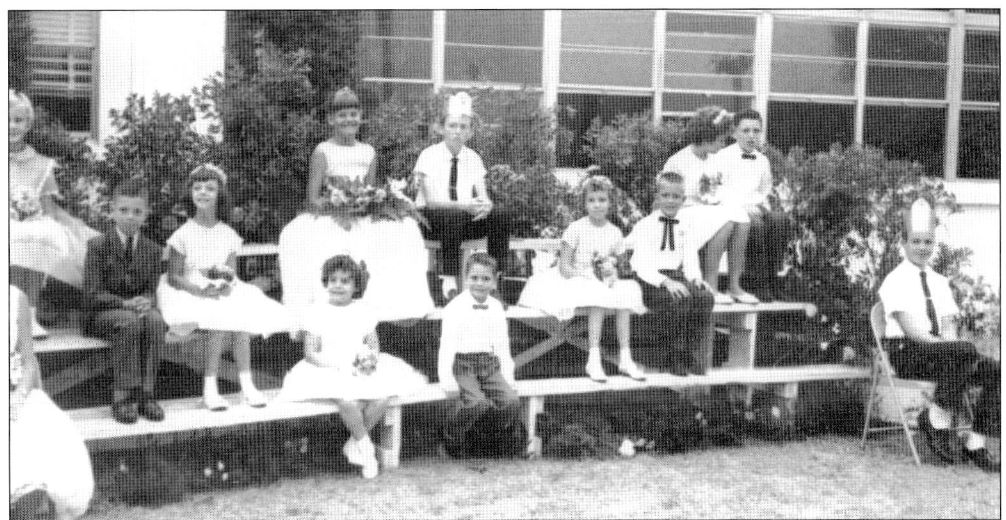

This 1962–1963 Alturas Elementary School May Day celebration is of the royal court at the coronation. Those pictured are, from left to right, (first row) Vicki Hielscher and Gene Watkins; (second row) John Emory Register, Sherry Hielscher, unidentified, and Brian Varner; (third row) Eleanor Odowski, Teresa Voigt, Bill Simmons, and two unidentified. (Courtesy of Sherry Hielscher.)

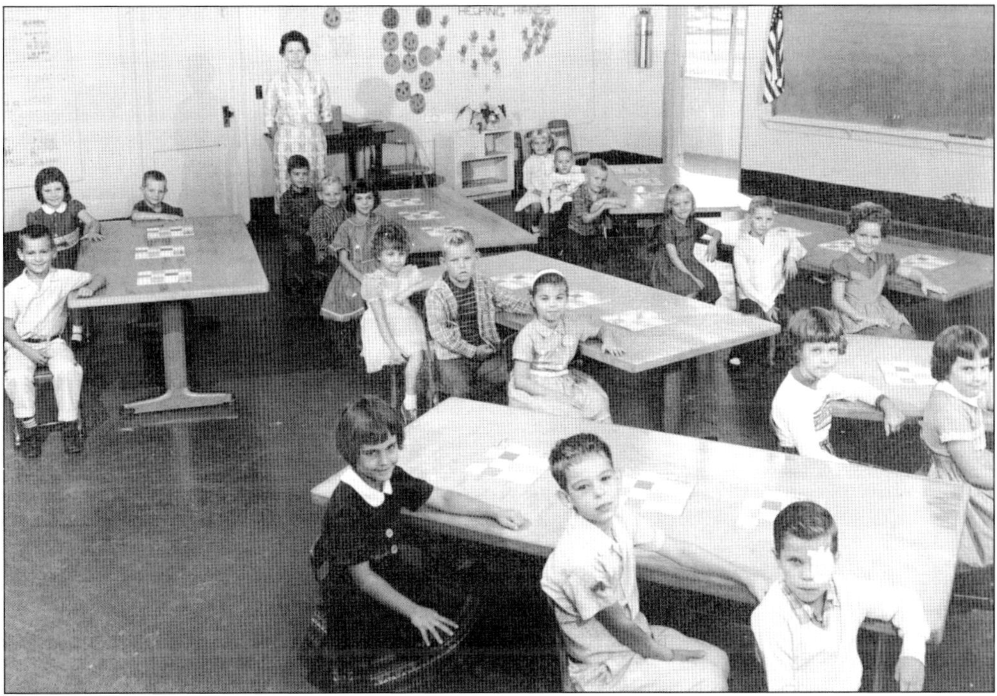

The Alturas Elementary first-grade class is pictured here in 1961. The teacher was Margaret Gressman. The students are (table one, front middle) Sheila Maddox, Ricky Staton, and Billy Green; (table two, far left) Joe Aycock, Kim Hurley, and Glenn Staton; (table three, far middle right) an unidentified girl and Frances Voigt; (table four, center) an unidentified girl, Reginald Palmer, and Vida Kay Luna; (table five, back center) Phillip Waters, Johnny Grace, and Sherry Hielscher; (table six, far right) Diane King, an unidentified boy, and Kathy Gillis; (table seven, far right rear) Kathy Morris, Kenneth Luna, and Bill Voigt. (Courtesy of Alturas Elementary.)

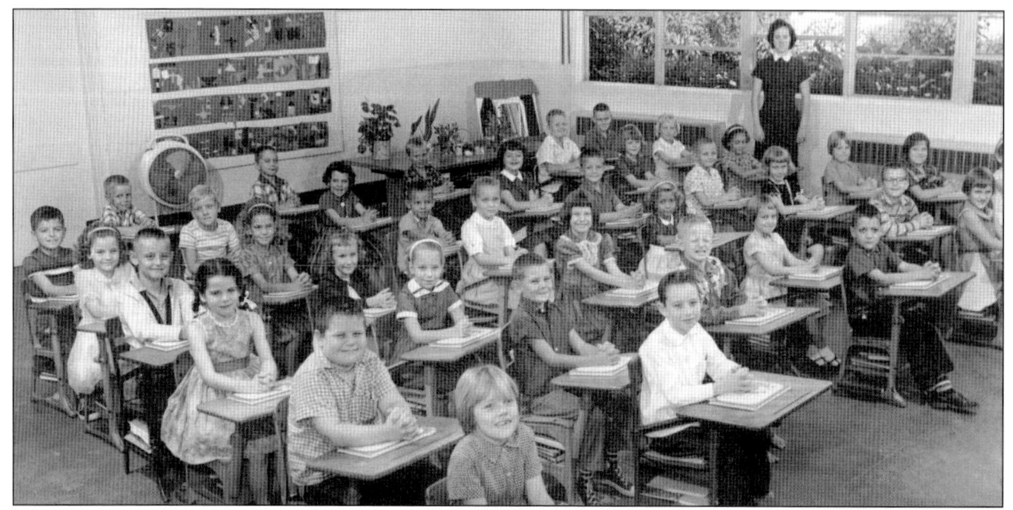

This second-grade class at Alturas Elementary School is pictured here in 1961. The teacher was Melissa Tyre. From left to right are (first row) Margaret Carmichael, Rocky Smothers, unidentified, Randy Hogan, and two unidentified; (second row) unidentified, Fred Hogan, Bonnie Murphy, Carolyn Wojteczko, Edith McGill, Randell Palmer, and unidentified; (third row) Danny Butts, Frances Sue Holloway, unidentified, Michal Aycock, Diane Aycock, and Harney Reynolds; (fourth row) unidentified, Harriet Reynolds, unidentified, Brian Varner, and two unidentified; (fifth row) unidentified, Pete Dickey, two unidentified, Debbie Tyson, and Glendale Martin; (sixth row) two unidentified, Evelyn Voigt, unidentified, and Frankie Taylor. (Courtesy of Alturas Elementary School.)

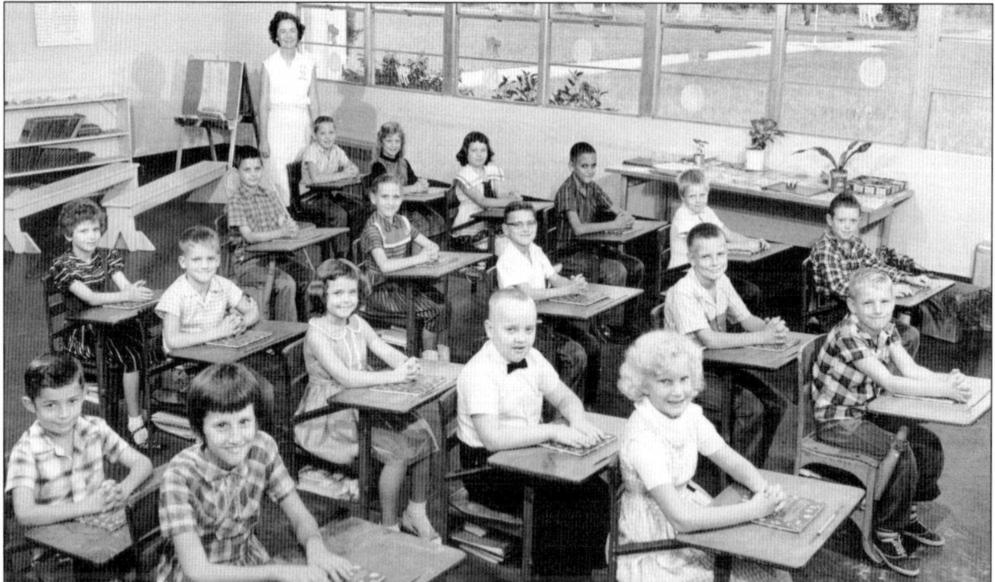

The Alturas Elementary School third-grade class is pictured here in 1961. Joyce Quigg was the teacher, and from left to right are (first row) students Barbara Holloway and unidentified; (second row) Eleanor Odowski, Teddy Young, Marilyn McDaniel, Wayne King, and unidentified; (third row) Tommy Grace, unidentified, Gary King, Rita King, and Lamar Colvin; (fourth row) Butch Tyson, Rex Carmichael, George Douglas, Linda Palmer, and two unidentified. (Courtesy of Alturas Elementary School.)

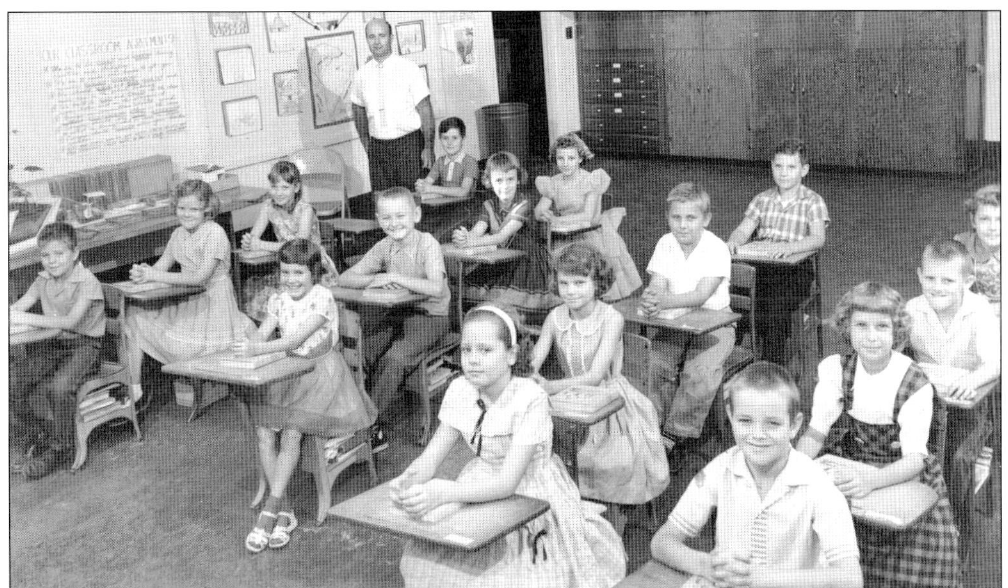

The Alturas Elementary School fourth-grade class pictured here in 1961 was led by teacher Arthur Gash Jr.. The students are, from left to right, (first row) Wendell McGill, Evelyn Joyce, Martha Butts, and unidentified; (second row) Rachel Daughtry, Charles Nelson, unidentified, and Joyce Grace; (third row) Shirley Annette Parrish, Marlene McDaniel, Jesse Jacobs, and Ricky Griner; (fourth row) David Young, Janice Colvin, Vincent Carmichael, and Loretta Hill. (Courtesy of Alturas Elementary School.)

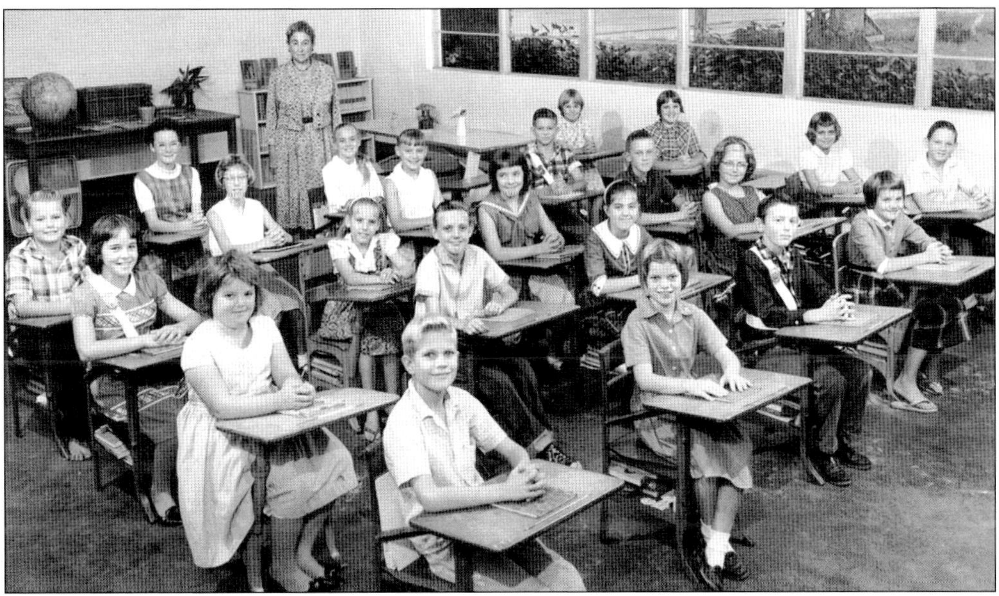

The Alturas Elementary School fifth-grade class is pictured here in 1961. The teacher was Ruth Graden. From left to right are (first row) Bobby Green, Susan Hicks, Bonnie Young, and James Jacobs; (second row) Karen King, David King, Edna King, Zenda Jenkins, and Gloria Richardson; (third row) Bill Simmons, Brenda Luna, Linda Gail Parrish, unidentified, and Sheila King; (fourth row) Teresa Voigt, Kathy Voigt, Leland Smith, and Tommy Voigt; (fifth row) Robert Werner, Debbie Reynolds, Patsy Garner, and Nancy Carmichael. (Courtesy of Alturas Elementary School.)

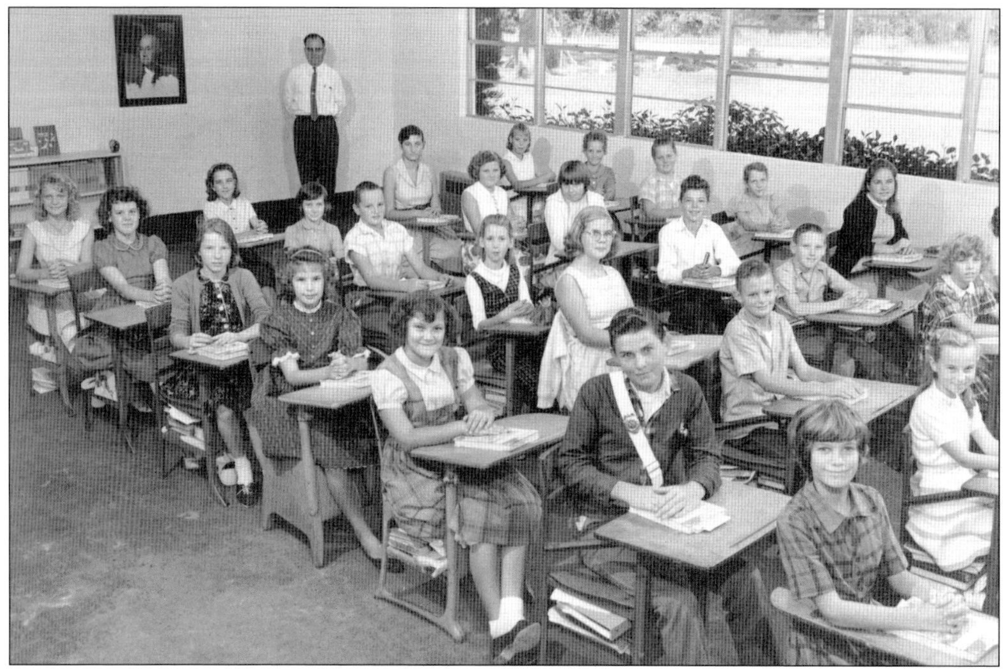

The sixth-grade class at Alturas Elementary School is pictured here in 1961. Principal and teacher Jack Skeen is standing at the back of the room. Student are, from front to back, (first row) Diane Green, Bob Simmons, Charlotte Register, Shirley Colvin, Ruth Lomaneck, unidentified, and Candy Voigt; (second row) Gail Staton, Bert Bennett, Shirley Watkins, Barbara Scarborough, Johnny McKinney, Dee Hielscher, and Elaine McGill; (third row) Susan Bullard, Floyd King, Raymond McGill, Barbara Carmichael, Eudell Joyce, and Carolyn Nicholson; (fourth row) Ann Holloway, Bobbie Jean Cannon, Charlotte Grace, Leon Seger, Lois Palmer, and Faye King. (Courtesy of Alturas Elementary School.)

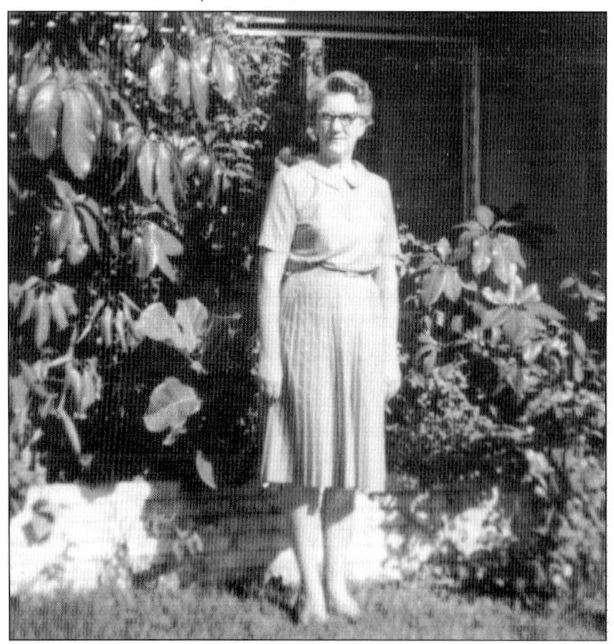

Ruth Hoaglin taught fifth grade at Alturas Elementary School in the 1960s. Students who were fortunate enough to have her as their teacher remember her fondly. She read stories after lunch every day and loved teaching history and grammar. She would correct anyone who used the word "stuff"—that was a lazy word. Hoaglin would hold up one hand with five fingers spread widely to remind her students that they were fifth graders and needed to act like it. (Courtesy of Alturas Elementary School.)

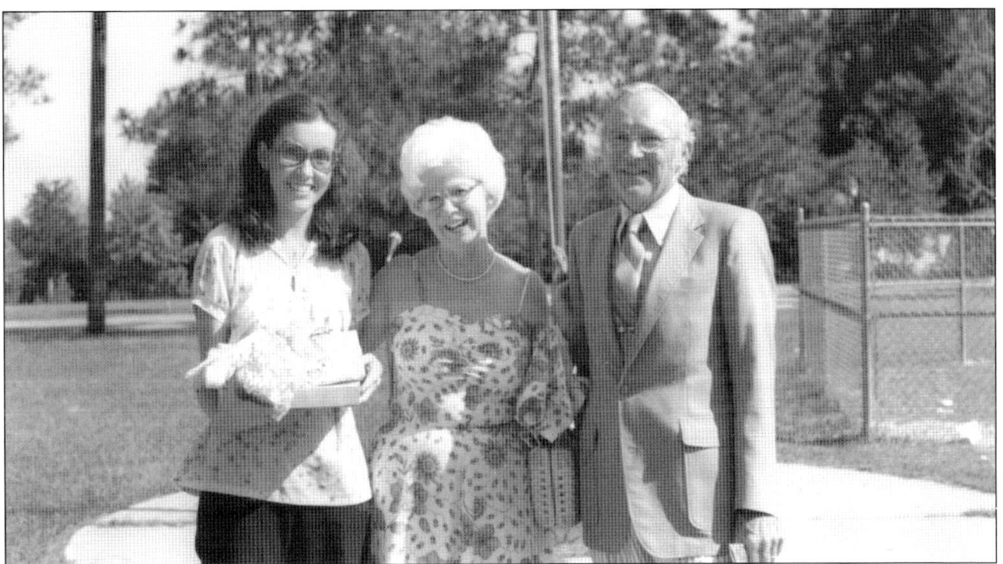

William "Bill" Whitney was the Alturas Elementary School principal from 1965 to 1982. He also taught sixth grade in the earlier years. Pictured beside him are his lovely wife, Kaye Schuck Whitney, and his secretary, Deborah Brantley Gainey. Several of the principals' names have been lost to history, but the following is a partial list: Ms. Rhoden (first principal), Mr. Teeter, Carlos P. Mullin, Bill Oster, Gerald Hatch, Jack Skeen, Billy B. Wright, Bill Whitney (17 years), John Barrow, Jack Cline, Ron Bush (16 years), Dodie Haynes, Anna-Marie DiCesare, and Charles Pemberton. (Courtesy of Alturas Elementary.)

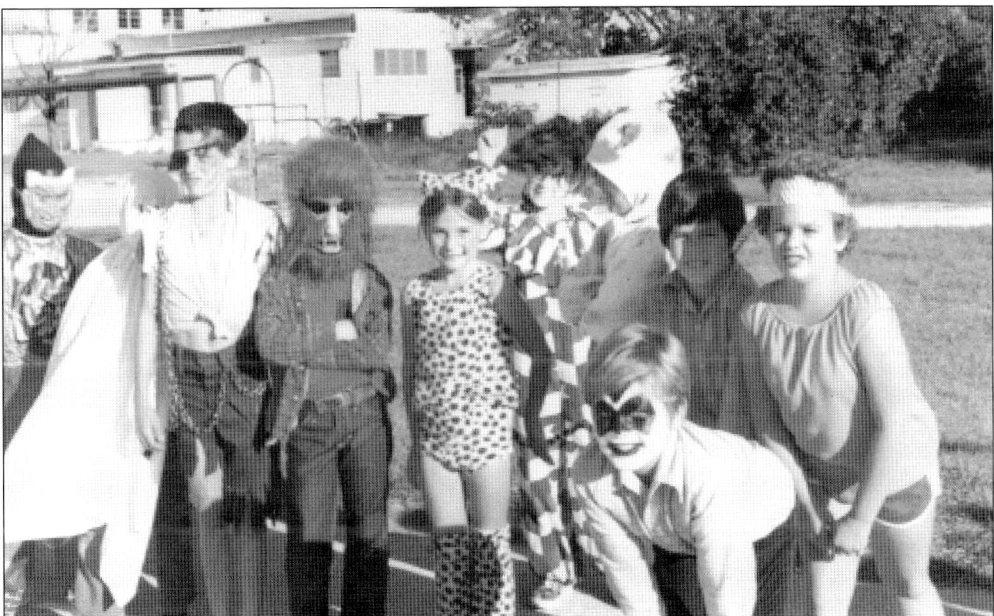

Throughout the history of the Alturas Elementary School, the Halloween Carnival was the event of the year for Alturas and the surrounding communities. The PTA worked countless hours making it a fun time for all. In this 1979 photograph, those pictured in costume, from left to right, are Billy Sander, Joseph Dowdy, Melissa Sellers, Doug Hardeman, Stephanie Finger, Timmy Fralic, Beth Gabriel, and Kevin Jenkins. (Courtesy of Alturas Elementary School.)

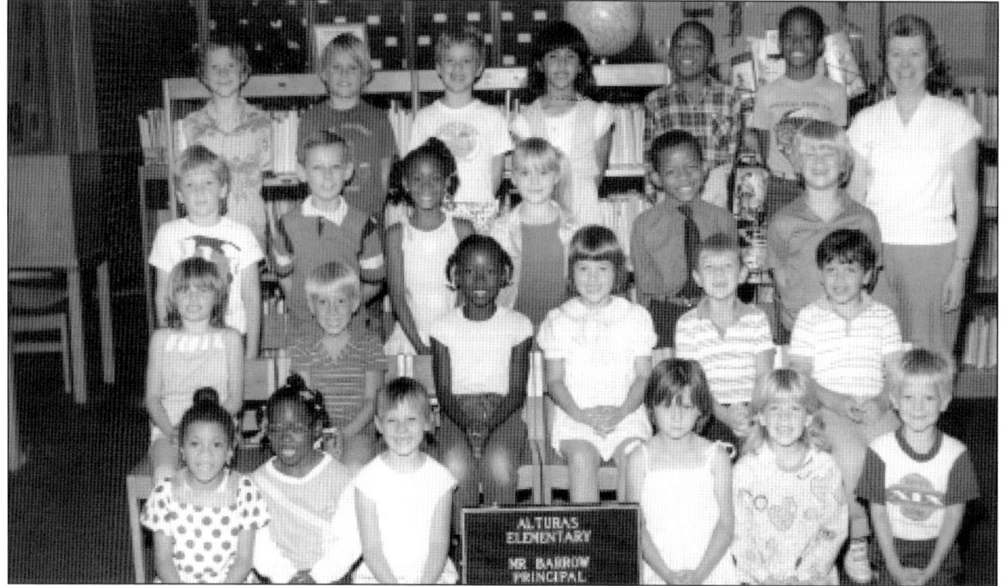

Jo DeYoung taught first grade at Alturas Elementary School from 1973 to 1993. This is DeYoung's first-grade class in 1986. DeYoung recounts a priceless story of when Masterpiece Gardens of Lake Wales, Florida, closed, and all the animals were released. Three monkeys ended up in Alturas, 15 miles away. One day, a surprised Jack Cline, the new interim principle, looked out his office window to see the monkeys playing near the school. DeYoung's class enjoyed watching the monkeys from their classroom windows, too. (Courtesy of Alturas Elementary School.)

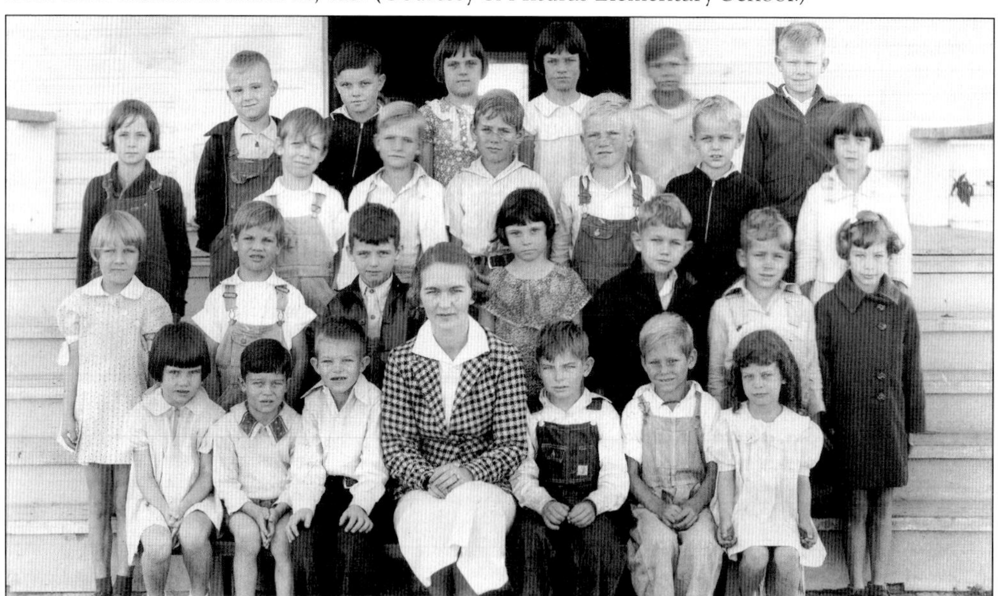

Lake Garfield had two schools, Polk Lake Elementary School (closed in the 1930s) and Lake Ann Elementary School (closed in 1953). No photographs were available for Polk Lake School, but Sam Waters and Louis Stenger attended there. This is a 1937 photograph of the first- and second-grade classes at Lake Ann Elementary School. Those identified are teacher Mary Faith Brice (first row, center), Bobby Yates (second row, third from left), Jimmy Keith White, (second row, fifth from left), and Patrick Huff (fourth row, far left). (Courtesy of W. Patrick Huff.)

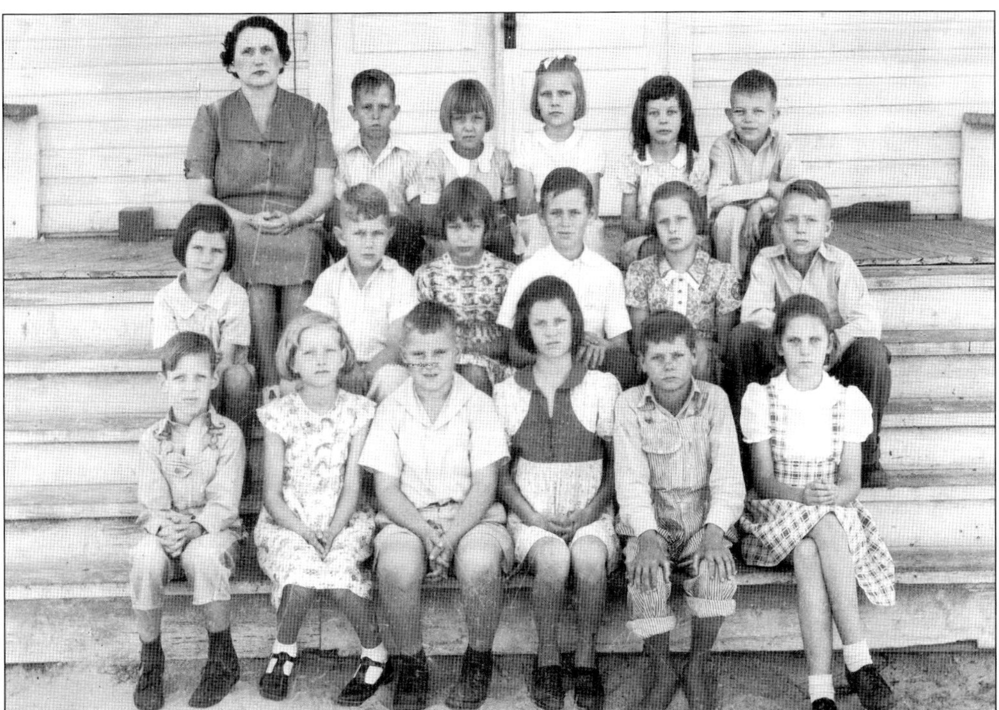

The third-grade class at Lake Ann Elementary School is shown in this 1938 photograph. The school was located on 80 Foot Road in Lake Garfield. The teacher was Meraba Boynton. It had a girls' and boys' outhouse, which was a privilege in those days. Those students identified are Patrick Huff (first row, third from left), Margaret Bush (second row, first student from left), and Jimmy Keith White (second row, second from left). (Courtesy of W. Patrick Huff.)

Lake Ann Elementary School

June 3, 1938

GRADUATING CLASS

ROBERTA MOORE - - - *Valedictorian*
SUE WILLIAMSON - - - *Salutatorian*

LUIE GENE BALLENTINE — ROY LOWERY
JEAN MCQUAIG — TOM JEFF KELLEY
FLOYD WIGGINS — DORIS DAVIS

PAGEANT: "THROUGH THE AGES"

The Voice of the Past .... Luie Gene Ballentine
Justice .... Patricia Sackett
Knowledge .... Roberta Moore
Spirit Interpreters .... Jean McQuaig, Sue Williamson, Doris Davis, Evelyn Goss.
Stone Age Men .... Earnest Fahrenback, Luie Thrailkill
Stone Age Women .... Lillian McDuffie, Edna Mae Smith
Flame Sprites .... Joy Gandy, Mertie Mae Loyd, Doris Ray, Louise Cumbie, Almetta Alderman, Frances Geiger.
King John .... Floyd Wiggins
Queen .... Sue Williamson
Pages .... Frances Alderman, Elwanda Sykes
Ladies-in-Waiting .... Jean McQuaig, Doris Davis
Courtiers .... Charles Rhame, Christopher Armstrong
Barons .... L. J. Creech, James Harrison, Carlie Brown
Edison .... Roy Lowery; Edison's Helper .... Charles Rhame
Power .... Joy Gandy; Automobile .... Mertie Mae Loyd
Airplane .... Carlton Wilbanks; Radio .... Janice McQuaig
White Fire Dancers .... Earnest Fahrenback, Luie Thrailkill, Albert Griffin, Carlie Brown, John Stenger, Carlton Wilbanks.
Lawmakers: Chairman .... Roy Lowery
Congressman Smith, Albert Griffin; Congressman Brown, John Stenger; Congressman Black, Tom Jeff Kelley; Congressman Jones, Earnest Fahrenback.
Music .... Lynn C. Armstrong; Art .... Carlynn Pirtle
Literature .... Mamie Lou Harrison

A Group of School Children.

OPERETTA: "LITTLE BLACK SAMBO"

By Henry P. Cross

Sambo—a little negro boy .... Pat Huff
Mumbo—his mother .... Ruth McQuaig
Jumbo—his slow-moving father .... Charles Lowery
Crocodile .... Billy Gandy; 1st Monkey .... Walter Griffin; 2nd Monkey .... Johnny Goss; Several Other Monkeys .... Billy Sykes, Stephen Armstrong, Lonnie Griffin, Bobby Wiggins, Kenneth Goss, Erwin White.
Several Negro Children .... Joyce Wilbanks, Wallace Wiggins, Carl Cannon, Margaret Bush, Arville Bush, Charles Loyd, Jewel Cannon, Margaret Cox, Vida Ray, Vivian McDuffie, Lois Cumbie.
1st Tiger .... Frances Baker; 2nd Tiger .... Ann Woodard; 3rd Tiger .... Phoebe McQuaig; 4th Tiger .... Mac Davis.

Act I. Sambo's Home at edge of jungle.
Act II. In the jungle.
Act III. Same as Act I.

Salutatory Address .... Sue Williamson
Presentation of Attendance Medals .... W. S. Moore
Valedictory Address .... Roberta Moore
Presentation of Diplomas .... J. W. Huff

Alas, no Clark Gable or Rita Hayworth were among the cast, although the playbill was worthy of Broadway. Edith Putnam, grandmother of former Florida agriculture commissioner Adam Putnam, was teacher and principal of Lake Ann Elementary School in Lake Garfield. She oversaw the pageant *Through the Ages* and the operetta *Little Black Sambo*, as shown in this June 3, 1938, playbill, which featured W. Patrick Huff in the star role. (Courtesy of W. Patrick Huff.)